THE SACRED THREAD

Gaṇeśa, the deity invoked to overcome obstacles at the start of an enterprise

THE SACRED THREAD

HINDUISM
in its
CONTINUITY
and
DIVERSITY

J.L.BROCKINGTON

for the University Press
Edinburgh

EDINBURGH UNIVERSITY PRESS
22 George Square, Edinburgh
First published 1981
Reprinted 1985, 1991
Printed in Great Britain by
Redwood Press Limited
Melksham, Wilts
ISBN 0 85224 393 6

Contents

Preface

In a single book, which examines the history and development of Hindu religious experience and thought from its earliest records to modern times, it is inevitable that much has been left out in order to make the broad outlines clearer. What has been passed over in silence is just as much part of the rich fabric of Hinduism. For Hinduism has never been a unitary phenomenon. In particular, there has always been a fascinating interplay between its more religious and more speculative elements. As a religion Hinduism tends towards the philosophical in its emphasis on the importance of knowledge, while Hindu philosophy sees that knowledge as having essentially a religious purpose in the achievement of the goal.

The history of Hinduism stretches over a vast time-span, during most of which the existing political boundaries of the Indian sub-continent did not exist. Accordingly the term India is used in this book in a geographical sense as referring to the whole sub-continent, except in those parts of the last two chapters where recent political events are referred to. The names of areas are generally those of the modern states of the Indian Republic, which in many cases have reverted to older names (e.g. Tamilnad for Madras State and Karnataka for Mysore).

The original terms, including names, retained in the book are presented in the standard transliteration for Sanskrit, from which most come (and are taken over virtually unchanged into the modern Indian languages). The basic point is that each sound has only one representation (unlike our clumsy English orthography). Long vowels are distinguished from short by the macron (ā), except that *e, ai, o* and *au* are long, all being diphthongs in origin. The letter *h* always signifies aspiration even in combinations like *th* and *ph* (to be pronounced as in *goatherd* and *uphill*). A subscript dot distinguishes retroflex consonants (*ṭ, ṭh, ḍ, ḍh, ṇ*), pronounced with the tongue far back in the mouth, from the dentals (*t, th, d, dh, n*) made with the tongue against the teeth. There are three sibilants, *s* pronounced as in English *sit*, and ś and ṣ both approximating to *sh*. In addition *c* is always pronounced as in Italian *cinquecento* (or *ch* in English *church*). For Tamil, the exact transliteration is also employed but on occasion a Sanskrit equivalent or an indication of pronunciation is added for the reader's guidance. The occasional translations included are my own (in three instances adapted from existing translations).

I should like to thank Mr A. R. Turnbull of the Edinburgh University Press, for suggesting that I write such a work, Professor R. E. Asher for various helpful comments, and those students over the years who have encouraged me to formulate my ideas about the nature of Hinduism. To my wife I am indebted for more than I can say; she has been directly involved in its production at every stage from first drafting to final typing.

J. L. Brockington
January 1981

The illustrations are reproduced by kind permission of: Edinburgh University Library, *frontispiece;* Department of Archaeology, Government of India, 1, 5; Gulbenkian Museum, University of Durham, 2; American Institute of Indian Studies, Varanasi and Sagar University Museum, 3; Victoria & Albert Museum, London, 4, 6, 7, 8, 9; Sanskrit Department, University of Edinburgh, 10; Office du Livre, Fribourg, 12, 13.

List of Illustrations

CHAPTER ONE

Prehistory of Hinduism

Many people's image of India is dominated by the Taj Mahal – a monument of Islamic not Hindu culture. Indeed, the Mughal period (1525–1761) as a whole bulks larger in popular assessments of Indian culture than the entire preceding period, despite the fact that it was basically as much of a foreign domination as the British Raj which followed it. Such an attitude is understandable in America whose own history has evolved over a similar period; but in Britain, where by popular stereotype history begins with the Norman Conquest in A.D. 1066, it has no real excuse. In fact, Indian culture and Indian religion can be traced back in some manner over five millennia. To survive and flourish over so long a period is a striking testimony to Hinduism's ability to adapt itself to changing circumstances, an ability which is often insufficiently appreciated because of the apparent dominance of traditional attitudes within the religion.

But what is Hinduism? The religion has an incredible variety of expression, to the extent that it has reasonably been suggested that it is not possible to characterise it as a religion in the normal sense, since it is not a unitary concept nor a monolithic structure, but that it is rather the totality of the Indian way of life. Certainly, there is no doctrine or ritual universal to the whole of Hinduism and what is essential for one group need not be so for another. Nevertheless, most people would accept that Hinduism is a definite, and definable, entity. What is it then that we are looking for or at when we are considering Hinduism? Is it the beliefs and practices of the uneducated villager or of the traditional intelligentsia? Are we cataloguing the minutiae of the ritual? Are we enumerating the dogmas held by those we (or their fellow Hindus) consider most orthodox? Or are we attempting to analyse the thought-structures of the religion? Quite apart from other factors, the sheer volume of the different ritual and other cultic practices makes it impossible to attempt an exhaustive description of the religion. Clearly, our concern must be with what is distinctive about Hinduism and what it is that sets it apart from the other great religions, while bearing in mind that to be too selective is to deny the diversity which is part of the essence of Hinduism. However, in a religion which manages very well without the cohesive effects of a common doctrine, a hierarchy of authority or a historical founder, its distinctiveness is only intelligible in terms of its history.

Nevertheless, attempts have regularly been made to lay down some criteria for Hinduism, either from the outside as a means of definition or from the inside as a test of orthodoxy. Views of Hinduism from the outside, especially at the popular level, tend very much to be stereotypes. Typical ones are that Hindus are excessively obsessed with religion (a trait that they are thought to share with much of Asia) and with the caste system, are vegetarian and non-violent, worship the cow, and see the world as an illusion, and that the religion itself is somehow conterminous with India. To take the last point first, although Hindu does basically simply mean Indian, Hinduism cannot be equated with India, despite being overwhelmingly found there. On the one hand other religions have originated within India (Buddhism, Jainism and Sikhism, to name only the major extant ones) and yet others have entered (notably Islam, but also Judaism, Zoroastrianism and Christianity); on the other hand Hinduism itself is to be found outside India, in Bali, as a result of cultural diffusion, and in the West Indies and East Africa, as a result of more recent population movements, not to mention certain bastard forms propagated by *gurus* capitalising on current uncertainties and malaise in Western society. Its spread to Bali was just part of a larger movement of economic and cultural expansion which affected most of South East Asia and Hindu elements are very apparent in the Buddhism of those countries. These extra-Indian adaptations are beyond the scope of this book, but it is worth observing here that the caste system is radically simplified and indeed in decline in these areas.

The question of religious fervour is also not as simple as it seems. To a Hindu, religion is all-pervading, but that is not quite the same as being obsessively concerned about it, for Hindus do not see religion as extraneous to their lives, nor as a duty imposed upon them from outside. Since life is an integrated whole with its various aspects interdependent, religion cannot be pondered over as a separate problem. Indeed, Sanskrit has no word which can simply be translated 'religion'; *dharma*, though often rendered thus for lack of a more comprehensive term in English, covers a far wider span, incorporating not only religious tradition but also social *mores* and the requirements of the law.

The very structure of Indian society in the caste system is widely felt to be part of the religion. Indeed, it is given a religious basis in the doctrine of *karma*, the belief that one's present position in society is determined by the net effect of all one's previous actions in past lives. To the extent that Hinduism is as much a social system as a religion, the caste system has become integral to it. But we have already noted that in Hinduism outside India caste is withering. More significantly, some elements in India would deny its validity; the devotional movement in general tends towards the rejection of caste and the famous Vaiṣṇava theologian Rāmānuja in the twelfth century A.D. coined for the untouchables the name *Tirukulattar*, 'the family of Śrī (Viṣṇu's consort)', which strikingly prefigures the name popularised by Mahatma Gandhi of *Harijan*, 'people of Hari (=Viṣṇu)'. The limitation on such attitudes to caste is that in general they were confined to the distinctly religious field, but that only reinforces the point here being made that caste, though intimately connected with Hinduism, is not necessary to it. Incidentally, the common preconception that belief in *karma* is tantamount to fatalism rests on a misconception: one's present state is determined by one's own past activities and one's future state is here and now being determined by one's present actions, and so basically a man is what he has made himself and can make himself what he chooses.

Similar over-simplification surrounds the issue of vegetarianism. It is the standard practice of the élite group, the Brāhmans, but has never been a universal practice, except in so far as many lower-caste Hindus can rarely afford meat. Its rationale lies in the theory of non-violence (*ahiṃsā*) which has come to play an important part in the religion. In its most extreme form this consists in a profound reluctance to kill any living being, though not necessarily in any positive concern for their well-being. But this can and does result in the use of a threat to fast to death as a form of moral blackmail, which subverts the whole intention of the concept, while the frequency of political murder in Calcutta a few years ago illustrates how little influence it has often had.

Veneration of the cow probably also has connections with the doctrine of non-violence but undoubtedly owes more to the economic importance of the cow at an early period as a source of milk and related products, which made the slaughter of productive animals an undesirable practice. However, belief in the sanctity of the cow, though a conspicuous aspect of popular Hinduism, is too superficial a feature to be considered fundamental, especially with this practical reason for its introduction. Similarly, many originally sensible hygienic practices were given religious sanctions in order to enhance their observance. Thus, for instance, the at first sight rather motiveless and even repugnant practice of using the urine and dung of cows as a purificatory material has a practical as well as a religious aspect, for there is a definite disinfectant value in its high ammonia content; indeed the ancient Iranians also used cow's urine as a cleansing agent and so have a number of other peoples. So too the rigid distinction between the right hand for eating and the left hand for cleaning oneself after defecation is at least some safeguard against diseases like typhoid. The problem is that such practices, once given a religious sanction, tend to fossilise into meaningless rituals.

If veneration of the cow is too superficial a feature, then the view of the world as illusory is too limited a one. For this view has never been true of Hinduism as a whole, either of its scriptures or of popular religion, but only of one school of philosophical thought. All the orthodox philosophical systems except the Advaita Vedānta are realist in outlook. The only justification for the view is that in general Advaita Vedānta is the form of Indian thought with which the West has become most familiar.

If external definitions are inadequate, do the internal criteria fare any better? The most usual ones put forward are acceptance of the authority of the Veda, observance of caste rules coupled with respect for Brāhmans, and belief in an eternal self (*ātman*) undergoing a continuous cycle of rebirth (*saṃsāra*). While each of these has some validity, they are not wholly satisfactory. From the remarks made earlier it will be clear that the caste system, though closely integrated into the religion, is not essential to it. Certainly, non-conformity to caste rules, rather than rejection of any particular doctrine or deviation from any particular religious practice, has traditionally been regarded as a serious lapse for a Hindu. This may entail the loss of one's caste status, but it does not necessarily involve the loss of one's religion; outcasting is not precisely equivalent to excommunication. Equally, respect for Brāhmans is normal among the more pious but there are nonetheless several sects which reject their claims to supremacy. Nor is it possible to find any sacraments that are obligatory for all Hindus.

Doctrines regarding the eternal self and the cycle of rebirth have become nearly universal in Hinduism. But this is too inclusive a criterion. The cycle of rebirth is also accepted not only by Buddhists, Jains and Sikhs (who, it might be argued, do not really count because they developed out of Hinduism) but also sporadically in quite separate religious traditions, such as Orphism and Neoplatonism, the Kabala and the Doukhobars. Conversely, there are a very few groups usually reckoned Hindu who deny it; the Liṅgāyats seem to reject the notion of rebirth, at least for those of their community, while the Deva Samāj (founded in 1898 by Shiv Narayan Agnihotri) rejects the pre-existence of the *ātman* and declares that at death it will either suffer extinction or go to a kind of heaven. Doctrines concerning *ātman* and *saṃsāra*, *karma* and *mokṣa* (release from the cycle) may be regarded as axiomatic by most schools of Hindu philosophy, but they are by no means universal or essential so far as its religious aspect is concerned, for a person can claim to be a Hindu without believing in them and acceptance of them does not in itself make one a Hindu. Hinduism has, after all, always been noted for its ability to absorb potentially schismatic developments; indeed, one of the prime functions of the caste system has been to assimilate various tribes and sects by assigning them a place in the social hierarchy. Thus, Hindu society is divided horizontally into castes and vertically into sects, although the vertical division is not as rigid or exclusive as the horizontal one.

Acceptance of the authority of the Veda is probably the most nearly universally valid criterion, but this is precisely because it has least content, often amounting to no more than a declaration that someone considers himself a Hindu. Certain Vedic hymns are still recited at weddings and funerals, though without any understanding of their meaning. The Veda has been considered in Hinduism as the sole source of true religion and rejection of its authoritativeness was a major factor in turning Buddhism and Jainism into separate religions. But, despite the fact that study of the Veda was made an absolute duty for men of the three higher classes, an accurate knowledge of it was lost at an early date and the works of mediaeval commentators give ample evidence of incomplete understanding. In particular, the *Ṛgveda,* to us the most important of the Vedic texts, though faithfully handed down in the schools of the reciters, remained unknown territory to most philosophers and religious teachers. Even those schools which professed to study the Veda did so from an extremely limited and one-sided point of view: the Mīmāṃsā deals at length with the ritual commands, ignoring the hymns and much else, and the Vedānta concentrates almost entirely on the Upaniṣads, which have admittedly contributed most directly to the development of later Hindu thought. The attachment of other philosophies to the Veda was very perfunctory. Indeed, it is reasonable to say that India had a very inadequate and incomplete knowledge of the Veda before it was discovered by European scholarship. Even the profession of belief in the authority of the Veda is not essential; many of the devotional trends in Hinduism tend to be critical of it, the various schools of Tantrism have at the least a very ambivalent attitude towards it, and Basava, the founder of the Liṅgāyats, definitely rejected the authority of the Veda and the Brāhmans along with much else.

Thus, although the Veda is regarded as the canonical scripture of Hinduism, in actual fact this canon is not read by the vast majority of Hindus, most of whom – the lower castes and all women – were in due course forbidden to read it. But this very inaccessibility has facilitated an almost endless reinterpretation of doctrine, for an appeal to the authority of the Veda may be used to lend respectability to any innovation. A particularly striking manifestation of this flexibility of Hindu tradition can be seen in the way that it has assimilated various heterodox movements; the concept of heresy in Hinduism is a relative one. The Jains, who originated out of the Hindu environment, adopt a relativistic view of reality and insist that we ought to preface any statement with a qualification like 'From this angle . . .', for any statement only has validity with reference to the particular standpoint from which it is made, but pragmatically accept that we do not bother with such qualifications in everyday conversation. Any study of Hinduism must involve many such generalisations, valid for a majority of Hindus but always liable to exceptions. In a way, it is a subconscious recognition of this diversity, which defies any simple definitions, that leads Hindus to appeal to their perceived origins in the Veda; it is a recognition that the unifying factor lies in their common history. The appeal to the Veda permits both an affirmation of the supremacy of tradition and an implicit acceptance of the reality of adaptation.

The earliest form of Hinduism still extant is recorded in the four Vedas. The religion exemplified by these collections of ritual hymns was brought into India by the Aryans who began to settle in North India some time between 1500 and 1000 B.C., but in their present form they were clearly composed over a long span of time. The oldest is the *Ṛgveda*, datable to around 1200 B.C. by its language and its obvious connections with the Iranian religion reformed by Zarathushtra before 1000 B.C. and recorded in the Avesta. Next comes the *Sāmaveda*, followed closely by the *Yajurveda*, and finally the *Atharvaveda*. The content of the Vedas was developed, also over a long period, by a further group of texts known as Brāhmaṇas, distinguished from them by their prose form and their characteristically later language; to the Brāhmaṇas are appended the Āraṇyakas, of which a further sub-division, the Upaniṣads, reveal a philosophy compatible with composition prior to the rise of Buddhism, that is before about 500 B.C.

The Vedas do not exhibit any fixed pantheon. The *Ṛgveda*, in common with Iranian tradition, recognises 33 gods connected with heaven, earth and the waters of the air, but also mentions others, while the lists given by the Brāhmaṇas vary in certain details. Images of the gods were not recognised in the Vedic cult, except in its latest forms, and then only in the domestic ritual. Nor was the ritual tied to any fixed sanctuary: eminently mobile, it used the sacrificer's house for the lesser rites and special terrains for the major rites, with the sacrificial stake assimilated to the Cosmic Tree connecting the three cosmic regions. As in Iran, the essential ingredients of the sacrifice were fire and *soma*, a juice used both as a libation and as a hallucinogenic drink for the worshipper; the gods Agni and Soma were thus accorded high prestige, for the sacrifice was the heart of the Vedic religion.

The hymns of the *Ṛgveda*, oldest and most important source for Vedic religion, were probably composed in the Brahmāvarta region (roughly modern Haryana), to judge from the climatic features they describe, although some scholars have located them in the Panjab, either west or east. Handed down in the early stages by oral tradition and long regarded as too sacred to be reduced to writing, the text itself provides ample internal evidence of the general accuracy of its preservation, corroborated by the other Vedas. Even so, they provide only a glimpse, albeit varied, of the religious thought and practices of their time. The hymns were used by priests in worshipping the major gods, and many are composed in highly refined poetry, but others are simple in thought and expression. Myths are frequently alluded to, but not recounted *in extenso*, and only the hieratic views are given much prominence; moreover, most deal with the *soma* ritual, and animal sacrifice is hardly noticed, apart from the rarest and most important, the horse sacrifice.

The 1028 hymns, equivalent in length to Homer's works, consist of stanzas, usually complete in themselves though often grouped in threes, composed in some fifteen different metres. The collection is divided into ten books, of which the homogeneous books two to seven form the core, with others as later additions. According to tradition, supported by internal evidence, each of the original books was composed by seers of the same family and they follow a standard arrangement of groups of hymns addressed to different gods in descending order of importance, Agni first, then Indra, then the minor deities, with hymns in each group arranged according to the diminishing number of stanzas they contain, and books arranged according to the increasing number of hymns. The earliest addition is the second part of book one; next comes its first part and book eight, which together form a unit comparable to the earlier 'family' books, but distinct from them particularly in metre and arrangement. The ninth book consists entirely of hymns to Soma, which are almost completely absent from the earlier books. The compilation is obviously late, but many of the individual hymns are as old as any, and were collected together from the earlier compilations for convenience of use in the ritual. The hymns in the tenth book, although a few are still early, generally reveal their later character by their language

1. Varuṇa, guardian of *ṛta*

and metre, though more particularly by their content. Some of the older gods, such as Mitra and Varuṇa and the Aśvins, decline in importance, to be replaced by more abstract deities, while several hymns speculate on philosophical questions. Others are concerned with popular religion, providing spells and family rites. Here, too, is reflected the changing pattern of society, with mention in one hymn of the four classes of society, and a theological explanation of the system.

The chief attribute of the Vedic gods is their power over the lives of men; moral values, though sometimes present, are of lesser importance. The gods also represent the chief powers of nature, such as fire, sun and thunderstorm, and respond benevolently to sacrifice. Only Rudra is regularly associated with destruction; other natural disasters, from disease to drought, are caused by powerful anti-gods such as Vṛtra, whose conquest is a prime concern of the gods. Varuṇa, and to a lesser extent the more arbitrary Indra, punish sin, and Agni is invoked among other things to free from guilt. Whereas major deities are invoked in all the earlier books, the distribution of the minor gods is patchy, suggesting that they were of importance only to limited groups of worshippers.

The gods of the *Ṛgveda* are called both Deva and Asura: both terms can be applied to one deity, Indra for instance, though sometimes the terms seem to be differentiated. Further confusion has been imported into the situation by the application in later mythology of the term Asura to anti-gods or demons. The Vedic term Asura seems to imply basically 'lord' or 'powerful' and to go back to a now almost obsolete Indo-European supreme god, perhaps reflected in the Iranian Ahura Mazdā. It is the meaning of the word which changes, not the character of the being to whom it is applied.

Indra was clearly the most popular deity among the poets of the *Ṛgveda* and no doubt of the Aryans in general, for almost a quarter of all the hymns are addressed to him. He is the dominant deity of the middle region, the region between Earth and Heaven. Indeed, some hymns attribute the eternal separation of Sky and Earth, Indra's parents, to their terror at their son's discovery of *soma*, drinking which made him swell to enormous size. A few make him the son of Tvaṣṭṛ, the Great Father and Creator of all creatures. He is described in anthropomorphic terms to a greater extent than other deities; his bodily strength and huge size are frequently alluded to, his arms are powerful to wield his weapons, his hair and his appearance generally are tawny, and changes are rung on the word for tawny in every verse of one entire hymn. His chief characteristic, accorded unstinted praise, is his power, both on the human plane as the god of battle aiding the Aryans in their conquest of North India, and mythologically as the thunder god who conquers the demons of drought and darkness, thus liberating the waters or winning the light. Accordingly, the weapon attributed exclusively to him is the *vajra*, or thunderbolt, fashioned for him by Tvaṣṭṛ. He is unsurpassed in power by men or gods, and words meaning 'mighty' (*śakra, śacīvat, śacīpati, śatakratu*) are applied far more frequently to him than to any other god. All the other gods yield to him in might and he is regularly presented as their king.

The most basic myth connected with Indra concerns his battle with the serpent Vṛtra, who is obstructing the waters and the sky. Here he is exhilarated by Soma and escorted by his companions the Maruts, and heaven and earth tremble with fear when he slays Vṛtra with his bolt, liberating the waters, generating the sun, and finding the cows upon which the nomadic Aryan herdsmen depended.

> Indra's heroic deeds now let me proclaim,
> which he who wields the thunderbolt performed at first;
> he slew the snake, cut a channel for the waters,
> and split the entrails of the mountains.
> He slew the snake as it clung to the mountain –
> for him Tvaṣṭṛ fashioned the sounding thunderbolt.
> Like lowing cows, the flowing waters
> made their way downwards straight to the sea.
> (ṚV 1.32.1–2)

The exact nature of this liberation of the waters has given rise to much speculation. In the nineteenth century it was interpreted as bringing down rain, a rare occurrence in the early homeland of the Aryans; an equally literal, though more fanciful, suggestion links it with the destruction of a dam, ruining the agriculturally-based civilisation in the Indus valley which preceded the Aryan incursions. But the Vṛtra myth is now generally accepted as a creation myth, with Vṛtra symbolising chaos. By killing him, Indra separated land from water, upper regions from nether, and caused the sun to rise in an act of creation repeated every morning and, at the winter solstice, every year. Thus, Indra destroys the resistance (*vṛtra*) or inertia of the pre-existing chaos, located on the primordial mountain, and activates the process of differentiation and evolution. Occasionally, Indra is declared thus to have turned the non-existent into the existent. The centrality of this exploit to Indra's nature is shown by the frequency with which he is called 'the slayer of Vṛtra', Vṛtrahan, and its antiquity by the occurrence of the parallel Vṛthragna, god of victory, in the Avesta.

Indra also engages in conflict with many other hostile forces, as well as aiding the Aryans in their battles; however, the Vala myth seems basically a priestly reworking of the Vṛtra myth, for Indra, the great warrior, is there depicted as overthrowing Vala with a hymn or other ritual means and thereby freeing the light from a cave in the mountain. Indeed, he is often joined or replaced in allusions to the myth by Bṛhaspati, a little mentioned deity who does not figure in the original pantheon, and accompanied by the priestly band of the Aṅgirases, who sometimes even play the major role. The term Bṛhaspati was no doubt originally an epithet of Indra, indicating his priestly functions as king of the gods, for the word means 'lord of *brahman* (the power of the ritual, but originally 'hymn' or 'formula')'; indeed the title is occasionally applied to Agni, the priestly god. Just as the Vedic king progressively relinquished his religious duties to professional priests, so Indra was replaced by Bṛhaspati in this context. Such functional deities, whose names are usually formed with the suffix *-pati* 'lord', seem regularly to originate from earlier divine epithets and belong especially to the tenth book of the *Ṛgveda*.

More remote than Indra, and possibly once superior to him in the pantheon, is the figure of Varuṇa, the guardian of the principle *ṛta*. With him is frequently associated Mitra – so much so that hymns invoking both jointly (as Mitrāvaruṇā) are much more frequent than those to either on his own (at least twenty-four to the pair, eight to Varuṇa alone and one to Mitra alone). This joint invocation goes back to the Indo-Iranian period, for Ahura Mazdā, 'the wise Lord', and Mithra are so linked in the Avesta; Varuṇa himself is several times called an Asura and described by terms meaning 'wise', so the difference in names is no problem. Varuṇa is called a king, ruling over heaven and earth, whose anger is feared and who deals out punishment but also mercy; he has at his disposal snares or bonds with which he fetters evildoers. Indeed Varuṇa's name has been explained by this property of binding, although the derivation from a root meaning 'oath' is more in keeping with his overall character, as well as with the clear meaning of Mitra's name as 'treaty, contract'. Both Varuṇa and Mitra watch over men to oversee their observance of truth, making use of spies everywhere and especially of their eye, the sun. In their guardianship of vows, they display not only the ethical concerns apparently denoted by their names but also their role as kings. In fact Dumézil and his school would see in Mitra and Varuṇa the representatives of the Indo-European 'sovereign gods', a view that does serve to highlight the imposing nature of Varuṇa's role. As the guardian of *ṛta*, the principle of order in the universe in both its natural and its moral aspects, and as such the representative of the static aspects of royal power, Varuṇa is the sovereign ruler of gods and men, who established heaven and earth and measured out the expanse of the earth, and he is the punisher of sin, the lord and upholder of fixed observances, who is implored to forgive and release from sin. Offence and forgiveness are frequent themes of the lofty hymns addressed to Varuṇa, who as a moral ruler surpasses other deities. One major qualification to this is that the cosmic order, *ṛta*, with which man's actions here on earth should be in accord, is not fully known to men, who may therefore unwittingly offend against Varuṇa's ordinances despite their wish to please him; in this respect Varuṇa's power and his creative activity, *māyā*, may be deceptive.

At first sight, at least, there is little mythology connected with Varuṇa, all the emphasis being concentrated on his sovereignty and moral rule. But he is not only an omniscient, celestial ruler, he is also associated with the waters and with the night, while both his occasional title of Asura and his decline in importance even within the *Ṛgveda* perhaps hint that he is connected especially with the period before the Devas established their dominance. Even more specifically it is said that the nether world is Varuṇa's realm and the abode of *ṛta*. Possibly Varuṇa as the god of the primordial, undifferentiated cosmos has been relegated by Indra's creative activities to the lordship of those aspects which survive from and still represent the original chaos: the nether world, the night-sky and the waters, whether under the earth or in the sky at night. Even the principle of *ṛta*, by which Varuṇa regulates the activities of the world and which must in some sense precede the evolution of the world, is replaced subsequently by the related principle of *dharma*.

As god of fire, Agni occupies a very prominent position in the *Ṛgveda*. He is invoked in over two hundred hymns, hymns which are the first group in each book (except the eighth and ninth), and he is frequently associated with Indra, to the point of occasionally being called, like Indra, Vṛtrahan, and of being invoked jointly with him as a dual deity more frequently than any other. His martial connections may be seen in exhortations to burn his devotees' foes, but he is also lord of the forest fire and the fire of cremation, he is able by the heat or power of austerity (*tapas*) to blast the impious who seek to use the ritual for evil purposes, and he comes to embody the heat of sexual desire. Fire was, of course, very important to early peoples and was not easy to acquire or control, as the myth of Mātariśvan fetching Agni from heaven and the Greek legend of Prometheus illustrate. Fire was thus of great significance in itself and it was only natural to elaborate rituals around it; the veneration of fire in the Iranian religion is well known. Within the Vedic tradition Agni is seen as present as a guest in every household on the domestic hearth, becoming identified with the householder; indeed, he has a particularly close association with mankind.

Agni's chief prominence, however, stems from his role as the sacrificial fire. He is the fire itself on the altar, and so is instrumental in conveying the sacrifice to heaven and, by extension, in bringing the gods down to the sacrifice. Personified, he is the mediator between men and gods, the divine counterpart of human priests in all their functions and often called by their various titles. He is the many-sided, universal priest who knows all the roles and functions of the sacrifice, the inner light placed among men to guide them through the mysteries and intricacies of the ritual, and thus omniscient and the author of wisdom and prayer; he is – like the human priests – poet, sage and seer. It is this priestly role which is most apparent in his association with Indra, whom he attends like a priest accompanying a human king, actively fighting the common enemy with his particular weapons of *mantras* and rites.

The ever-present physical basis of Agni's nature inevitably

2. Agni, god of fire and sacrifice

limited the growth of any mythology, but there is speculation about his origin and form. He is spoken of as reborn daily from his parents, the kindling sticks, whom he promptly devours; he is also regarded as being born from himself, from which comes his epithet Tanūnapāt, or somewhat paradoxically from the waters as Apāṃ Napāt, an ancient concept shared with Iranian religion and sometimes addressed as a separate deity, which probably symbolises the lightning flashing from the clouds. Agni is thus simultaneously both one, as deity, and many, as the individual fires, both primordial, as the celestial fire, and ever young, being kindled daily. In one late hymn to Agni in his universal aspect, Agni Vaiśvānara, the poet in conclusion broaches the problem of the relationship between the many manifestations and the one universal deity and indicates that it is just part of a wider problem (10.88.17–19).

Next in frequency to Indra and Agni comes Soma. In the oldest parts of the Veda Agni and Soma have much in common because of their basis in the material equipment of the sacrifice, for Soma is the personification of a plant, the extraction and drinking of whose juice formed the centre of the Vedic ritual. The anthropomorphism of both gods is constantly impinged on by their physical basis, and so remains undeveloped. The deeds given to Soma are simply borrowed from the other gods, especially Indra and Agni, with whom he is closely associated, since Indra is the great *soma* drinker and Agni is also a god of ritual. On the other hand, the *soma* is the great object of priestly interest, and the most elaborate imagery seems to have formed round the simple operations of pressing and straining the juice. In its present form the whole of the ninth book of the *Ṛgveda* is devoted to Soma (deity and plant) and he has six hymns in other books.

The preparation and offering of *soma* was a feature of Indo-Iranian worship, and there are numerous similarities between the Soma and Haoma cults, although the belief in an intoxicating beverage of the gods, a kind of honey or mead, probably goes back to the Indo-European period. The parallelism of the legends of the eagle and *soma*, the nectar-bringing eagle of Zeus, and the eagle which fetched the mead and which was really Odin, is obvious, especially since the term *madhu* 'honey' is often applied to *soma*. In a ritual performed thrice daily, the plant is made to yield its juice by being pounded with a stone or pressed with stones which lie on a skin. The pressed juice passes through the filter of sheep's wool, and in this form is offered to Indra and Vāyu. The filtered *soma* next flows into jars or vats where it is mixed with water and milk to sweeten it. This admixture brings Soma into a special relationship with the Waters; their father as well as their son, he seems sometimes to be considered to be rain, an indication that the earliest ritual concerned rain-making. Again, as a thunderer and a loud-sounding god, Soma is a bull and the waters are his cows whom he fertilises.

The exhilarating power of *soma* is stressed; it is a divine drink conferring immortality on gods and men; it is called *amṛta*, the 'draught of immortality'. As a deity, Soma is a wise seer, a poet, who stimulates thought and inspires hymns. The fact that Soma invigorates Indra in his fight with Vṛtra is repeated so often that Indra's exploits and cosmic actions come to be attributed to him. Again Indra makes the sun to rise when he has drunk *soma*, so that Soma is credited with this feat also. From this it is a short step to becoming a great cosmic power, who generates the two worlds and wields universal sway. Soma is not only lord of plants but also king of the gods, of the whole earth and of men. The priest who crushed the *soma* stalks knew that this ritual meant the killing of King Soma in order to set free his victorious, invigorating and life-promoting power. *Soma* pressing early took a central place in the mythology, particularly in the cosmogonic myth. The Veda seems to view Soma and Agni as originally dwelling within the primordial hill, guarded by a snake or dragon embodying the power of 'resistance' (*vṛtra*). Agni and Soma represent contrasting but complementary elements: fire and liquid, heat and coolness; in a few of the latest hymns of the *Ṛgveda* Soma is identified with the moon, just as Agni is with the sun.

The identity of the *soma* plant is subject to considerable dispute. Both the Avesta and the Veda state that it grew on the top of mountains. It may have been *Amanita muscaria*, the fly agaric, a hallucinogenic mushroom growing in the mountains of Afghanistan, but not in the plains of India. The Aryan incursion into India by this route resulted in progressive loss of contact with the areas from which the *soma* plant was acquired and consequent loss of knowledge of its actual nature, which seem to have coincided with a steady increase in elaboration of the ritual. It may be that there is more to this than just a temporal link. The authentic plant was replaced by an ineffectual substitute, and its absence may have been increasingly compensated for by the expectations built up through the ritual which created their own fulfilment; the sense of ecstasy and communion with the gods was now produced by purely ritual means. This may even have set a pattern for the later development of the religion, where the emphasis on the achievement of certain states by manipulation of one's consciousness comes more and more to the fore.

The major figures of the pantheon are complemented by a number of minor deities, each with his own particular characteristics. Prominent among them, Dyaus (Heaven) and Pṛthivī (Earth) are almost inseparable. Often addressed as 'father and mother', they are the parents of the gods and, by a symbolic act of procreation, of all living creatures; the fixing of Earth out of the original chaos represents the beginning of order, both physical and spiritual.

A nature goddess with a much wider field of operation is Aditi. Her name may best be translated 'freedom', and she represents ideas of breadth and boundlessness throughout the free, limitless space of the universe, combined with the inner space of the gods. Thus comprising everything, she is called the mother and father of all the gods and of all creation. This aspect as the Great Mother is the only physical characteristic much expressed, and provides the reason for her identification with the earth, and also with the cow, India's great symbol of motherhood. She is frequently invoked to confer freedom, both from physical illness and spiritual sin, and indeed from all kinds of harm. Her sons, called as a group by the derivative title Ādityas, comprise the major figures among the Devas, and likewise confer benefits on mankind in response to their worship.

Dyaus's son Sūrya is the most specific of the solar deities, for his name refers both to him as god and to the physical sun. He drives his chariot across the sky to drive away darkness from gods and men, but is sometimes also conceived of as a shining white horse or as an eagle. Another great natural force, the wind, is rarely invoked, being represented in concrete fashion by Vāta and in more abstract form by his doublet Vāyu; Iranian tradition accords Vayu much greater importance. Closely associated with Indra and privileged to drink the *soma*, he was the breath of god and impelling principle of the whole cosmos. Uṣas, the dawn, sometimes protrayed as Sūrya's wife, is another female member of the otherwise almost exclusively male pantheon. She is a great goddess who represents the victory of light over darkness, of life over death. She is invoked in about twenty hymns of great beauty, where the poets link the natural splendours of the dawn to the benefits she confers on man.

The twin gods known as the Aśvins have obvious links with the Greek Dioscuri. In the *Ṛgveda* both participate jointly in their roles as warrior and fertility deities, yet they have different fathers, and there is evidence, both internal and from Iranian tradition, to suggest that originally at least these functions were differentiated. Yama, ruler of the dead, occurs almost exclusively in books one and ten, the latest parts of the *Ṛgveda*; the poets of the earlier books tell us little of their ideas of death and the after-life. He associates with gods and is by implication divine, but is only expressly called king of the dead. He has a particularly close relationship with Agni, who bears the dead to his kingdom. He also has a twin sister Yamī, which recalls the Indo-Iranian myth of a pair of primeval twins who produced the human race.

The figure of Viṣṇu provides further evidence that the hymns of the *Ṛgveda* do not provide a complete picture of the religious attitudes of the Aryans. He clearly occupied a position of importance in men's minds, but is not referred to frequently in the hymns. His basic personality, however, is remarkably consonant with that revealed in later mythology, where he assumes an increasingly prominent role. He is benevolent and never inimical to man, willing and able to bestow abundant riches on his worshippers, and concerned to assure the continuance of the human race. In one aspect he is a solar deity, engaged like the sun in sending blessings from heaven in the form of all-pervasive, life-giving energy.

Viṣṇu is a friend and ally of Indra, helping him in his battle against Vṛtra, and in spreading out the spaces between heaven and earth. Indeed, in one hymn it is Viṣṇu who opens Vala's cowpen. As representatives of the two great beneficent forces of sun and rain, they co-operate as equal partners, though Viṣṇu's is the less active role. Sometimes the two gods are so intimately associated as almost to form one dual deity, Indrāviṣṇū, participating in each other's qualities and activities.

The major mythological exploit attributed to Viṣṇu is his striding through the universe with three steps, an action which has given rise to the frequently applied epithets 'wide-going' and 'wide-striding'. At the earliest stages, these three steps symbolise his might and omnipresence, traversing the earth and sky, and the regions beyond the knowledge of man, and may be considered to represent the sun's progress across the sky. Thus his abode, *viṣṇupada*, at his highest step, is located at the meridian. The epithets 'dwelling in the mountains' and 'standing on the mountains' applied in one hymn are thought to allude to the sun looking down from the mountain-tops, though others see in them a reference to mountains as stores of water and the home of beneficial plants. Later these three steps are explained more fully as Viṣṇu fixing the boundaries of the world and claiming it for man to inhabit.

A further feature of Viṣṇu's all-pervasiveness is that he may also represent the cosmic pillar, the mystic centre of the universe which leads to and supports the heavens. His home is in the mountains, which seem to uphold the firmament, and to him belongs the *yūpa*, the stake to which the sacrificial victim is tied, which is a symbol of the cosmic pillar. Thus intimately linked with the sacrifice, he is implored to bestow heavenly gifts on men and to lead man upwards so as to rescue him from all evil: indeed, by ritually imitating the god's three strides, the duly consecrated sacrificer becomes Viṣṇu and attains the highest goal.

The destructive character of Rudra provides a striking contrast to Viṣṇu's benevolence. He is a sinister figure, living in the mountains, clothed in skins; his hair is braided, his colour brown, his belly black and his back red. He is dreaded for his ever-present wrath, whether offended or not, and the blessings he is implored to bestow on man consist largely, though not entirely, of averting his anger. This end is often sought by means of euphemisms such as 'What are we to say to Rudra, the attentive one, the most kind and liberal one, the extremely powerful one, that makes his heart as glad as possible?' (ṚV 1.43.1), and the epithet *śiva*, 'auspicious', applied rarely to Rudra in the *Ṛgveda*, became the name of his successor in post-Vedic mythology. Nevertheless, the worshipper took care to ask Rudra to spare men and cattle, but not to come in person.

Rudra occupies a subordinate position in the *Ṛgveda*. The origin of his name and functions is obscure, but he is sometimes regarded as a storm-god. Though malevolent and aggressive, he is not warlike, and does not engage in conflict with the demons. Although the father of the Maruts, he is never, unlike Indra, associated with their martial exploits. He is also closely associated with Agni. The standard interpretation of his name translates it as 'the howler', but it may derive from roots meaning 'heavenly', 'bright' or 'red' – a colour closely associated with death. In any case, it seems to be an epithet applied only secondarily to him, his personal name having been presumably considered taboo.

Altogether, Rudra appears something of a misfit and a stranger in the *Ṛgveda*. He is not even offered the same sacrifices as the other gods but has to be satisfied with a ball of food thrown down on the ground, the sort of offering made to various local and possibly malevolent spirits. There is every likelihood that Rudra is indeed an incomer to the Vedic pantheon, taken over as the result of contacts with some indigenous group, either the descendants of the Indus Valley Civilisation, looked at later, or some other even less known source.

Unlike the *Ṛgveda*, the *Sāmaveda* is of interest chiefly for its form rather than for its literary or historical content. As ritual became more elaborate – a tendency already apparent in the later parts of the *Ṛgveda* – the functions of different priests came to be demarcated, and the *Sāmaveda* comprises a handbook of the chants or *sāmans* used by the group of priests called *udgātṛs* at the Soma sacrifice. In addition to the text of the verses used, there are four collections of chants (*gānas*) which indicate how they were to be sung. Although, in common with the Vedas as a whole, the notation was not written down until relatively modern times, it seems that the music has been preserved almost as faithfully as the words, and that in style it resembled Western mediaeval plainsong, similarly based on a heptatonic scale. In the *gānas* the words are filled out with various interjections, to make them fit the melodies. The verses themselves are isolated, arranged not into hymns but according to the requirements of the ritual. They are derived almost invariably from the eighth and ninth books of the *Ṛgveda*, though with the variations of detail to be expected from the different purposes of the two collections.

The *Yajurveda* is a more original compilation of ritual material drawn partly from the Ṛgvedic hymns, although in this case the older verses, often adapted to their new use, are supplemented by material which had to be composed to accommodate the wealth of new ceremonies and extraordinary development of ritual detail now taking place. The *yajus* of its title are formulae in prose or verse, muttered (not chanted like the *sāmans*) by the *adhvaryu* priest and his assistants as they actually carried out the sacrifice. Developments from the practices of the *Ṛgveda* include a greater emphasis on the mechanics of the sacrifice itself rather than on the deities behind it, with the consequent emergence of invocations to the sacrificial utensils as symbolising the powers of the gods; spells and riddles occur similar to those to appear in the *Atharvaveda* and the Upaniṣads respectively, and syllables of mystical significance are to be found, such as *oṃ* and *vaṣat,* which later developed into the magical formulae of the Tantras. The gods are still invoked, sometimes in litanies such as the *Śatarudrīya,* a hymn praising Rudra by pronouncing his many names and epithets, thus also allowing the devotee to identify himself mystically with aspects of the deity's nature. Viṣṇu's link with the sacrifice leads to some increase of his prominence.

The *Yajurveda* is not a single work, but has come down to us in two recensions, each with its own sub-recensions. The major recensions are known as the *Black* and the *White Yajurvedas,* though 'pure' might render the latter more accurately; the names are thought to refer to the fact that the *yajus* of the former version have been interspersed or 'adulterated' with prose commentary material, while in the *White Yajurveda* similar material has been collected together into a Brāhmaṇa. A further distinguishing feature is that the second half of the *White Yajurveda* is of demonstrably later date than the first and corresponds to nothing in the more homogeneous *Black Yajurveda.*

The *Atharvaveda* is, like the *Ṛgveda,* a collection of complete hymns rather than isolated verses, but its general lack of connection with sacrificial ceremonial led to some reluctance to accept its authority alongside the other three Vedas. It takes its title from one of the great priestly families (partly mythological) of the *Ṛgveda,* while an older name for it links the Atharvans with that other notable priestly family, the Aṅgirases. It consists of a diverse compilation of spells for every purpose, whether to secure success and wealth, or to procure health and offspring. There is, of course, little basic difference in purpose between the spell and the sacrifice, for both seek to achieve similar ends, and the distinction of subject-matter between the Vedas is by no means absolute; the *Ṛgveda* contains, for instance, a hymn likening the chanting of Brāhmans to frogs croaking (ṚV 7.103), often misunderstood as satirical but in fact a rain charm and used as such up to modern times. So too, the spells of the *Atharvaveda* have been given a priestly veneer throughout, some spells have been included which do pertain to the sacrifice, and its last and latest book, book twenty, seems to have been added specifically to link the work to the sacrificial cult.

There are two recensions of the *Atharvaveda*, with considerable variation between them; the version normally cited is that of Śaunaka. The contents are diverse in date and style, in part due to a conflict between popular origins and subsequent priestly influence. Some of the material may be older even than the *Ṛgveda*, and one seventh of its hymns are drawn from that source (especially the tenth book), but a considerable development in thought took place before the latest parts were composed. Language and metre, too, essentially follow the *Ṛgveda*, though with somewhat greater freedom of versification and some substantial passages of rhythmic prose. Divergences from the linguistic norm are also found, which should be attributed as much to the material's popular origins as to lateness of composition. The style is similarly varied, ranging from obscure, repetitious incantations peopled with a host of evil spirits and demons – the universal stock-in-trade of the commonplace sorcerer – to hymns showing real poetic feeling, sometimes clumsily grafted on to a magical formula, and often adapted to this use from their original purpose. A particular example is a prayer to Varuṇa as overseer of the human conscience (4.16), an imposingly solemn prelude to a banal spell.

The pantheon of the *Ṛgveda* is preserved in the *Atharvaveda*, although the character of Rudra is further developed, with increasing emphasis on his fearsome aspect. His title 'lord of the animals' is indicative of the way in which his character is evolving towards that later attributed to Śiva. Other powers invoked are all manner of spirits, in addition to demons, diseases, animals, healing plants and amulets, with some remarkable hymns addressed to Earth. There is as yet, however, no major female divinity, although bad qualities and disasters tend to be personified as goddesses.

Philosophy in India has always been firmly rooted in practical aspirations, so the presence in the *Atharvaveda* of a greater amount of philosophical speculation than occurs in the other three Vedas is not inappropriate. Knowledge of the true nature of things was seen not merely as a liberating force for the individual concerned, but as a means of acquiring ascendency over his fellows, particularly his enemies, and thus of gaining wealth and temporal success. Cosmogonic themes developed in mystical terms include a eulogy of Virāj, the principle of extension (8.9–10), a hymn on the creation of *puruṣa*, the cosmic man sacrificed by the gods (10.2), the glorification of *skambha*, 'support', a form of the cosmic tree (10.7–8) and of the *brahmacārin*, the Vedic student (11.5), all of them creative principles. *Kāla*, Time, is celebrated as the primordial power (19.53–4), and the *ātman* concept gains in prominence (11.4). Altogether, the *Atharvaveda* provides important evidence of older Vedic thought and, as a forerunner of the oldest Upaniṣads, presents a valuable insight into the continuity and development of Indian speculative reflections.

It must not be forgotten that the religion of the Vedas was an alien culture brought into India by the Aryans. Long before their arrival, probably from about 2500–1700 B.C., there flourished in the Indus basin a highly developed urban culture of which we know in some respects tantalisingly little. Evidence for this Indus Valley Civilisation has been provided by the excavation of several cities, notably Mohenjo-daro and Harappā, now in Pakistan. Interpretation of the extant remains is fraught with difficulty, for no written records have been discovered, and the few brief inscriptions cannot be deciphered with any certainty or plausibility. The civilisation seems to have come to an end a considerable time before the Aryan invasion; nevertheless, it is at least a possibility that some of the beliefs of these people lingered on in popular form, with elements eventually being absorbed into Hinduism alongside those inherited from the Vedas.

Speculation as to the religious ideas of the Indus Valley people centres on a few buildings, a large number of terracotta figurines and an enormous number of carved steatite seals. Various buildings have been identified as temples, largely because they are imposing structures consisting of a large open space, some containing statues; even if these suggestions are correct, the extant remains are as yet insufficient to furnish us with any details of the cult practised there. More significant is the elaborate Great Bath complex at Mohenjo-daro. The tank itself (measuring as much as 39 ft by 23 ft by 8 ft deep) was surrounded by porticoes and sets of rooms, with a stairway which apparently led to an upper storey. Water in suitable quantity is the prime necessity of life, and most primitive religions are concerned with securing the supply. The Indus Valley economy was based on arable farming, rendered possible by a certain amount of artificial control of the river, and while this bath seems to have been for ritual bathing rather than for any practical purpose of water storage, it emphasises the centrality of water to the people's lives. The use of such tanks, and frequent bathing, are important features of modern Indian ritual, and may well continue a custom carried on since the earliest times.

Various stone statues found in the public buildings have sometimes been thought to be cult images. There is little supporting evidence, but even if the identification is valid, it tells us little more about the religious pattern. One bust of a bearded, robed figure has a grave dignity of demeanour more appropriate to a ruler or public official. This uncertainty extends equally to the system of government; the usual assumption of some kind of priestly control rests on the apparent existence of twin capitals (thought impossible under a single ruler) and on the conservatism of so many features of life from urban planning downwards, but other explanations are by no means ruled out.

Numerous other small statues or figurines, mostly of terracotta, have been found, some of which represent a standing female figure with an elaborate head-dress. If these have a religious significance, they probably relate to a domestic cult of a mother goddess, a feature found in many early religions but largely absent from the Vedas. Once again, the evidence is not clearcut: many figures have the bloated shape generally characteristic of fertility deities and considered to represent pregnancy, but it cannot always be determined whether the Indus Valley figures are male or female, and many are also part animal.

The steatite seals present potentially the largest volume of evidence, but the various decorations and inscriptions carved on them may or may not have a religious significance. Some are adorned with patterns or symbols, others depict human or animal figures, or more elaborate scenes. The animals represented are diverse and not always easy to identify, but they include wild and domestic animals of all kinds, including tigers, buffalo, rhinoceros, elephant, goat and cobra. Prominent among them, but by no means all-important, is the bull; occasionally humans are depicted leaping over it. Often we find composite figures of male or female humans with horns and other animal features. One seal, which shows a seated human figure surrounded by animals, has given rise to the confident assertion that it represents a prototype of Śiva Paśupati, 'lord of the animals', but again the sex of the figure cannot be established beyond doubt, and it has been linked with some of the figurines and pronounced a fertility goddess. A number of seals seem to depict a tree deity of indeterminate sex, sometimes with suppliants; one apparently shows the production of vegetation from the spirit's very womb. Other scenes have been interpreted as human sacrifice. In general, the evidence afforded by the material remains of the Indus Valley cities can only be regarded as insufficient to give a true picture of the religious beliefs and practices of their inhabitants, except to demonstrate their total dependence on the forces of nature.

Another possible source for those elements of later Hinduism obviously not from a Vedic background is the Deccan Neolithic culture, which flourished about 2000 to 750 B.C. This culture is known from a number of often sizable ashmounds found in Karnataka and Andhra Pradesh. These ashmounds have resulted from the periodic firing of the dung in the stockades where the pastoral and partially nomadic people involved penned their cattle; some are associated with settlements and some not, presumably representing a seasonal shifting of pasture. These people evidently were very dependent on their cattle and it has been suggested that the firing of the cattle-pens may have been related to some ceremonial connected with the seasonal migrations, just as the worship of cattle and the lighting of lamps or bonfires are associated in the modern festivals of Holī and Dīvālī in the north and Pongal in the south. The use of ash for ritual purposes by followers of Śiva could also conceivably be connected. These conjectures would certainly provide sources for certain aspects in Hinduism of non-Vedic origin but can scarcely be considered as established.

That there was a large influx of deities and spirits from non-Vedic sources into the religion during and after the Vedic period is however indisputable. Perhaps the most obvious feature is their evident local character, for they have fixed places of worship, often outside the settlements on a hill or in a grove. The earliest term to denote such beings, found even in the *Ṛgveda*, is *yakṣa*, essentially denoting some kind of apparition or manifestation of the numinous, perhaps also pointing to the fact that such powers were often represented visibly from an early stage. The term could be applied to anything mysterious, it seems, on the evidence of episodes from two later works treated in subsequent chapters; in one passage of the *Kena Upaniṣad* the gods are puzzled by an apparition, a Yakṣa, who is revealed to be Brahman, the Supreme, while in one episode from the *Mahābhārata* the Yakṣa, at first an invisible water deity, finally declares that he is Dharma, the divine father of Yudhiṣṭhira. Both in the epic *Mahābhārata* and in early Buddhist texts Yakṣas are fairly well known, reflecting the more popular background of both sources by comparison with the Vedic tradition. In fact, Buddhism tended to group under this term several classes of supernatural beings, which the Hindu tradition kept separate, and so to give them an ambivalent character. Within Hinduism the Yakṣas were regarded as generally benevolent and were most commonly honoured by a stone tablet or altar placed under a sacred tree, suggesting an origin in vegetation cults analogous to those which may perhaps be postulated for the Indus Valley Civilisation; within Buddhism, the tree-cult was incorporated into the cult of *caityas*. In later times the Yakṣas' chief is Kubera, the god of wealth and regent of the north, who also has connections with the Rākṣasas, a class of definitely malignant and deceptive beings.

A similarly important element is the veneration of Nāgas, sometimes represented purely as snakes (especially the cobra) and sometimes half human. Of course, even in the *Ṛgveda* Vṛtra is represented as a snake or serpent, but the use of a new term and the attitudes involved in the post-Vedic period indicate a quite different source. Despite the lack of early textual evidence (although Nāgas do occur in the Sūtras, treated in the next chapter), from the wide diffusion of their cult as a subordinate element in many forms of Hinduism it is clear that Nāgas were very ancient objects of worship, a type of chthonic deity obviously significant for good or ill to the peasants themselves. At subsequent periods, Nāgas are incorporated in subsidiary roles into Buddhism in the form of the snake king Mucalinda, into Jainism as the symbol of Pārśva, into Vaiṣṇavism as the cosmic serpent Ananta on whom Viṣṇu rests, and into Śaivism as a garland for Śiva and a weapon for Gaṇeśa; in short they penetrate all the more developed forms of religion, as well as remaining regular objects of worship by the villagers. The earliest evidence so far for temple worship of Nāgas goes back to the first century B.C.

Such are the types of influence that entered the main stream of the religion, blending with the Vedic traditions to form an ever evolving synthesis. Though only fully under way in the periods following the hymns, there is nonetheless, especially in the *Atharvaveda*, evidence that elements from non-Aryan sources were already being absorbed within the Vedic period.

CHAPTER TWO

Impersonal Trends

An inevitable result of the *Ṛgveda*'s long period of composition is that the religious practices and ideas it depicts undergo a considerable development, so that the tenth book diverges from its predecessors in several respects. The earlier books present two basic analogies or metaphors in their cosmogonic myths, one deriving from the craftsman's activity, the other from natural parentage. In addition to some examples already given, we may note their combination in the role of Tvaṣṭṛ, the divine carpenter or architect, who in some hymns is declared to have fashioned Heaven and Earth, Dyaus and Pṛthivī, themselves regarded as the divine parents. These views persist in the tenth book, as when one poet asks, 'What was the wood, what was the tree out of which they shaped heaven and earth?' (ṚV 10.31.7ab=81.4ab), but increasingly the tendency is to indulge in more nearly philosophic than mythological speculation. The transition is seen in hymns such as 10.72, where the poet announces his intention of proclaiming 'the births of the gods' and speaks of Bṛhaspati as a smith, but then goes on to say: 'In the first age of the gods, being was born from non-being', before relapsing into more mythological imagery. In the pair of hymns 10.81–2 addressed to Viśvakarman, the 'maker of all', a term applied on occasion to Indra is turned into a more abstract deity, represented as creating the world through sacrifice and as having on all sides eyes, faces, arms and feet, but another explanation is also offered in terms of a 'first embryo', a world egg floating on the waters of chaos, out of which Viśvakarman apparently arises. The theme of an original sacrifice comes more clearly to the fore in the hymn 10.90 to *puruṣa*, the cosmic person. This *puruṣa* is first described, in similar fashion to Viśvakarman, as having a thousand heads, eyes and feet, and then it is declared that only one quarter of him is manifest in creation; there is thus maintained here and elsewhere – as in 1.164.45 where Vāc, sacred speech, similarly has only one quarter manifest – the understanding that divine reality is greater than the world, a panentheistic rather than a pantheistic approach. But overall the emphasis is on the creative function of sacrifice and ritual in general, revealing the continuing links between the ritualistic and speculative approaches. From this primeval man, sacrificed by the gods, are produced Indra, Agni and Vāyu, the atmosphere, heaven and earth, and the compass-points, animals and birds, and man; specifically the four classes of society are said to issue from different parts of his anatomy, the only mention of this system in the *Ṛgveda* and in itself an indication of the lateness of this hymn. Dissatisfaction with existing solutions is still more pointedly expressed in hymn 10.121, which gives in successive verses an impressive description of a creator deity, beginning with the concept of the golden embryo or germ, but ends each verse with the question, 'to which god shall we offer worship with an oblation?' as if to ask which god measures up to such a description, an impression strengthened by its partial imitation of an earlier panegyric to Indra (2.12). Its force has been somewhat blunted by the later addition (betrayed in its textual transmission) of a final verse naming Prajāpati, 'the lord of creatures', a deity otherwise unknown to the *Ṛgveda* but frequent in the Brāhmaṇas.

The culmination of this trend is seen in 10.129, which begins: 'Non-being did not exist, nor did being at that time; there was no atmosphere nor firmament beyond it. What enveloped it, where, whose the protection? Was there water, profound and deep?' The agnosticism and scepticism here apparent are reinforced in the last two verses which, after declaring that the gods are later than creation, assert that 'he who is its overseer in the highest firmament, he no doubt knows or else he does not'. Thus, instead of the gods or even one supreme creator deity as agents of creation, we now have *asat*, non-being or the unreal, and *sat*, being or the real, evolving together (by contrast with 10.72.2–3) under the impulse of desire from That One, a pre-existing indefinable entity, which is their common origin and in which there is no duality or differentiation.

Such trends originated earlier, of course, and are also to be found in other parts of Vedic literature. The verse of hymn 1.164 already mentioned which declares that only one quarter of Vāc is manifest on earth is followed by the often quoted, and misunderstood, verse in which she, as the principle of ritualistic utterance, is declared to be That One, which seers speak of variously as Indra, Mitra, Varuṇa, Agni and so forth

(1.164.46). Thus here in the context of the ritual and in the form of the riddling contests (*brahmodya*), in which the nature of the sacred power *brahman* was enigmatically revealed as part of such rituals, the same tendency was earlier manifest of reducing all phenomena, including the gods, to some unitary principle. This same hymn occurs virtually in its entirety in the *Atharvaveda*, as hymns 9.9–10, while one of its images, that of the two birds perching on the same tree, one of which eats while the other looks on (1.164.20–2), is taken up in the Upaniṣads and later.

The *Atharvaveda* does indeed include rather more speculative hymns than the *Ṛgveda*. Interestingly, it uses the term *brahman* both to denote its own incantations and to name the universal principle, or rather it would be more accurate to say that the term now possesses both meanings simultaneously, for example when Brahman is the origin of both *sat* and *asat* and is also linked with Vāc (AV 4.1.1–2); the linkage lies in the emphasis on ritual activity and in particular on its expression through ritual speech. The *Atharvaveda* also employs other images or descriptions of the ultimate cosmic principle, several of them of a relatively material and even mechanical nature. A pair of hymns (AV 10.7–8) are devoted to the extolling of *skambha* 'support' or more generally 'framework' as the basis on which the universe is erected and within which are both the non-existent and the existent; the second hymn also passes on to other themes, concluding with an apparent declaration of *ātman* as the cosmic principle. Another hymn on *prāṇa* 'breath' (AV 11.4) sees that both as the breath of life in the individual and as the wind animating the universe. Exceptionally within the Indian tradition, another pair of hymns (19.53–4, in fact artificially divided) make of *kāla* 'Time' a first principle, declaring that it is by Time that everything has been created and set in motion, from the sun's course onwards, and thus even Prajāpati, 'the lord of creatures', was produced in the beginning by Time; the image of the chariot is transferred to him from Sūrya and includes the striking figure of immortality pictured as the axle around which everything revolves.

However, despite the speculative aspect of such hymns, the ritual emphasis is still in general the dominant one and is itself also tending towards a more impersonal view.

The next stage of the Vedic literature following the hymns consists of the Brāhmaṇas which, as their name indicates, deal with and expound *brahman,* the sacred power above all now manifested in the sacrificial ritual. They are voluminous prose works which collect together a large mass of views and discussions on the ritual and also on the stanzas of the hymns employed in the various rites. Each is linked to the requirements of a particular priest in the ritual, as are the hymn collections to which they are assigned; thus the Brāhmaṇas of the *Ṛgveda* are intended for the use of the invoking priest (*hotṛ*), those of the *Yajurveda* for the officiating priest (*adhvaryu*) and those of the *Sāmaveda* for the chanting priest (*udgātṛ*), while later in imitation of these a Brāhmaṇa was attached to the *Atharvaveda.* While the Brāhmaṇas of the *Yajurveda* closely follow the ritual and the *Black Yajurveda* shows an intermingling of hymns and Brāhmaṇa, those of the other Vedas are less tied to it. This indicates that the Brāhmaṇas began as appendices to the liturgical parts of the hymn collections but later became independent, growing by addition and possibly reworking to their present bulk. The exponents of this tradition are indeed often members of the same families which were prominent as 'seers' of the *Ṛgveda.*

The Indians themselves usually divide the contents of the Brāhmaṇas into two major categories: rules and explanations. The texts primarily give rules for the performance of the individual sacrificial rites and from this central theme of ritual all discussions start. The compilers' aim, however, was not just to describe the rites – in fact they assume an audience well acquainted with the course of the ritual – but to explain the origin, purpose and meaning of the ritual acts and to establish their validity and significance. Consequently, the texts also include much mythology and legend, and involve speculative etymologies and speculations on the connection of ceremonial details with each other and with the hymns, as well as dealing with local variations in performance and variations due to circumstance. The Brāhmaṇas are indeed extremely discursive texts, taking in much that is only marginally relevant to their basic concern of ritual but often of considerable interest for charting the development of Indian culture.

The number of Brāhmaṇas is reputed to be very great and certainly many quotations from lost Brāhmaṇas are preserved in other literature, but the number even of those extant is by no means small. The Brāhmaṇas of the *Black Yajurveda* are generally considered the oldest, with the *Taittirīya Brāhmaṇa* forming a continuation of the *yajus* section, though not necessarily later, for both parts are complementary as though each presupposed the other. Next come the two Brāhmaṇas attached to the *Ṛgveda*; the more important is the *Aitareya*, the essential part of which deals with the Soma sacrifice, the other sacrifices being reserved for the *Kauṣītaki Brāhmaṇa*, which, besides repeating the description of the Soma, covers the setting up of the sacred fire, the daily morning and evening offering, the new and full moon ritual, and the four-monthly sacrifices. Then follow the major Brāhmaṇas of the *Sāmaveda*, the *Pañcaviṃśa* and *Jaiminīya Brāhmaṇas*. To the *White Yajurveda* belongs the *Śatapatha Brāhmaṇa*, the best known, most extensive and probably most important of them all. Unusually for the Brāhmaṇas, which are mostly fairly uniform but not unified texts, there is considerable internal difference within it. In part this reflects two separate traditions, one of which cites as its authoritative teacher Yājñavalkya and the other Śāṇḍilya, who is the authority for the construction of the fire-altar dealt with in sections six to nine of the more commonly cited of its two recensions. The last of the major Brāhmaṇas is the *Gopatha Brāhmaṇa* associated with the *Atharvaveda*, which is divided into two sections; the first shows considerable originality, especially in its glorification of the *Atharvaveda* and its priests, whereas the second is a collection of more or less literal borrowings from other Brāhmaṇas compiled to fit it into the accepted pattern.

Many of the legends preserved among the 'explanations' of the Brāhmaṇas have their parallels elsewhere. The story of the nymph Urvaśī and her love for the mortal prince Purūravas embodies a near universal theme and provides the plot of one of the greatest plays of Sanskrit literature. The story of Manu who on the advice of a fish that he has helped builds a boat and so saves himself from a deluge that overwhelms all living creatures has obvious analogies to the Middle Eastern flood myth. Another dramatic legend is that of Śunaḥśepa: he is the second of three sons of an impoverished Brāhman, who agrees to sell him as a substitute for the son whom a king has vowed to sacrifice to Varuṇa in return for healing; the story has a happy ending in that Śunaḥśepa, about to be slaughtered by his father (who has agreed to do the deed for further reward), sings hymns of praise to the gods and thus moves Varuṇa to compassion. Here the sacrificial context is obvious and it also explicitly provides the framework of a well-known aetiological myth of how Agni escaped from a king and his priest as they were sacrificing, and burnt up the country stretching down the Ganges basin, an interesting combination of Agni's aspects as the forest fire clearing ground for cultivation and as the sacrificial fire ceremonially purifying such newly-cleared territory.

Such material is in one sense peripheral to the main concerns of the Brāhmaṇas but it nevertheless attests an important factor in their thinking. In Vedic thought, as in the Iranian tradition, there was a conception of the world as due not to a chance encounter of elements but as governed by an objective order, inherent in the nature of things, of which the gods are only the guardians. By the period of the Brāhmaṇas, these fundamental laws of the universe came increasingly to be identified with the laws of sacrifice. *Dharma,* which replaces the older term *ṛta,* is then supremely the sacrificial act which in effect conditions and maintains the cosmic order. Originally an act of homage to the deities of the cult, consisting of a gift or oblation made in order to obtain certain benefits, the sacrifice has become ever more complex and its significance correspondingly enlarged. The Brāhmaṇas elaborate a classification of sacrifice into three types, the vegetable and other oblations, the animal sacrifices and the Soma sacrifice, although the animal sacrifices were often subsumed under the Soma sacrifices. The sacrifice is performed on behalf of an individual householder, technically called the sacrificer, accompanied by his wife, but all the ritual acts are performed by priests, varying in number from one to sixteen and ultimately seventeen officiants in the full Soma sacrifice; there were also certain regular and simpler rituals which the householder performed himself. A special area is consecrated for each performance of a ritual and the sacrificer undergoes a consecration setting him apart from the profane world. In essence the sacrifice can be regarded as a periodic ritual by which the universe is recreated, with the sacrificer like his prototype Prajāpati incorporating the universe.

Indeed, the construction of the altar is conceived as a creation of the world from the basic elements of earth and water.

In this cyclical process the gifts to the priests in attendance originally represented the redistribution involved but inevitably as concepts changed came to be seen as the fee paid for the performance of the ritual, for in the course of development the cyclical ritual was broken up into separate sacrifices. Thus the original pattern of the redistribution of impurity was disrupted and the sacrifice became more and more the exclusive domain of purity opposed to the impurity outside. This is shown in the marked aversion to killing visible in the texts; according to their descriptions the animal is killed by suffocation outside the sacrificial site proper, not as no doubt originally by decapitation at the sacrificial stake, which nevertheless continues to be endowed with great symbolic significance as the symbol of the cosmic axis and simultaneously a form of the tree of life. Originally, as indeed in the myth of the cosmic sacrifice of *puruṣa* (ṚV 10.90), the sacrifice was a sacrifice of the sacrificer himself and then successively of increasingly remote substitutes. This evolution is mentioned in more than one Brāhmaṇa, which tell us that the gods first killed the man (*puruṣa*) as the victim, but when he had been slain, the sacrificial essence in him went to the horse; then from the horse it similarly went to the ox, then to the sheep, then to the goat, where it remained for a very long time; then it entered the earth and from the earth entered the rice of which the sacrificial cake is made; thus, the sacrificial cake contains the sacrificial essence. There could hardly be a clearer statement of the history of its transformation.

This is not of course to say that animal sacrifice had been abolished by substitution in the Brāhmaṇa period, simply that this was the trend being encouraged by their authors who would have been drawn from among the more reflective Brāhmans. Indeed, there is ample evidence that animal sacrifices continued for centuries. The great horse sacrifice is a case in point, where its direct links with the values of a warrior aristocracy and specifically kingship would have opposed their more robust attitudes to the Brāhmans' sensibilities. In a sense it represents the peak of Indian sacrificial pageantry, being spread out over a full year and involving thousands to some extent in its performance. By this horse sacrifice the king asserted a claim to sovereignty over his neighbours, a claim directly embodied in the wanderings of the sacrificial horse, which was ceremonially set free to roam for a year before its ritual immolation. Throughout the year various ceremonies took place leading to the climax when, after an elaborate consecration undergone by the king, the horse was slaughtered at the end of a three-day ritual along with numerous other victims. The horse is an image of fertility and a symbol of power; both it and the king had to abstain from sexual intercourse throughout the year and immediately after its slaughter the chief queen mimed intercourse with it, thus channelling its energies for the prosperity of the kingdom.

Overall, however, the understanding of the sacrifice was changing. The symbolism involved was being developed into an elaborate system of correspondences. Systems of classification have always played an important part in man's attempts to understand and control his environment, just as they still do in modern scientific enquiry. As soon as man exercises his mental abilities to draw inferences about and gain an understanding of the various phenomena around him, he begins to classify those categories which seem most significant on the basis of supposed common features and to study their interrelations. For knowledge of the relevant interrelations enables the extension of influence or control from one category to another. In the Brāhmaṇas the idea already found in some of the later hymns that sacrifice created the world is developed into the view that the correct performance of sacrifice regulates the maintenance of the world and that the rituals produce their effects by their own power, often designated *brahman,* which resides in the connections between the ritual process and the cosmic order. Observing that certain effects seem regularly to follow preceding events, the Brāhmaṇas attempt to exploit the assumed cause-effect relationship (and modern medicine similarly exploits the effects of some drugs without a full knowledge of the mechanism involved). Concentration on the sacrificial ritual as such is in these terms entirely rational. However, it alters the balance between the various parties involved. The gods, to whom the sacrifice was once directed for their gratification, become increasingly irrelevant as the act itself assumes greater significance and correspondingly the importance of the priestly officiants increases. As one of the Brāhmaṇas so succinctly puts it: 'Truly there are two sorts of gods, for the deities indeed are gods and the Brāhmans who have studied and teach religion are human gods; sacrifice to them is of two sorts: oblations form the sacrifice to the deities and gifts to the priests that to the human gods' (Śat.Br.2.2.2.6). The pretensions of the Brāhmans, who alone were qualified by birth and training to act as officiants, were practically unbounded and of course served to reinforce the trend towards regarding the sacrifice as the centre of everything.

The older gods to whom the sacrifice was offered inevitably decline in importance and those more intimately connected with the ritual and its symbolism become more prominent. Thus Prajāpati becomes in some ways the chief god, while Viśvakarman is identified with him, for the creative principle is now concentrated in Prajāpati, 'the lord of creatures'; but his role is completed in the act of creation, which empties him of his substance. Prajāpati creates the world by 'heating' himself through asceticism (*tapas*), whereby he splits himself in two or mates with a female deity produced from himself, sometimes Vāc 'Speech' or his daughter Uṣas, the dawn; from this initial creative act everything then emerges through a series of transformations. Viṣṇu, who had already risen in importance in the *Yajurveda,* is regarded as the personification of the sacrifice and it is also stated that Prajāpati in his creative activity imitated Viṣṇu, who is thus directly equated with Prajāpati, elsewhere similarly identified with *puruṣa*; the elements which will make up developed Vaiṣṇavism are beginning to coalesce. Rudra, now often called Śiva, is also mentioned quite frequently and now has a benign aspect, although in general his malevolence is still more prominent. In contrast to the other gods dwelling in the east, Rudra lives in the inauspicious north.

In other respects the Brāhmaṇas more obviously represent a transition phase. There is no single view about the future life and the texts rarely give any detail of the way in which man is rewarded or punished after death. The dominant view is that of immortality in heaven, the abode of the gods. At times we find ideas of how man dissolves into various natural phenomena; the funeral fire is occasionally called the third birth of man; and one text, in the context of the annual reawakening of nature, declares that a man who knows this is indeed born again in this world but it is more probable that continuity through descendants is meant than personal rebirth. The very evident cyclic pattern in nature has come to have a profound influence on all aspects of thought in India. Nonetheless the Brāhmaṇas contain hints for the development of the doctrine of rebirth, even though individual immortality is the main tendency. But there also appears the doctrine of repeated dying (*punarmṛtyu*), the possibility that the future life may also have a limit, that the literal meaning of immortality, freedom from death, may not be gained so easily.

However, even in their main concerns of the ritual, the Brāhmaṇas show a development that goes beyond themselves. In later parts of the Brāhmaṇas and in the Āraṇyakas appended to them is seen a growing pre-occupation among their composers, and presumably among the officiants generally, with the ultimate basis of this ritually maintained cosmos. This ultimate is identified with certain ritualistic principles (whether Vāc or Agni) or with a divine creator embodied in the sacrifice, given personal attributes in some circles but more and more identified among the officiants with the creative principles of ritual. Indeed the Brāhmaṇas, for all their ritualism and formalism, are closer in spirit to the Upaniṣads than to the *Ṛgveda* in so far as they emphasise the importance of knowledge, of a real understanding of the inner meaning of the matters discussed. Their elaborate debates on the ritual and its significance in a very real sense give rise to the cosmic and metaphysical speculations of the Upaniṣads.

The ritualistic concerns of the Brāhmaṇas, however, were not exclusively theoretical and on their more practical side were continued in the areas of study which became known as the six 'limbs of the Veda' (*vedāṅga*), phonetics, metrics, grammar, etymology, ritual practice and astronomy, probably developed between the eighth and fourth centuries B.C. It is interesting to note that four of them are concerned with language, illustrating the degree of concern shown for the exact wording of the hymns and their correct recitation. The texts concerned with ritual practice were sub-divided into three: the Śrautasūtras, so called because the major public ceremonies detailed in them are literally those in accordance with *śruti* (the heard or revealed scripture of the Veda), the Gṛhyasūtras, detailing the more domestic rites, and the Dharmasūtras, dealing with the customary law and practice and in some ways forming a continuation of the Gṛhyasūtras. These Sūtras (literally 'threads', strings of rules) were regarded as part of human tradition, authoritative only so far as they were based on *śruti.* As manuals for the actual performance of the ritual, the Sūtras are terse in expression in marked contrast to the discursive style of the Brāhmaṇas but nevertheless occasionally preserve material not found in the Brāhmaṇas. In general the ritual detailed in them agrees with that discussed in the Brāhmanas but sometimes reveals a later stage of development.

The rituals dealt with in the Śrautasūtras are the major ceremonies which in general were not obligatory but might be undertaken for the fulfilment of certain wishes. Even more clearly than in the Brāhmaṇas such rituals present a highly rationalised system of symbols for the relations governing the cosmos, enabling the officiant who understands them to manipulate the universe. These rites were to be performed with three or five fires set up at a special rite by the sacrificer and his wife, whereas the domestic rites were performed on a single fire, kindled at marriage and constantly maintained thereafter. The Gṛhyasūtras and Dharmasūtras are of interest because they preserve the more domestic side of religion practised by the ordinary householder. The actual domestic rites are fairly simple, some to be performed regularly and some on important occasions, but the Gṛhyasūtras also include a large number of traditional rules for the religious life of the household, typically laid out in accordance with the different stages of a man's life, from marriage through the ceremonies connected with the conception and birth of children to the funeral rites and memorial rituals; the investiture with the sacred thread, which marks the formal initiation of a young man as a member of one of the three higher classes, is a particularly important rite and forms the start of the student phase of life.

The aim of the Dharmasūtras is to teach *dharma,* the rules of conduct producing spiritual merit, in accordance with each individual's situation. For his religious duties vary according to a man's status and thus the texts broadly speaking formulate those for a Brāhman at different stages of life and then note the different requirements for the other three classes. The difference from the Gṛhyasūtras lies in the treatment of the material. Whereas, for instance, the Gṛhyasūtras typically start with marriage as the sacrament that begins the householder stage (and thus the domestic rites), the Dharmasūtras, having given the regulations governing life as a student, then reach the rules about marriage and lay down conditions for the validity of a marriage. But this is still, as it were, canon law rather than civil law and similarly penalties laid down are in the form of penances, unenforceable except by conscience or public opinion. Ethical and ultimately legal elements enter in, but the overall framework is still the ritual requirements derived from the Brāhmaṇas.

A further development of the Vedic literature proper is the Āraṇyakas which form the concluding portions of several Brāhmaṇas. Their name Āraṇyaka 'forest book' indicates that they were not for general circulation and so studied in seclusion in the forest because of their abstruse nature or perhaps their dangerous mystical power; they are not particularly connected with the third stage of life, of retirement to the forest. Most of them are composite works, containing hymn, Brāhmaṇa and Sūtra elements, and in both language and content they form a transition between the predominantly ritualistic Brāhmaṇas and the predominantly speculative Upaniṣads, which are either incorporated within them or more usually form their conclusion.

There are two Āraṇyakas attached to the *Ṛgveda*, the *Aitareya* and the *Kauṣītaki*, included in the Brāhmaṇas of the same name. The five sections of the *Aitareya Āraṇyaka* are sometimes designated as separate Āraṇyakas: the first deals with the Soma liturgy from a purely ritual point of view, the second contains speculations on *prāṇa* ('breath') and *puruṣa* as cosmic principles (and concludes with the *Aitareya Upsaniṣad*), the third deals with the symbolic meaning of the methods of recitation of the *Ṛgveda*, and the last two are really Sūtras in style and content. In the *Black Yajurveda* tradition, the *Taittirīya Āraṇyaka* shows a mixture of verse, on the horse sacrifice, the human sacrifice and the fire altar, and prose; in the *White Yajurveda* the last book of the *Śatapatha Brāhmaṇa* is termed an Āraṇyaka, the name of which also applies to the Upaniṣad which completes it, the *Bṛhadāraṇyaka Upaniṣad*.

The Āraṇyakas in effect concede that the exact performance of a highly complex ritual as developed in the Brāhmaṇas could not be expected from all. They do not on the whole lay down rules for the performance of sacrifice or comment on the ceremonial detail but mainly expound the mysticism and symbolism involved; meditation and understanding rather than performance is the theme of their teaching and they tend to substitute a simpler ceremonial for the complex Brāhmaṇa ritual. The earlier equation of austerity or asceticism (*tapas*) with sacrifice is extended and instead of the external offerings of the sacrifice there is developed the concept of inner sacrifice, in which physiological functions replace libations and ritual objects; the *Kauṣītaki Āraṇyaka* in particular expounds the *prāṇāgnihotra*, 'the fire oblation through breath', as a substitute for the basic rite. This idea of the inner, mental offering as distinguished from the outer, formal sacrifice is an important element in the transition from the Brāhmaṇas to the Upaniṣads.

Although formally continuations through the Āraṇyakas of the Brāhmaṇas, the older Upaniṣads can also be regarded as a natural continuation of the creation hymns in the tenth book of the *Ṛgveda* and of certain cosmological hymns of the *Atharvaveda*. Their name is interpreted as meaning either 'a sitting down near' as of pupils around their teacher, often with a hint of esotericism, or as 'a setting alongside', that is a comparison or connection, the establishment of mystical equivalences and symbolic identities. The closeness of their connection with the preceding Vedic literature varies. The oldest Upaniṣads, from perhaps as early as the eighth century B.C., are properly Vedic in that they are closely associated with their Brāhmaṇas and are in the same prose style, with some gnomic verses and occasional lyric passages. This group, consisting of the *Bṛhadāraṇyaka*, *Chāndogya*, *Aitareya*, *Taittirīya* and *Kauṣītaki Upaniṣads*, contains the teachings of approximately a hundred individuals, of whom many also appear in the Brāhmaṇas and who appear from their interrelationships to span five generations or something over a century in time. The *Bṛhadāraṇyaka* and *Chāndogya Upaniṣads* in particular originated from the combination of several texts which were probably once separate Upaniṣads, and basically the same texts are sometimes found in several Upaniṣads.

A second group consists of Upaniṣads which are similarly incorporated into Brāhmaṇas but where the link is nonetheless not so intimate; the earliest in this group are metrical but this gives way to a mixture of prose and verse and then prose. In their probable chronological order, the Upaniṣads in this group are the *Kena*, *Īśa*, *Kaṭha*, *Śvetāśvatara*, *Praśna*, *Muṇḍaka*, *Mahānārāyaṇa*, *Māṇḍūkya* and *Maitrī*. These two groups between them contain the fourteen Upaniṣads which, with minor variations, are those usually considered early and significant. A third group of Upaniṣads, of which the connection with Vedic schools is purely nominal or altogether lacking, are undoubtedly later, many of them being of sectarian origin, and indeed works entitled Upaniṣad have continued to be produced up to modern times.

Most of the Upaniṣads are in dialogue form and there are also occasional records of great set debates where many individuals competed for a prize. These recall the enigmas and debating contests (*brahmodyas*) set in the ritual context occurring in earlier literature. Indeed, one of the earliest and most famous of such occasions in the Upaniṣads takes place when King Janaka performs a sacrifice and organises a debating contest, at which the prize is a thousand cows each with ten gold pieces on her horns (BĀU 3.1.1). Incidentally, this episode, like many others, shows that those who took part in the Upaniṣadic debates were by no means regularly those who had renounced society to dwell in the forest. Yājñavalkya, the victor on this occasion, who stakes his claim to the cows even before the contest starts, is a prominent figure in the Upaniṣads and is clearly very much in society until the point, also recorded, when he does retire to the forest after making an equitable distribution between his two wives; is there indeed a hint of sarcasm when the king asks Yājñavalkya next time he presents himself 'What is your reason for coming? Do you want cattle or subtle debate?' Equally, other debaters beside King Janaka himself, who figures elsewhere more directly (a feature which goes back to the *Śatapatha Brāhmaṇa*), are of aristocratic rather than Brāhman background. It is noteworthy that the idea of rebirth, which appears as a decided novelty in the two oldest Upaniṣads, is taught by a *kṣatriya*, a member of the ruling class. There are several other clear indications that these speculations were not the exclusive preserve of the Brāhmans. Indeed, the passages associated with the *kṣatriyas*, which often contain the greatest innovations, may well be distinguishable from the brāhmanic material by their inclusion of verses in *śloka* metre, the standard metre of the martial epics. It seems plausible that ideas from outside the Aryan community were filtering in through the medium of the less conservative *kṣatriyas*.

On the other hand, the Upaniṣads inherit from the Brāhmaṇas and earlier the propensity to relate one line of speculation to another, continuing the definitely magical element found alike in the ritual and speculative material. Speculation at the cosmic level now centres on the identity and nature of Brahman, the sacred power which resides in the sacrificial ritual and thus, with the claim that the sacrifice maintains the world, comes to be regarded as the power underlying the universe. Nevertheless, the early speculations in the Upaniṣads on the nature of Brahman are basically materialistic with this principle identified either as food or as breath or as both. But it is from this type of ultimately ritual speculation that there comes this aspect of Upaniṣadic thinking, that the world has Brahman as its inner essence and emanates from Brahman, which is therefore the underlying reality behind everything.

The other main aspect of Upaniṣadic thought clearly owes much to a tendency towards inwardness, fostered by dissatisfaction with the externals of religion; this is the concept of the *ātman*, the permanent self or soul lying within. One of the commonest terms also for *ātman* is *prāṇa*, 'breath', and several passages deal with this *prāṇa* or with its relations to the organs of the self (speech, breath, sight, hearing and thought), which correspond to the five natural forces (fire, wind, sun, the directions and the moon). For the thinkers of the Upaniṣads still attach the greatest importance to systems of correspondences. Indeed, this underlies the identification which comes to be made between the basic principle in man and the basic principle of the universe; in a real sense the identification of *ātman* with Brahman is simply the logical outcome of older types of thinking. Nevertheless, once made such an identification has profound implications which the Upaniṣads themselves only begin to explore. Although use of the term *ātman* in something like this sense goes back at least to the *Atharvaveda*, there is a definite possibility that an emphasis on a plurality of selves enmeshed in rebirth but capable of achieving liberation from it, which is found in Jainism and is elaborated within Hinduism by the Sāṃkhya system, is a contribution to Hinduism from non-Aryan sources here brought into a synthesis with the other speculations of the Upaniṣads in the Brahman-*ātman* equation, with the subsequent tendency to suggest that there is only one *ātman*. The nature of this inner essence of man is by no means fully explored but as early as the *Bṛhadāraṇyaka Upaniṣad* there appears the view that the *ātman* is of the nature of pure consciousness, which is the ground of all our experiences.

While Brahman and *ātman* are the main preoccupations of the thinkers found in the Upaniṣads, there are many other speculations put forward and there is nothing like a consensus. The later claims by the Vedānta system that the Upaniṣads teach a single consistent doctrine (on which however the system's sub-schools disagree), should not blind us to the fact that they contain a heterogeneous assortment of speculations, ranging from the relatively primitive to the sophisticated, which is the more remarkable in the light of the early stage of development as yet reached by Indian culture generally. The only way to do justice to this variety – and to appreciate the evolution of ideas over the period – is to examine, however briefly, the individual Upaniṣads.

The *Bṛhadāraṇyaka Upaniṣad*, belonging to the *White Yajurveda*, illustrates very well the link between Brāhmaṇas and Upaniṣads. The opening sections of its first part unfold the elaborate and awesome symbolism of the horse sacrifice and identify the sacrificial horse with Prajāpati in his cosmogonic self-immolation. This exaltation of the horse and also of the *arka* plant, followed by the *mṛtyu* (death) theme, is basically of the Āraṇyaka type and is obviously linked with the thirteenth section of the *Śatapatha Brāhmaṇa*, which closes with just such speculations and is associated with Śāṇḍilya. By contrast, the central part of the Upaniṣad (2–4) forms an extension of the fourteenth section of the *Śatapatha Brāhmaṇa* and is essentially the Upaniṣad of the Yājñavalkya school, to which are appended two sections of more miscellaneous origin. It is quite in keeping with such a background, and with its probable priority among the Upaniṣads, that the *Bṛhadāraṇyaka Upaniṣad* moves from the theme of the horse to that of death and presents the view that repeated death – a concept first appearing in the Brāhmaṇas – is something which the possessor of certain kinds of knowledge can ward off (B Ā U 1.2.7 and 1.5.2.).

The idea of rebirth as such appears first in an account found in its supplementary section and also in slightly fuller form in the *Chāndogya Upaniṣad* (B Ā U 6.2 and Ch.Up.5.3–10). Śvetaketu, son of Uddālaka Āruṇi, comes to the court of a Pañcāla ruler, presumably seeking reward for sacrificing or for teaching, and is asked by the prince a series of five questions about a person's fate at death. Śvetaketu cannot answer them and neither can his father, to whom he hurries back. So Uddālaka goes to ask the answers from the prince who is reluctant to reveal them, claiming that this knowledge has not hiterto been imparted to any Brāhman, and only relents when Uddālaka declares that he comes to him as a pupil to a teacher, a significant role reversal. The prince, Pravāhana Jaivali, then propounds in terms of fire as the underlying principle a theory of transmigration in which the conditions of rebirth are exclusively determined by one's knowledge. However, a more developed view is given in another passage (BĀU 4.4) where, using among others the image of the caterpillar looping itself from one blade of grass to another, Yājñavalkya roundly declares that rebirth is determined by one's actions (*karma*) and that release is achieved through knowledge. So too in the *Chāndogya Upaniṣad* version, Pravāhana declares that *karma* is what controls one's rebirth, while in another version of the story in the *Kauṣītaki Upaniṣad* (the prince is differently named) the progression from death to rebirth is simplified and knowledge and action combined determine the conditions of rebirth.

The great intuitive and mystical thinker, Yājñavalkya, is especially associated with King Janaka of Videha and thus with the east of North India. He appears only in the *Bṛhadāraṇyaka* and *Chāndogya Upaniṣads.* whereas his teacher Uddālaka Āruṇi figures also in the *Kauṣītaki Upaniṣad*; Uddālaka tends to be critical of traditional views and to take a scientific attitude towards nature. Among the teaching which Yājñavalkya propounds to Janaka is that concerning the three states of the self (BĀU 4.3). In its normal waking state the self exists in the mundane world, influenced to the greatest extent by externals; in the state of dreaming, the self creates for itself and inhabits its own interior world; beyond these and even more important is the state of deep sleep in which alone a man achieves the greatest bliss possible, for it is only in this state that the dichotomy of the world into a conscious subject and an external object is superseded by a unitary experience. This is indeed a characteristic insight of Yājñavalkya and in the famous discourse to his wife Maitreyī, after asserting that everything else is dear to us because the *ātman* is dear to us, he shows that everything comes together in it, which consists of nothing but knowledge and yet transcends knowledge in its essential unity: 'For where there is indeed duality, there one sees another, there one smells another, . . . there one knows another; but where the whole of this has indeed become the *ātman*, then how and what would one see, . . . then how and what would one know? How would one understand him through whom one knows all this? That *ātman* is not like this or like that. . . . How assuredly can one know the knower?' (B Ā U 4.5.15 cf. 2.4.14).

The *Chāndogya Upaniṣad*, after two introductory chapters expounding the mystery of the *sāman*, embarks on various speculations about *ātman* and Brahman in the course of which the declaration is made 'This is my *ātman* within the heart, this is Brahman' and attributed to Śāṇḍilya, after whom this equation of *ātman* and Brahman was subsequently known. Śvetaketu, who was unable to answer Pravāhana's questions, appears also in the next episode where, after twelve years study of the Vedas, he fails to answer his father's question about that 'by which the unheard becomes the heard, the unthought becomes the thought, the unknown becomes the known' (Ch.Up.6.2.3). Uddālaka then in the rest of this sixth chapter, often called the *sadvidyā* 'the knowledge of the existent', teaches his son the identity of *ātman* and Brahman. In the first section Uddālaka declares that individual objects are only the matter of which they are made and that only formless matter is real. In the opening words of the second section he takes issue with the hymn 10.72 of the *Ṛgveda* declaring: 'Originally this was Being, one alone; some say that this was Non-being originally, one alone and that from Non-being Being was born.' Uddālaka thus challenges on the grounds of logic the view that existence came out of non-existence, denying the possibility of creation *ex nihilo*. These first two sections are perhaps one source of the later Sāṃkhya theory of causation that the effect pre-exists in its substantial cause. This Being, *sat*, is then expounded also in the next two sections as the essence of the universe, producing the three basic components of fire, water and earth, followed in sections five to eight by the doctrine of its being the essence of man; then in the second half of the chapter, Uddālaka begins a series of examples, mostly taken from the natural world, to inculcate his insight, concluding each with his famous dictum

'You are that' (*tat tvam asi*). This Being is here particularly identified with the *ātman* and with Truth, *satya* (sections eleven and fifteen) and the text does not use the name Brahman, but Vedānta later holds that the Being referred to is Brahman. The enacted images in sections twelve and thirteen are particularly effective: Uddālaka tells Śvetaketu to break open a banyan fruit, then to divide one of the seeds inside, asks him what he sees and declares that the subtle principle which he cannot perceive is the essence of the banyan, and similarly he tells him to put some salt in water then later to fetch it and, when he cannot recover it, to taste the water, thus revealing the salt's pervasion of the water.

This more profound instruction is imparted by Uddālaka after his son has finished his Vedic studies and to humble some of his pride in his learning. Still more pointedly in the next chapter Sanatkumāra dismisses all Nārada's Vedic learning as mere verbal knowledge, incapable of providing the clue to liberation, before leading him through a lengthy series of ever more basic aspects to an understanding of the primacy of the self. This critical attitude towards Vedic learning is something of a feature of the *Chāndogya Upaniṣad*. The final eighth chapter, on the 'city of Brahman' within which is contained all creatures and all desires, interestingly reverts to a more mythological setting for its final instruction: Prajāpati accepts as pupils Indra from among the Devas and Virocana from among the Asuras, but only Indra goes beyond his preliminary identification of one's *ātman* with one's reflection and perseveres till he reveals the *ātman* as purely spiritual, while Virocana is satisfied with externals and so goes to destruction.

The brief *Aitareya Upaniṣad*, belonging to the *Ṛgveda*, is probably almost as old as these first two. Its three chapters each address a different aspect of the *ātman*: the first contains a cosmogony with the *ātman* as creator, which retains something of the Brāhmaṇa approach; the second deals with the threefold origin of the *ātman*; and the third defines the *ātman* as intelligence (*prajñā*). The *Taittirīya Upaniṣad*, the oldest of several Upaniṣads of the *Black Yajurveda*, is also in three parts, which in its case are largely autonomous. The first part (*Śikṣāvallī*) comprises precepts and prayers for students with their teacher. The second part (*Brahmānandavallī*) is the best known; it begins with the definition of Brahman as truth, knowledge and infinity, before analysing man on five levels – the five sheaths – from the physical, vital, mental and intellectual aspects up to the blissful aspect of the real self, which is ultimately identical with Brahman. This series is notable for subordinating intellect to bliss in the ascending series but perhaps harks back to ritual contexts where all desires or bliss represent the supreme level. The third part (*Bhṛguvallī*) is a series of identifications of Brahman, especially as food.

The *Kauṣītaki Upaniṣad* is somewhat later; indeed, whereas the common themes of the *Bṛhadāraṇyaka* and *Chāndogya Upaniṣads* are readily explained by their close contemporaneity, the substantial passages of the *Kauṣītaki Upaniṣad* shared with them are obviously borrowings, presumably to give the *Ṛgveda* tradition a similarly comprehensive Upaniṣad. In particular its fourth chapter is an almost literal reproduction of the teaching of *Bṛhadāraṇyaka Upaniṣad* chapter two concerning Brahman. It starts also with a more advanced version of the teaching given to Uddālaka Āruṇi on rebirth first given in the two oldest Upaniṣads; here even more clearly the moon, with its own periodic 'death', is conceived as the prototype of the dead and their return linked with its cycle of waxing and waning. Reincarnation and other eschatological views occupy its first part and then it moves on to theories of *prāṇa* and *ātman*, concluding with a progressive definition of Brahman in a dialogue between Bālāki Gārgya and King Ajātaśatru (Kauṣ. Up.4, cf. BĀU 2.1), where again the *kṣatriya* shows the limita tions in the Brāhman's views and proceeds to instruct him through the analogy of deep sleep, a state apparently of nothingness in which yet consciousness persists to be roused when we are wakened.

The *Kena Upaniṣad* (so called from its opening word 'by whom') is in two distinct halves. The first two sections in verse emphasise the inscrutability of Brahman, which is yet everywhere: 'He who thinks it not thinks it, he who thinks it knows it not; it is not understood by those who know and known by those who do not know' (2.3). The last two sections in prose present an allegory of how even the gods are ignorant of Brahman. Brahman appears before the gods, who do not know what this apparition (*yakṣa*) is. So Agni and Vāyu go out to challenge it but find their powers of burning and blowing nullified. When Indra goes to find out what the *yakṣa* is, Brahman has gone and he finds instead Umā, daughter of the Himālaya (and later wife of Śiva), who reveals to him that it was Brahman. Thus it is clear that Agni and Vāyu lost their power by divorcing themselves from Brahman, the essential power in everything.

Although entirely metrical, the *Īśa Upaniṣad* also belongs to the transition phase from prose to verse; indeed it marks a transition in more than one respect. Its name, 'the Lord' (more fully *Īśāvāsya* 'enveloped by the Lord', again from its opening word), indicates the new emphasis. In eighteen verses it seeks to teach the essential unity of god and the world and emphasises the union of the contemplative and active sides of life. It is perhaps natural that it quotes from the *Bṛhadāraṇyaka Upaniṣad*, since both belong to the *White Yajurveda*, but the fact that no less than a third consists of more or less direct quotations suggests a definite appeal to tradition, precisely at the point of innovation in the stressing of a theistic approach. It is also interesting to note, although the explanation is obscure, that its last four verses still form part of the Hindu funeral ritual and that probably the next Upaniṣad in date, the *Kaṭha Upaniṣad*, has the god of death himself as its interlocutor and similarly has a more personal, though not theistic, element to its speculations.

However, as always, the shift to a new outlook did not take place all at once and some later Upaniṣads continue the more impersonal approach of the earliest ones. The three Upaniṣads assigned to the *Atharvaveda*, the *Praśna*, *Muṇḍaka* and *Māṇḍūkya Upaniṣads*, all broadly continue the impersonal trend. The *Praśna Upaniṣad* is in the form of the replies given by Pippalāda – the founder of one *Atharvaveda* school, just as Śaunaka, who receives the *Muṇḍaka* from the legendary Aṅgiras, is of the other – to six questions from his pupils; the last on the sixteen constituents of a person leads into the assertion that all the parts of the individual return to their inmost essence, losing their identity, just as rivers merge into the ocean. The *Muṇḍaka Upaniṣad* is chiefly notable for the clear distinction it makes between the higher knowledge of the supreme Brahman and the lower knowledge of the empirical world, including the ritual. It declares that performance of Vedic rites leads to heaven but the real goal, the uncreated world of Brahman, cannot be gained in this way but only by the higher knowledge, obtainable by the one who renounces everything – a definite shift towards the concept of the world-renouncer, the *saṃnyāsin*. Intriguingly, as part of its stress on the two levels of truth (later to be seized on by Advaita Vedānta), it utilises the old-established but popular image of the two birds on the same tree (3.1.1, cf. ṚV 1.164.20, Śvet.Up.4.7 and BhG.15.16) and in that context introduces the concept of *īśa*, the Lord, as the Supreme. The *Māṇḍūkya Upaniṣad* develops, in twelve sentences, the older waking-dreaming analogy in three stages (cf. BĀU 4.3.9–32, Ch.Up.8.9–13) by the addition of a fourth stage, which in one sense is the sum of the others and in another stands over against them. These four stages are also equated with the four quarters of the sacred syllable *oṃ*, its three phonetic elements (a+u+m) and a fourth soundless quarter, and with the three times and what transcends temporality. Thus, after successively realising the correspondences of the first three quarters, the seeker arrives at a fourth state, which is rather the indefinable whole, and 'enters with his *ātman* into the *ātman*', merging the immanent with the transcendent. Its ideas have been particularly important for the development of Advaita Vedānta.

CHAPTER THREE

Theistic Trends

The theistic trend which we noted as an innovation of the *Īśa Upaniṣad* is more clearly apparent in the *Śvetāśvatara* and *Mahānārāyaṇa Upaniṣads.* Slightly earlier than them, but equally belonging to the *Black Yajurveda,* is the *Kaṭha Upaniṣad,* which shares however with the *Īśa Upaniṣad* some link with death. The mythical framework of the Upaniṣad is also found in the *Taittirīya Brāhmaṇa* (11.8), though in a much shorter form, and may be alluded to in a hymn to Yama in the *Ṛgveda* (ṚV 10.135). A Brāhman is engaged in a sacrifice involving the giving away of all he has and, when his son Naciketas persistently asks to whom he will be given, the father says in effect 'To hell with you'. So Naciketas dutifully goes off to Yama's realm but, as the *Taittirīya Brāhmaṇa* account makes clear, he has to wait without food for three days until Yama returns. To make amends, Yama then offers him three boons. Naciketas' first request is to be able to return to his father as before, the second is the knowledge of the Nāciketa fire, and in the Upaniṣad the third is the higher knowledge of *ātman,* whereas in the Brāhmaṇa it is identical with the second and deliverance from repeated death (*punarmṛtyu*) is the highest aim. More exactly, Naciketas' third question is about man's destiny after death and Yama's reply is in terms of the *ātman* which is not born and does not die, but is eternal and indestructible, for death is now seen as part of the life-cycle and deliverance is sought from the cycle of births and deaths (*saṃsāra*). Yama's teaching leads to an enumeration of the various stages to be ascended in this quest: 'Beyond the senses are their objects, beyond objects is the mind (*manas*), beyond mind is intellect (*buddhi*), beyond intellect is the "great self" (*mahān ātmā*), beyond the great is the unmanifest, beyond the unmanifest is the *puruṣa,* beyond the *puruṣa* there is nothing; he is the limit, the supreme goal' (Kaṭha Up.3.10–11, cf. 6.10–11). Thus, the old ideas about some great cosmic *ātman* undergoing a process of self-division is subordinated to the state of non-differentiation, which is equivalent to Brahman, but that in turn is lower than the supreme *puruṣa,* in which the personal element is undoubtedly present, together with the view that 'he can be grasped only by the one whom he chooses' (2.23).

In the *Śvetāśvatara Upaniṣad* the personal element is subsumed in the theistic for, though a composite and eclectic text (belonging to the fifth or fourth century B.C.), it is concerned overall to establish the existence and supremacy of the Lord. In so doing it quotes and reinterprets older Vedic texts, including verses from some of the creation hymns of the tenth book of the *Ṛgveda,* to indicate that Agni, Prajāpati, Viśvakarman and Hiraṇyagarbha are all aspects of this great Lord and that it is he who is really meant when they describe the creator whose face, eyes, arms and feet are everywhere. It thus teaches a personal deity as creator of the universe and proceeds to name him unequivocally as Rudra or Śiva, as well as describing him by the more abstract titles of *deva, īśa* and *maheśvara* 'the great Lord'; indeed, whereas the terms *īśa* and *īśvara* continue to be used to denote the supreme deity as a concept (without identifying him with one particular deity), *maheśvara* and the similar *mahādeva* soon come to be used of Śiva almost exclusively and thus become names for him.

The beginning of the *Śvetāśvatara Upaniṣad* reveals its position clearly, for it mentions the different views of creation then current – that it is due to time, nature, necessity, chance, the elements, the *puruṣa,* or a combination of them – and rejects them in favour of the power of the supreme. It next speaks of the world as a wheel, centred on the deity, in which the soul (pictured as a wild goose) flutters trapped until it realises its true nature; both this image and that of the deity as a river of five streams sandwiched within it illustrate the view of the deity and the world which considers *prakṛti* 'nature, matter' to be a part of the deity himself. Elsewhere, however, using the image of the two birds on one tree which goes back ultimately to the *Ṛgveda* (1.164.20), it propounds a dualistic separation of spirit and matter, as well as suggesting that simply by being seen the deity is responsible for the release of the soul (*puruṣa*). Nevertheless, it immediately reverts to its own characteristic viewpoint when it declares that nature (*prakṛti*) is creation (*māyā*) and the great Lord is the creator (4.10); it is exceptional among the Upaniṣads in using the term *māyā* but undoubtedly employs it still in its Vedic sense of 'creative power'. Here and subsequently it makes clear that the personal deity transcends both the perishable and the imperishable which together constitute Brahman. In the body of the Upaniṣad it is expressly stated that through the grace (*prasāda*) of the creator alone one sees the Lord and his majesty, being freed from sorrow (3.20). Yet Rudra's mythological aspect is not entirely suppressed; he is still the dweller in the mountains, who wields the arrow, and is besought not to hurt the speaker and his relatives. Again in the conclusion Śvetāśvatara is said to have declared his views by the power of his asceticism (*tapas*) and the grace (*prasāda*) of the deity.

Several of the quotations from older Vedic literature in the *Śvetāśvatara Upaniṣad* are shared with the *Mahānārāyaṇa Upaniṣad*, and similarly are employed to buttress with traditional material the belief in a personal supreme deity. However, there is a big difference in that this deity is here named as Nārāyaṇa, a name of Viṣṇu. Though slightly later in date, the *Mahānārāyaṇa Upaniṣad* is in some respects archaic, with its attempt to harmonise the ritual and reflective ways of life in similar fashion to the Āraṇyakas; thus, it too gives considerable prominence to the mental and internal 'fire oblation through breath' (*prāṇāgnihotra*) as a substitute for the ordinary rite. Towards the end, the sacrifice and its elements are interpreted in terms of the mental cult of the Brāhman who renounces the world, to the extent that life is an initiation – a state of sacrificial consecration; this both looks back to Brāhmaṇa ideas of Viṣṇu as the embodiment of the sacrifice and looks forward to the doctrine expounded in the *Bhagavadgītā* of all activity as a sacrifice.

The central part, which gives the Upaniṣad its name, praises Nārāyaṇa as the Absolute, dwelling in the hearts of men, who is the highest lord, the all, the highest light, the all-pervading one, identified with Brahman (201–69). There is some uncertainty about the figure of Nārāyaṇa. He is traditionally the author of the hymn to the cosmic man, *puruṣa* (ṚV 10.90), but by the time of the *Śatapatha Brāhmaṇa* is identified with that figure and so himself the original sacrifice which produced both the gods and all creation. The *Mahānārāyaṇa Upaniṣad* itself gives a sequence of identifications from Prajāpati to Brahmā to Nārāyaṇa which clearly links up with this theme of cosmic sacrifice and which presumably is the reason for his eventual identification with Viṣṇu. For the *Śatapatha Brāhmaṇa*, in addition to calling Nārāyaṇa *puruṣa*, elsewhere conflates *puruṣa* and the creator god Prajāpati, who is described as imitating, that is identifying himself with, Viṣṇu. Within an apparently more orthodox framework, then, and for all its archaism in some respects, the *Mahānārāyaṇa Upaniṣad* stands at the beginning of the Vaiṣṇava expression of this new theistic trend, which by contrast with the older polytheism amounts virtually to monotheism.

However, this trend towards a theistic outlook found expression in other forms than the rise of Śiva and Viṣṇu; there is evidence that Indra maintained some kind of supremacy in more popular belief longer than most Vedic deities and a personalised form of the abstract Brahman, the deity Brahmā, achieved prominence for a time. Still, for the evidence concerning these, we need to pass beyond the Vedic literature. In particular, the two great Sanskrit epics, the *Mahābhārata* and the *Rāmāyaṇa*, are a major source for understanding the substantial transformation now taking place in the religion. This is of great interest for, as epics, they belong in their origins to the culture of the *kṣatriya* aristocracy, whose different outlook on religion they undoubtedly reflect. The role of the *kṣatriyas* in some of the innovations of the Upaniṣads has already been seen. Originally secular works, recited at courts by bards attendant on the kings, both epics grew over a long period to include much other traditional material and acquired religious significance as an important figure in each was identified as an incarnation of Viṣṇu; in the process their transmission and amplification passed into the hands of the Brāhmans, the established guardians and teachers of tradition. The core of each work was composed in about the fifth or fourth century B.C., but was subject to a process of expansion and accretion which continued at least until the beginning of the Gupta period in the fourth century A.D. However, the political situation they reflect is substantially older, going back perhaps another five centuries in the case of the *Mahābhārata*. There is need therefore for discrimination in utilising the evidence from the epics.

In their earliest layers Indra is still a prominent and frequently mentioned deity; his exploits in defeating Vṛtra, Bali, Namuci and the like are frequently made the standard for assessing the strength and bravery of human heroes; he is normally the most active and influential of the gods and as king of the gods is the ultimate comparison for any king. His prominence and his martial nature are seen in the symbolic scheme of the five Pāṇḍava heroes being the sons of various gods, for he is the father of Arjuna, while in the *Rāmāyaṇa* its sole hero Rāma is compared far more frequently to Indra than to any other deity, and at the climax of the whole story in his duel with Rāvaṇa receives the aid of Indra's charioteer. At a slightly later stage however the deity Brahmā becomes important and is credited with some of the cosmogonic myths associated in the later Vedic period with Prajāpati; essentially he is a fusion of a creator deity with the impersonal absolute, Brahman, of the Upaniṣads in a more popular and therefore personalised form. There is other evidence, though scanty, beside the epics to indicate that Brahmā was a major figure, seen as the supreme deity by some, during the last century or two B.C. and the first centuries A.D. He even finds a mention in one of the Upaniṣads (Maitrī Up.4.5), alongside the two deities who eventually are to oust him from supremacy, Rudra and Viṣṇu, though admittedly all three are subordinate to Brahman; this grouping of the three, the so-called *trimūrti,* perhaps reflects a transition phase in the relationship of the three gods but becomes fossilised and retained mechanically in later Hinduism, where conventionally Brahmā is considered the creator, Viṣṇu the preserver and Śiva the destroyer.

In their middle and later stages, however, both epics amply attest the supremacy of Viṣṇu and Śiva, some passages favouring one and implicitly or explicitly demoting the other and vice versa. Since ultimately they became Vaiṣṇava works, the Vaiṣṇava emphasis tends to dominate but Śaiva elements are by no means absent. At the same time Indra particularly but also to some extent Brahmā suffer a decline in prestige. Instead of Indra's martial exploits, stories of his amours become current, just as in the later formalised stages of classical mythology Zeus and Jupiter become notorious for their affairs. One of the best known stories, told in later parts of both epics, is his adultery with Ahalyā, wife of the sage Gautama, whose form he takes and who curses him with impotence. In the same way Brahmā's creative activity becomes trivialised into a readiness to grant boons to any who perform penance or asceticism regardless of the consequences.

A pivotal role in this change is undoubtedly played by the *Bhagavadgītā* (Mbh.6.23–40), the sermon which Kṛṣṇa delivers to Arjuna on the eve of the battle which is the climax of the *Mahābhārata*. However, it is hardly likely that the *Bhagavadgītā*, at least in its present form, was a part of the original epic narrative and there is textual evidence for the process of insertion. It may well have originated as a separate composition, for it not only presupposes the epic setting but itself contains a reasonably full description of Arjuna's dilemma. It is commonly assigned to about the second century B.C. – it is certainly no older, if indeed it is as old as that. Whereas the slightly older *Mahānārāyaṇa Upaniṣad* makes Nārāyaṇa its supreme being, in the *Bhagavadgītā* Kṛṣṇa presents himself as the supreme, identical to or more often superior to Brahman. To Vaiṣṇavas and indeed to most Hindus the *Bhagavadgītā* is their main religious text and the real source of many of their beliefs. Nevertheless, as part of one of the epics, it falls outside the Vedic literature, though calling itself an Upaniṣad, and so has no inherent authority. Yet its setting at the heart of the *Mahābhārata* in fact provides its strength, for Kṛṣṇa is answering a real-life dilemma for Arjuna and in the process propounds a view of life and a way to liberation with which in large measure the ordinary man in the world can identify. The *Bhagavadgītā* thus holds out the hope of real spiritual progress to those who are nonetheless still very much involved in the affairs of the world.

Arjuna's dilemma is that the leaders of the army which he and his brothers are about to fight are their cousins, for the conflict is over the possession of their ancestral kingdom. In the first chapter Arjuna gives vent to his despondency and ends up declaring that he will not fight. In the rest of the *Bhagavadgītā* Kṛṣṇa demonstrates to Arjuna the limitations of his view and stresses the need to fulfil one's role in society. He begins in the second chapter by teaching that the *ātman*, being eternal and indestructible, does not die when the body is killed but transmigrates from body to body until it achieves final release; thus, death for the *ātman* is impossible, for 'just as a man throws away worn out clothes and puts on new ones, so the embodied self abandons worn out bodies and acquires other new ones' (BhG.2.22). Quoting from the *Kaṭha Upanisad* to reinforce his point, Kṛṣṇa then applies it to Arjuna's own situation, declaring that since death is not final there is no need for sorrow over the imminent deaths in battle, and he is not averse to including an appeal to Arjuna's fear of being called a coward. It is possible to recognise this eternal *ātman* through the practice of Yoga, that is by learning to detach oneself completely from the results of actions; this leads on through emphasis on the abandoning of desires to declarations that such a person reaches peace and the stillness of Brahman (BhG.2.71–2). As this already shows, the *Bhagavadgītā* draws heavily on the Upaniṣads, as well as other parts of Vedic literature and other less clearly identifiable ways of thinking. It is not a completely consistent text but rather seeks to combine and synthesise into an overall theistic framework the various strands of thought then current; it is undoubtedly a work of popularisation and its inclusion in the *Mahābhārata* with its massive audience is not coincidental.

Kṛṣṇa next in the third chapter expounds the view that all activity is a sacrifice if undertaken in the right spirit which he goes on to show is one of complete detachment; he thus simultaneously provides a reinterpretation of sacrifice and of the renunciatory way of life. For he makes it clear that withdrawal into inactivity is not only useless but even misguided. Just as Kṛṣṇa, as the supreme deity, has no need to act but is incessantly engaged in activity, since otherwise the universe would collapse, so men should help to maintain the world order – now by sacrificially-motivated activity rather than the sacrifice itself. Thus Arjuna should perform his caste duty (*dharma*) of fighting the enemy, but in a spirit of complete detachment without concern for the outcome.

The *Bhagavadgītā* thus provides a new aspect to the doctrine of *karma* and meets the problem in a simple yet convincing manner, by stressing the motivation involved. There had already been suggestions in the Upaniṣads that it is desire that leads to actions and it was a prominent feature of the Buddhist analysis. The *Bhagavadgītā* goes on from this to declare that, since desire is more basic than action, actions as such have no particular effect, provided one acts unselfishly and without interest in the result. In fact such disinterested action, rather than mere inactivity, is the true opposite to action. Thus renunciation is not the way forward and the *Bhagavadgītā* rejects the practice of asceticism in favour of disciplined activity in the world, suggesting that in any case complete cessation of activity is impossible and the ascetic way of life therefore untenable. Action without attachment is action in accordance with one's *dharma*, one's religious and social duties which vary according to one's particular situation. In Arjuna's specific situation, as a member of the *kṣatriya* caste, he has a duty to uphold law and order and for that reason to take part in the forthcoming battle; thus, the *Bhagavadgītā* tends definitely to support the status quo. Moreover, Arjuna should not think that he is responsible for his actions, for in reality they are performed by the constituents of nature which are entirely separate from the *ātman*.

After thus examining the way of activity (*karma*), Kṛṣṇa takes up the way of knowledge (*jñāna*), the type of intuition going back as far as the speculative hymns of the *Ṛgveda* but here carefully defined as knowledge of the deity; interestingly, it is within this chapter that he declares: 'Whenever there occurs a decay of righteousness (*dharma*) and a springing up of unrighteousness, then I send forth myself. To protect good men and to destroy evil-doers, in order to establish righteousness, I come into being from age to age' (BhG.4.7–8). However, after this emphasis on the deity come two chapters on Brahman and *ātman* respectively, reverting to ideas of meditation as the means to achieve insight.

The middle six chapters of the *Bhagavadgītā* are then mainly concerned with the nature of the supreme deity and his attributes, although the eighth chapter again presents the method of meditation in Yoga as the way to release. Even within that chapter, however, the supreme deity is equated with Brahman, the mystical syllable *oṃ* and the supreme *puruṣa*. Emphasis on the deity culminates within this section in the awe-inspiring theophany in the eleventh chapter, where Kṛṣṇa reveals to Arjuna his universal form, having just before identified himself with the most essential aspects of every part of the cosmos. Although Viṣṇu is mentioned, he is not especially prominent (and indeed Kṛṣṇa also identifies himself as Indra among the gods) and Kṛṣṇa himself is rather the supreme deity. This revelation produces in Arjuna a spirit of humble adoration, summed up as the way of devotion (*bhakti*).

The last six chapters, which are quite probably later in date than the rest, deal with a variety of topics, gradually leading back through a good deal of practical moral teaching to the concept of *bhakti* with the declaration at the end of the whole poem of Kṛṣṇa's attachment (*bhakti*) to Arjuna and the promise that by his grace he can be reached and entered into. The nature of this devotion in the *Bhagavadgītā* is rather different from later views; sacrifice and discipline are its hallmarks and there is little room for spontaneity. Indeed, the stress on duty (*dharma*) as specifically the role appropriate to one's station in life leads in the opposite direction. Nor is there any real suggestion of intimacy, except as part of the goal, but rather the attitude of the devotee is one of subservience, typified by Arjuna's humble response to Kṛṣṇa's divine self-revelation. This way of devotion, available to all, is ranked higher than the way of knowledge, which because of its difficulties only a few can achieve, and that in turn is superior to the way of action, the performance of deeds without attachment to their results but merely out of duty. These ways are not rejected, but a definite order of value is established; this is perhaps the first clear appearance of this principle of ranking. It might even be said that, by its stress on the happiness secured by detachment here and now, the *Bhagavadgītā* begins the shift of emphasis in the theistic movement away from the idea of release (*mokṣa*) in some distant future to an immediate and direct relationship with the deity; in this as in much else, the *Bhagavadgītā* stands at the very beginning of what is a long process of development.

Important as the *Bhagavadgītā* is for Vaiṣṇavism, it is not the earliest record of worship of Kṛṣṇa Vāsudeva. One or two references to a Kṛṣṇa in Vedic literature should probably be discounted, since there is nothing really to connect them with the Kṛṣṇa of later worship. There is possibly an allusion to followers of Vāsudeva in the grammarian Pāṇini (fifth to fourth century B.C.) but the clearest mention is by the Greek ambassador to the Mauryan court at the end of the fourth century B.C., who records that the people of the Mathurā area held Heracles in special honour, since Heracles would be the nearest Greek equivalent to Kṛṣṇa. Elsewhere in the *Mahābhārata* Kṛṣṇa appears as a chief of the Yādava clan of Dvārakā who sides with the five Pāṇḍava brothers and acts as their counsellor in the war against their cousins, the Kurus. His advice is cunning to the point of unscrupulousness and with the inclusion of the *Bhagavadgītā* in the epic it was felt necessary to attempt some justification. Even after his self-revelation in the *Bhagavadgītā*, he continues to be treated as a human ally rather than the supreme deity. The historical character of Kṛṣṇa Vāsudeva, as the son of Vasudeva of the Yādava clan, is quite possible in view of his considerable human role in the epic story. Presumably this hero of the Yādavas became – or was identified with – the leader of a religious movement, was deified as a result and called Bhagavat, 'the blessed one'. From this title are then derived the names of both the *Bhagavadgītā* and the sect that worshipped him, the Bhāgavatas.

Inscriptional evidence for the Bhāgavata cult comes from Western India around 100 B.C.; the more interesting of the two inscriptions records the erection of a pillar to Vāsudeva by a Greek from Taxila who calls himself a Bhāgavata. Inscriptions also indicate that there were temples of Bhagavat Vāsudeva in the Mathurā area itself in the middle of the second century A.D. and that by the same period Vāsudeva was revered in the Western Deccan. Over the course of time this Bhāgavata cult amalgamated with the cult of Nārāyaṇa. Indeed the next substantial evidence for the doctrinal development of either movement comes from a late section of the *Mahābhārata*, the *Nārāyaṇīya* (Mbh.12.321–39), of uncertain date but later than the *Bhagavadgītā* and probably no earlier than the third century A.D. Here Nārāyaṇa, the supreme deity, explains to his devotee Nārada, an ancient seer, that Vāsudeva is the supreme *puruṣa*, the inner ruler of all. Interestingly, Nārāyaṇa performed asceticism by which he became Brahmā and saw Śiva who granted him superiority to everyone, including Śiva himself. The *Nārāyaṇīya* describes the worshippers of these figures by various names, including Bhāgavata and Pāñcarātra, which later was to become the name of a definite Vaiṣṇava sect; it also mentions several groups of hermits or ascetics, among them the Vaikhānasas, who later also are a Vaiṣṇava sect. The variety of names no doubt indicates the existence of slightly differing groups. Altogether, the picture given is of a state of flux as several influences merge and evolve. The doctrines also of the *Nārāyaṇīya* show a blend of Upaniṣadic monism, dualistic elements similar to Sāṃkhya and Yoga, and ritualistic features from the Brāhmaṇa tradition with the devotional worship of a personal deity – a synthesis analogous to that of the *Bhagavadgītā* but not identical, differing especially in the higher value assigned to ritual and asceticism.

In the developed mythology of Vaiṣṇavism, however, the warrior figure of the *Mahābhārata* proper plays little part, except as the expounder of the *Bhagavadgītā*, and the focus of attention is on the pastoral Kṛṣṇa, first presented in the supplement to the *Mahābhārata*, the *Harivaṃśa* ('the dynasty of Hari' i.e. Kṛṣṇa), which is usually assigned to the early centuries A.D. and presents a complete account of Kṛṣṇa's life and death. The pastoral Kṛṣṇa is perhaps not completely unknown to the *Mahābhārata* but the Kṛṣṇa Gopāla, 'cowherd', portrayed in the *Harivaṃśa* is rather different. Equally his older brother Balarāma appears in a minor role in the *Mahābhārata* but appears in the later work as a much more important figure. He seems originally to have been a non-Aryan agricultural deity, whose cult reveals many features of Nāga worship; he is regarded as an incarnation of the cosmic snake, Śeṣa, and at his death a snake – evidently his self – issued from his mouth. Other names for him are Saṃkarṣaṇa and Halāyudha, both alluding to ploughing and emphasising his connection with agriculture; he is regularly as light in colour as Kṛṣṇa is dark. The two brothers grow up in the free and easy atmosphere of the pasturage on the banks of the Yamunā in the company of the cowherds and their cattle. They wander from forest to forest despatching the demons in animal form that infest them. But Vṛndāvana, the forest near Mathurā, is their favourite spot, where they and the other young men on special occasions dance and sport with the young women of the clan, the *gopīs*. The other members of the clan are supposed to be ignorant of Kṛṣṇa's divine nature and in the *Harivaṃśa* the narrative does presuppose this, unlike many later works.

The story of Kṛṣṇa's childhood is narrated, of which perhaps the most notable incident is his uprooting of two *arjuna* trees by dragging a mortar between them, obviously a mythological expression of the supplanting of a local tree cult by worship of Kṛṣṇa Vāsudeva. Only at a much later date do his childhood pranks become a focus of attention, when also a decidedly erotic aspect is elaborated out of his youthful contacts with the *gopīs*. The narrative leads up to his slaying of his evilly disposed maternal uncle Kaṃsa, the story possibly representing a conflict between maternal and paternal systems of inheritance. Then, in his adult life, come various martial exploits, including the wars against Jarāsaṃdha, and his activities as leader of the clan, such as the founding of the city of Dvārakā. The second half of the work narrates the deeds of Kṛṣṇa's son and grandson, Pradyumna and Aniruddha.

Although ultimately Kṛṣṇa alone is the central figure of worship, other members of his family originally shared this deification. An inscription of the first century A.D. from near Mathurā records the setting up of images of the five heroes of his clan and references in the Purāṇas include their enumeration as Saṃkarṣaṇa, Vāsudeva, Pradyumna, Aniruddha and Sāmba, of whom all except the last also figure in later theology. But there are also traces of the worship of Kṛṣṇa's sister Ekānaṃśā, which may again point to earlier matriarchal traditions; Ekānaṃśā is said to be identical with Subhadrā, the goddess still worshipped in association with Balarāma and Kṛṣṇa at Purī in Orissa, but some later texts declare her to be an emanation of Durgā or Pārvatī.

Kṛṣṇa is not the central figure in the *Mahābhārata* and his deification is obviously directly related to his expounding of the *Bhagavadgītā*. But Rāma is the eponymous hero of the *Rāmāyaṇa* and his deification is as obviously the result of the portrayal of his character there. Although he is clearly a martial hero and the climax of the whole epic is his defeat of the Rākṣasa king Rāvaṇa, from the beginning important issues of conduct were central to the plot. When, on the eve of his installation as heir apparent, Rāma is suddenly sent into a fourteen year exile through the machinations of a stepmother, his reaction is not anger but calm acceptance of his father's will – an impressive demonstration of filial obedience. So too, in similar displays of wifely devotion and brotherly affection, Sītā and Lakṣmaṇa insist on accompanying him. Once in the forest, Rāma as a *kṣatriya* fulfils his duty by offering protection to the various hermits living there. The underhand abduction of Sītā by Rāvaṇa leads inexorably to the climax of the poem in the siege of Rāvaṇa's capital Laṅkā and his eventual defeat; this is easily represented as a conflict between good and evil, while the long search for Sītā amply demonstrates Rāma's devotion to his wife.

Thus, the elevation of Rāma's character, combined with his standing as a prince, made it natural to compare him to the gods. Initially and regularly compared with Indra, the king of the gods and a natural comparison for martial heroes, Rāma later is seen increasingly as himself divine. Although he is still compared to Indra and his brother Lakṣmaṇa as his close helper to Viṣṇu, by the later parts of the epic's development Rāma is directly identified with the now more prominent Viṣṇu. This is first clearly seen in the first and last books which were added round the earlier core. In the first book is recounted, among the events of Rāma's youth, how he and his three brothers are born as incarnations of Viṣṇu, while various deities engender other leading figures of the story, and how he wins the hand of Sītā, daughter of King Janaka of Mithilā, by drawing till it breaks the great bow given to Janaka by Śiva.

In the last book, Rāvaṇa's genealogy and past exploits are developed, making him into an adversary of the gods who has indeed won from Brahmā by his asceticism the boon of invulnerability from all beings more powerful than man. The older struggle between the Devas and Asuras for power is here not only transposed to the mundane sphere but also given definitely moral aspects. Rāma's defeat of Rāvaṇa has been assigned the same cosmic significance as Indra's defeat of Namuci and Viṣṇu's of Bali. With this change of interpretation of the story, various features undergo modification. Originally the epic ended in a joyful reunion followed by a triumphant return, the fourteen years of exile having conveniently expired; in a reworking which is similar in outlook to the first and last books the text now extant has Rāma recognised as divine (first by identification with various deities and then by identification with Viṣṇu) by a contingent of the gods led by Brahmā, while Sītā has to undergo an ordeal by fire to prove her chastity before Rāma will accept her back.

At the same time other episodes of the original story receive a moralistic gloss to adapt them to this new outlook, for when Rāma is perceived to be a god, moral lapses are unthinkable. His killing of the Vānara chief Vālin while the latter was engaged in combat with his brother Sugrīva, now Rāma's ally, receives elaborate but rather unconvincing justification. Even his martial activities to protect the hermits as they pursue their religious activities are seen as slightly suspect, and emphasis is placed on his duty as a *kṣatriya* and a ruler to uphold *dharma*, law and order as well as religion. Indeed, the ethical polarisation apparent in the development of the *Rāmāyaṇa*, proceeding from within the plot itself, leads naturally to a stress on Rāma's activity on behalf of *dharma* and his defeat of evil in the person of Rāvana. The reasons for his eventual identification with the benevolent activity for mankind of Viṣṇu are thus easily discerned, more so than with Kṛṣṇa, although it is the *Bhagavadgītā*, with its already quoted declaration of the deity's periodic manifestation, that provides the theoretic framework for the doctrine of Viṣṇu's *avatāras*, incarnations (literally 'descents').

Viṣṇu himself, of course, right from the Vedic period possessed a pronounced benevolent aspect, which was more definitely channelled into an active, creative capacity through his association with the sacrifice in the Brāhmaṇas. There too is seen his linking with Prajāpati (who subsequently is more often identified with Brahmā) and thus indirectly with the *puruṣa*, who is also called Nārāyaṇa. Nevertheless, the process of fusion of the various cults is still somewhat obscure, for in the *Mahānārāyaṇa Upaniṣad* and the *Bhagavadgītā* Viṣṇu is only mentioned in passing, by contrast with Nārāyaṇa and Kṛṣṇa respectively, while Rāma's identification with Viṣṇu is secondary to his deification. Viṣṇu's pervasiveness may well be significant as well as the fact that his strides and other activities brought him into association with Indra. His junior partnership with Indra persists into the epic period but there we see Viṣṇu develop from an assistant into the greater god, until Indra even appeals to Viṣṇu to help him. The connecting link is perhaps to be seen in the elaboration of his three strides in the Brāhmaṇas by making Viṣṇu become a dwarf before taking them in order by artifice to recover the earth for the Devas from the Asuras – the assumption of a particular form for a particular purpose. However, Viṣṇu's original traits of benevolent activity towards mankind combined with resistance to evil powers and readiness to pervade or penetrate the earth are obviously consonant with the view eventually formulated of the purpose of his incarnations, to destroy the wicked and to protect the righteous.

Viṣṇu's *avatāras* begin to appear during the later phases of development of the epics, although they are not yet classified as systematically as in later literature. A varying number of animal and human heroes, some of whom appear in the Vedic hymns, come to be viewed as exemplars of the god's benevolent activity

3. Varāha: Viṣṇu as the boar rescuing Earth

on earth, and eventually to be identified completely with him. Several of the stories have had to undergo some modification to fit this theme, even to the extent of being taken over from other gods, at whose expense Viṣṇu is now becoming more prominent. The number of incarnations varies: it seems to have started from a nucleus of four (Mbh.12.337.36), but in later works as many as 24 and 29 are mentioned; by the eighth century A.D. the standard number was accepted as ten, namely *matsya*, *kūrma*, *varāha*, Narasiṃha, Vāmana, Paraśurāma, Rāma Dāśarathi, Kṛṣṇa, Buddha and Kalki, but earlier lists include different characters. Attempts were briefly made to date the *avatāras* according to the system of mythological ages, but that system, representing a steady decline from original perfection, can hardly be reconciled with the repeated descent of saviours who restore righteousness.

Four of the *avatāras*, *matsya*, *kūrma*, *varāha* and Vāmana, make use of cosmogonic myths from the Vedas and Brāhmaṇas, pointing to a similar cosmogonic role for them as incarnations of Viṣṇu. None of the first three, however, is associated with Viṣṇu in Vedic times. *Matsya*, the fish, protects Manu, the first man, during the great deluge, and *kūrma*, the tortoise, supports the earth on his back at the time of the churning of the ocean, an early creation myth. The Brāhmaṇas identify both creatures with the god Prajāpati (=Brahmā) and mention the tortoise as lord of the waters, and thus a representative of Varuṇa; it is also a traditional symbol of the sacrifice. Though mentioned in the *Mahābhārata*, it is not until the Purāṇas that fish and tortoise are linked to Viṣṇu. Viṣṇu's third appearance, as *varāha*, the boar, was to raise up the Earth after she had been submerged in the ocean. This story seems to incorporate some pre-Aryan cult of a sacred pig, centred around the Vindhya mountains and connected with fertility rites; like the fish and the tortoise, the boar was possibly the totem of some non-Aryan tribe. Like them, too, it was identified by the Brāhmaṇas as Prajāpati, although in a late passage of the *Mahābhārata* the boar has become Viṣṇu.

Narasiṃha, the man-lion, who frees the world from a demon, does not appear in Vedic literature, but there are noteworthy similarities to the story of Indra and Namuci. In both cases the demons have received what they are satisfied is an all-embracing promise of inviolability, and are only overcome by subterfuge. Both legends represent the specifically Indian adaptation of the universal motif of the ineluctability of fate, typified in such stories as Achilles' heel and Balder and the mistletoe. Here the Asura Hiraṇyakaśipu has gained invulnerability from man or beast, by day or night, within or without his house, so Viṣṇu, to punish him for the excesses into which his false security leads him, manifests himself as the man-lion at twilight on the veranda and tears him apart. Later still, the motive for intervention is an appeal by Hiraṇyakaśipu's pious son Prahlāda who has become a devotee of Viṣṇu – as it were the white sheep of the family. The first few centuries A.D. saw a popular cult of Narasiṃha in parts of the Panjab, as a protector against thieves, wild animals, malign stars and all forms of evil.

By contrast, the incarnation as Vāmana, the dwarf, has developed from the feat attributed to Viṣṇu in the *Ṛgveda* of striding through the universe. Now the world and the gods are being threatened by the demon tyrant Bali; Viṣṇu, in the guise of a dwarf, begs as much land as he can cover in three strides, transforms himself into a giant, and wins back the whole world. A significant stage in the growth of Viṣṇu's prestige at the expense of older gods can be seen in the version of this myth found in a late part of the *Rāmāyaṇa*: here, after winning back control of the world, Viṣṇu presents it to the still prominent Indra.

It is not immediately obvious why the list of *avatāras* should include Rāma Jāmadagnya or Bhārgava, known from the sixth century A.D. as Paraśurāma ('Rāma with the axe') to distinguish him from Rāma Dāśarathi, the hero of the *Rāmāyaṇa*. He figures in Vedic literature only as the traditional author of one hymn (ṚV 10.110) and appears first in an active role in the epics, particularly the *Mahābhārata*; his story is then taken up by the Purāṇas, though never particularly popular outside the *Mahābhārata*. By no stretch of the imagination can his activities be considered as saving the world from catastrophe. Reclaiming some land along the west coast by throwing his axe at the sea and frightening it into retreat is not an exploit comparable to the earlier cosmogonic myths. His blind obedience to his father's command (Jamadagni orders him to behead his mother Reṇukā, and he obeys after his brothers have refused, although he later asks for her to be restored to life) compares ill with his namesake's self-sacrifice. Paradoxically, a clue may be provided by the third story associated with him, which shows him in an even less benevolent light. As a Brāhman, he determines to annihilate all the *kṣatriyas*, or warrior class, to avenge his father's murder; that he does so (no fewer than twenty-one times!) using the weapons of a warrior rather than a priest points to an origin for this legend at a time when the functions and status of these two classes were fiercely disputed. As his name Bhārgava indicates he is the hero of the Bhṛgu group of Brāhmans who were responsible for inflating the *Mahābhārata* and through it bolstering the pretensions to superiority of the Brāhmans.

Some partisanship between groups of Brāhmans with differing allegiances may be detected in the very different portrayal of the next *avatāra*, Rāma Dāśarathi. His character and actions are, as we have seen, in stark contrast to Paraśurāma's, and this contrast is heightened by an incident added to the already late first book of the *Rāmāyaṇa* where the two *avatāras* meet. The belligerent Paraśurāma comes out of retirement to challenge Rāma Dāśarathi, only to be humiliated by his youthful counterpart. In some later versions of the story, from Bhavabhūti's eighth-century drama, the *Mahāvīracarita*, onwards, this hostility is attributed to Paraśurāma's indignation at the insult offered to Śiva when the younger Rāma breaks the god's bow. In other late versions, Rāma and his ally Hanumān are also sometimes depicted as devotees of Śiva. It is clear that these epic heroes, including Kṛṣṇa, the eighth *avatāra*, have been taken over to serve the interests of several different sects, but that in their origins at least they are independent.

The appearance of the Buddha as the next *avatāra* of Viṣṇu is not as bizarre as it first appears, for his role is to mislead the unwary and his inclusion represents an attempt by Vaiṣṇava theologians to absorb heterodox elements. In any event, he does not figure in the lists until the fifth century A.D. at the earliest. Considerably later still, one Purāṇa turns a leading figure of another heterodox movement, Ṛṣabha, the first of the 24 Jain saviours, into a partial *avatāra*, illustrating once again the all-embracing nature of Hinduism and its propensity for dealing with heresy and the like not by opposition but by absorption. Other figures sometimes regarded as *avatāras* include Kṛṣṇa's brother Balarāma who, in addition to his Nāga characteristics, also has some Śaiva attributes, and another relatively early figure Dattātreya, who was the object of a largely tantric cult localised in Maharashtra and is represented in the Purāṇas as a forester with a taste for wine, women and song. However, all of these were probably too divergent from the standard pattern established to remain popular, whatever the reasons for their initial inclusion.

Kalki was early recognised to be Viṣṇu's last intervention in the affairs of the afflicted world. He will appear at the end of this present age, a millennial figure, who probably owes his main inspiration to the Buddhist doctrine of Maitreya, the future Buddha, and thus ultimately to Zoroastrian ideas of the future Saviour. He will punish the wicked, reward the righteous, and establish a new era symbolising the ultimate triumph of Brāhmanism. He will appear as a warrior riding a white horse; indeed, in South Indian popular tradition he actually is a horse, apparently representing some ancient animal god of the region. His martial aspect may reflect a reaction to a historical event such as the invasions of north-west India between the second century B.C. and second century A.D.

With the rise of the *bhakti* movement, religious interest switched from the theme of a god's occasional intervention in the world's affairs by direct incarnation to that of his abiding presence through grace in the heart of each devotee, and so the mythology of the *avatāras* underwent no further development.

Although the evidence of the *Śvetāśvatara Upaniṣad* shows that Śiva was being viewed as the supreme deity at least as early as any of the figures who combine into the developed Viṣṇu, the rise of a definite religious sect worshipping Śiva as such is even less easy to trace. However, the *Mahābhārata* in its latest parts refers to the Pāśupatas, the worshippers of Śiva Paśupati 'the lord of the animals', as a distinct group along with the Vaiṣṇava Pāñcarātra and certain others. But any detailed information on this or other Śaiva sects belongs to a later period.

Many of the characteristics making up the later complex nature of Śiva can be traced back into the Vedic pantheon, but not only to the figure of Rudra, for Śiva also grew by a process of accretion and aggrandisement at the expense of other deities. However in his case they were amalgamated into a single ambivalent and even paradoxical figure. Although Śiva is occasionally said to have undertaken several *avatāras*, these play no significant role in either the mythology or theology of Śaivism. From Rudra, Śiva inherits the awesomeness and even malevolence of character which made him feared, as well as the exclusion from orthodox sacrifice which marked his outsider status. Indeed, in later parts of the *Mahābhārata,* this is developed into the myth of Dakṣa's sacrifice, explaining both how Śiva was excluded and how he was then accepted into the orthodox pantheon; Dakṣa, a Prajāpati figure who is also Śiva's father-in-law, begins a sacrifice from which as usual Śiva is excluded but Umā, Śiva's wife and Dakṣa's daughter, is upset at this slight to her husband and so Śiva attacks the sacrifice, until at length he is pacified by Brahmā who declares that the gods will give him a share of the sacrifice. Here the god's destructive aspect inherited from Rudra is also prominent, as it is in another late *Mahābhārata* myth where, however, it is harnessed to help the gods; this is the myth of his destruction of the triple city of the Asuras, where he is appealed to after Indra's failure to conquer them and uses Brahmā as his charioteer. Symbolically then Śiva supersedes Indra and Brahmā but in fact he takes over from both other aspects of his character.

There is in fact a direct link between Indra and Śiva in the Maruts, the storm gods attendant on Indra who are also called Rudras; whereas in the *Ṛgveda* they are Indra's companions, later they are called Indra's brothers and sons of Rudra. But it is rather the adulterous side of Indra's character that ultimately appears in some of the legends concerning Śiva, although the best-known myth, that of Śiva's real or apparent seduction of the wives of the ascetics in the pine forest, is attributed in the *Mahābhārata* to Agni, from whom Śiva draws something of his connection with the heat (*tapas*) of asceticism and of sexual desire. In succession to Brahmā Śiva takes over the creative attributes of the late Vedic Prajāpati. Indeed, this may be a particularly early feature, for an interesting passage in one of the Brāhmaṇas, dealing with Prajāpati's creative activity, gives a newly born deity eight names corresponding to elements or other important entities (Kauṣ.Br.6.1); this is very close to the eight forms of developed Śaiva theology. These eight forms of Śiva and a similar grouping of his five faces or manifestations are each given a name and a function (possibly in some cases representing local deities incorporated into the cult), through which the Purāṇas begin to identify Śiva with the totality of

4. Hanumān, Rāma's Vānara helper

creation ; the five faces are rulers of the five directions (the four points of the compass and the zenith) and other groups of five such as the senses, while the eight forms represent the five elements, the sun, the moon and the sacrificer or individual self, representing between them the spatial extension and physical expression of the universe. Elsewhere in the Brāhmaṇas the stress is still on Rudra's malevolence and his dwelling in forests or other lonely places and he is said to reside in the north, the ill-omened region. However, the identification with Agni is already beginning to be made. Śiva is still regarded as fierce and uncanny, frequently angry, in the *Mahābhārata*, but the main body of the epic also knows him as an ascetic absorbed in contemplation, who nonetheless grants favours to his worshippers, while some later parts show acquaintance with his phallic aspect, which from archaeological evidence is known to have been in existence in the first century B.C.

The tension between Śiva's ascetic and erotic aspects visible here later becomes a definite feature of his portrayal in the Purāṇas. The contrast between Śiva as the lord of Yogins, smeared with ashes and meditating in a cremation ground, and Śiva making love for a thousand years with his wife Pārvatī represents however not just an apparent paradox in the nature of the deity but also a basic problem for the ordinary worshipper, who has to reconcile the conflicting claims of celibacy during studentship and of reproduction as a married man. The resolution of the conflict on the human plane must be in such temporal terms through successive stages. But at the divine level there is no such successive or cyclic assumption of different aspects. Rather there is a perception of Śiva as the totality, an omnipresent cosmic power, ever changing and thus ever creating and destroying. Śiva can be described as the reconciliation of opposites – good and evil, auspicious and malignant, active and quiescent – but more exactly he is the expression of the ultimate nature of reality manifest in the world in the many apparent polarities of life and death, creation and destruction, the ascetic and the erotic, which are however not separate states but mutually dependent pairs on whose interrelationship the whole of life depends.

Perhaps the most widely known and appreciated form of Śiva is that of the 'lord of the dance', Naṭarāja, which embodies just this insight. For, while he is thereby the patron of music and dance, its real significance is that as the cosmic dancer Śiva embodies the energy manifest in the universe in five activities – the emission of creation, its maintenance and destruction, the concealment of his nature through the world-process and the granting of grace to his devotee. Śiva's association with the dance is found in late parts of the *Mahābhārata* and further developed in the Purāṇas. In the typical iconographic form of this aspect of Śiva he is surrounded by a ring of fire symbolising the life-process of the universe within which Śiva dances incessantly: all is subject to constant change and Śiva alone, the ultimate cause of transient beings, is immutable. As an image of the rhythm of the universe it is undeniably powerful, containing as it does the notion of an equilibrium which could so easily be disturbed, as when Śiva performs his wild Tāṇḍava dance, shaking the world to pieces. The continued emphasis on the destructive aspect takes us back to the Vedic Rudra, while the stress on power or energy is reminiscent of the depiction of the Vedic gods in general; despite elements from outside the Aryan milieu which have contributed to the developed Śiva and the synthesis that has taken place within it, his ambivalent and even paradoxical nature reflects a continuing strand in Hindu thought.

CHAPTER FOUR

Unorthodox Movements

Although the rise of Vaiṣṇavism and Śaivism can be traced back to the theistic trends of the Upaniṣads and forward to become the dominant religious trends within Hinduism, the period of their origin was also, broadly speaking, that which saw the most divergent trends arising to test its absorptive abilities to the limit, with the appearance in the sixth to fifth centuries B.C. of Buddhism, Jainism, the Ājīvikas and other less well documented heterodox movements. However, distinct movements divergent from the main stream are much older than that, quite apart from more popular features filtering in to the hieratic religion, such as the cult of Nāgas and Yakṣas already mentioned.

The *Atharvaveda* has quite a lot of information about the Vrātyas, devoting its fifteenth book to the Vrātya who is the type figure for the whole group. They were evidently a sizable group who were quite distinct from the general Aryan population and a special ritual is prescribed in later Vedic texts for their admission or restoration to society. Their precise nature has been much discussed but certain features about them are quite clear: they had a distinctive style of dress, including turban and ramskins, they carried a bow and other weapons, their chariots were of great significance, and some of their practices recall the breath-control which is a regular feature of asceticism. In texts of all periods there is more than a hint of violence as part of their way of life and by the time of the *Mahābhārata* they were classed among various groups despised for their violence and evil ways. Nevertheless, their relationship to Aryan society must have had a sufficient basis to require the elaboration of a whole *vrātyastoma* ritual to purify them; they were not complete outsiders. The oldest references to their violence are in association with some kind of expeditions and this fact, together with the importance of the warrior's chariot to them, may well indicate that they were some kind of raiding party, whether as a first wave of Aryans who differed somewhat in customs from the Vedic Aryans (for the Aryan arrival was not a single event but more probably a succession of groups filtering in) or as a special group of young warriors set apart from within the community as a whole, a feature which is known in other early Indo-European societies. In that case the *vrātyastoma* of which a major feature is the distribution of wealth would represent the purification of the group from ritual impurities contracted in their expeditions by distribution among the rest of the community of the goods thereby won; this fits well with the original pattern of the sacrifice as the redistribution of impurity, and the decline in esteem of the Vrātyas would follow inevitably with the change in religious and social conditions brought about by a more settled way of life.

On the other hand, this still leaves the links with Śiva and with asceticism. Other views would make of the Vrātyas prototypes of the yogin or of the Śaiva ascetic. A connection with Śiva would also help to explain the obvious fertility elements in parts of the *vrātyastoma*, including ritual intercourse with a prostitute, but this can also be interpreted as the celibacy appropriate to a military expedition and the abandon after its conclusion, and it is not irrelevant that the horse sacrifice, the most *kṣatriya*-oriented of the orthodox rituals, includes ritual intercourse. The explanations are not necessarily exclusive. Some elements of Śaivism might well have entered more orthodox Aryan tradition through such relatively informal advance parties.

A similarly enigmatic figure is that of the long-haired *muni* 'inspired one' (later an ascetic under a vow of silence) described in one late hymn of the *Ṛgveda* (10.136). Although the ecstacy experienced is similar to that depicted in another late hymn (ṚV 10.119), where it is produced by *soma*, in this hymn the *munis* have drunk from the cup of Rudra and the whole ethos is different from the sacrificial cult. The *munis*, wind-girdled and wearing yellow robes, soar into the atmosphere and the company of the gods, seeing everything and transported everywhere. The emphasis on inner meditation and various kinds of asceticism leading apparently to experiences of ecstasy in both Vrātyas and *munis* has as much to do with certain trends in the Upaniṣads as with later Yoga techniques, but of course the development of thought in the Upaniṣads may in part be explained by the impact of such new ideas from outside the traditional orthodoxy.

In the Upaniṣadic period (eighth to fourth centuries B.C.), among the individuals of varied backgrounds who contributed to the discussions were some who had renounced society for life in the forest. Substantial numbers of such wandering ascetics, sometimes forming loose groups, form the background to the emergence in the sixth to fifth centuries of Buddhism, Jainism and the Ājīvika movement. Evidently social and political conditions were conducive to such a trend and specifically the rise of great monarchical states in the Ganges basin was subverting the older tribal way of life, in which each individual had a definite place. All these wanderers professed the religious life and adopted various speculative doctrines; they rejected their ties with relatives and society at large to live a wandering existence by begging or by gathering their own food in the forests, not settling down anywhere except in the rainy season, when of course movement became virtually impossible. Some retired right into the forests to indulge in various forms of self-torture by hunger and thirst, heat and cold, and other privations, while others undertook spectacular penances on the outskirts of settlements aimed in part no doubt at impressing the ordinary people and gaining alms thereby. But others were less committed to such physical self-discipline and were concerned more with techniques of meditation by which they could master their surroundings mentally. For underlying all the manifestations of asceticism was still the same concern for power and control over the world which was so entrenched in the thinking of the Brāhmaṇas. The ascetic was believed, as he advanced in his spiritual practice, to acquire supernatural powers from clairvoyance and levitation to the ability to destroy anyone who opposed him; in more spiritual terms, he acquired an insight into the nature of the cosmos and through this knowledge reached a state of freedom transcending all mundane limitations. The existence of a sizable body of individuals who had thus rejected society suggests a considerable malaise at the period and there are several indications in the events of the Buddha's life that the expansion of the state of Magadha, where most of his preaching took place, was seen as a threat to the tribal states along the foothills of the Himālaya, from which the Buddha himself had come.

Siddhārtha Gautama, who was to become the Buddha, the

'enlightened', lived probably from 563 to 483 B.C. and was born as the son of a leading figure among the Śākyas, a small tribe in the area of modern Nepal. The later traditions about his birth and youth are in large part legendary but from the point when at the age of 29 he 'went out from home to homelessness' the record becomes more precise. However, one story from his youth, implausible as it is in its extant form, does vividly depict the psychological background to the Buddha's teaching. This is the story of the successive chariot drives in which the previously carefully secluded youth comes face to face with the realities of life in the form of a decrepit old man, a diseased man, a corpse accompanied by mourners, and a serene wandering ascetic; from this he draws the lesson that all existence involves suffering, conquest of which is the chief religious goal.

Such pessimism was undoubtedly a feature of the period, even though Buddhist teaching has given it a characteristic expression. Ājīvika doctrines are permeated by the same outlook and it also affected the Upaniṣadic tradition. The *Maitrī Upaniṣad* has regularly been considered to show Buddhist influence because it commences with an expression of world-weariness which might almost have been taken direct from Buddhist meditations on the loathesomeness of the human body and includes a list of great kings who have vanished into oblivion and a picture of cosmic decay with 'the drying up of oceans, the collapse of mountain peaks, the wandering of the pole star', and so forth. That such a complaint should have been inserted into the latest of the major Upaniṣads illustrates very well the shift in general attitudes.

After his abandonment of the world, Siddhārtha Gautama at first begged his food but soon adopted the life of a forest hermit. For a time, he became a pupil of two named teachers in succession, in each case finding that their teaching, which seems basically to have consisted of techniques to achieve psychological states of interiorisation similar to Yoga, did not lead to liberation. After further wanderings he joined another five ascetics engaged in austerities consisting mainly of fasting but again decided that this was getting him nowhere and so left them. The recording of these details in the Buddhist scriptures strikingly attests the prevalence of this way of life. Thereafter, Gautama resolved to remain seated in meditation under a tree until he had resolved the problem of suffering; after traditionally 49 days, passing through successive stages of contemplation, he finally understood why the world is full of suffering and what the remedy is – he became enlightened, the Buddha. By this enlightenment he achieved the release from the unsatisfactoriness of worldly existence which Buddhists call Nirvāṇa, the cessation of the flux of becoming and its replacement by a state of permanence.

In relation to the history of religion in India, one of the most striking features of Buddhism and the contemporary systems of Jainism and of the Ājīvikas is that they accept as axiomatic the belief in transmigration – seen in the earliest Upaniṣads as a novel and esoteric doctrine – and the associated view of the religious goal as release from rebirth. So swift an acceptance of the doctrine probably conceals the fact that it was current in those circles from which the Buddha came before it penetrated orthodoxy. This is the more striking in that early Buddhism denied other basic tenets of the Upaniṣads with its theories of impermanence and non-self which, together with the emphasis on suffering or more exactly on the general unsatisfactoriness of life, can be viewed as a deliberate antithesis to the understanding gradually developed in the Upaniṣads of a permanent, blissful self. However, the early Buddhist scriptures show little direct acquaintance with the newer strands of orthodox thought in the Upaniṣads or antagonism towards them, by contrast with the Jains or Ājīvikas, for which their more easterly place of origin probably provides the explanation.

There is also evident in the teaching ascribed to the Buddha himself a critical attitude to all authority – the Buddha went so far as to stress that what he himself said should not be taken for granted but tested, since the only criterion is whether it is effective. In consequence, early Buddhism had a distinctly empirical or pragmatic tendency and the Buddha laid out his basic teachings in the form of a diagnosis in the Four Noble Truths, ascertaining the symptoms in the impermanent and unsatisfactory nature of existence, identifying the cause in the desire for pleasure and for existence, giving a prognosis and declaring it curable by removing ignorance, and finally prescribing a remedy in the way of life summed up in the Eightfold Path.

The critical attitude to authority led inevitably to the rejection of claims to absolute authority for the Vedas or for a special status for all Brāhmans regardless of qualifications. Indeed, some pronouncements of the Buddha seem to elevate the *kṣatriyas* above the Brāhmans, reflecting the old rivalry between them for the top position in society. In the long run this rejection of the Vedas served to mark the separation of Buddhism from Hinduism as a distinct religion. But even in the Buddha's own lifetime the efforts to gather together a group of committed followers and the vigorous polemics against other such groups indicate an intention to establish a distinct sect at the least; it was such features more particularly that served to set Buddhism apart from Hinduism, although how far lay-people in general recognised the distinction is open to question.

One of the most obvious features from the beginning was the organisation of the Buddha's followers into the Saṅgha, the 'community', which was modelled to a considerable extent on the constitution of the fast disappearing tribal groups which were called by the same name. Nostalgia for the old order may well have been a potent factor in recruitment to the Buddhist Saṅgha and to the other similar groupings which were emerging out of the diffuse body of wandering ascetics. Thus, in addition to the Buddhist Saṅgha, the Jains and the Ājīvikas were forming their own communities and possibly other groups were coming together which were reabsorbed into more orthodox Hinduism; for instance, the later Vaiṣṇava sect of the Pāñcarātra may well have originated from such a group, whose distinctive feature of a maximum of five nights' stay in a habitation gave them their name. Certainly, various rules of the Buddhist Saṅgha seem designed to preserve its distinction from other groups; the use of an ochre robe (even if related in some way to the attire of the *munis* in ṚV 10.136) has become absolutely characteristic. The stress on regular meetings of the Saṅgha and the need for all decisions to be reached by the unanimous assent of all the assembled monks look back to tribal organisation.

In other respects Buddhism reveals indebtedness to the popular cults of the time. The worship of the *caitya*, the sacred spot often marked by a tree but occasionally by a tumulus, was taken over and adapted to the veneration of the *stūpas*, tumuli built over the divided ashes of the Buddha and subsequently over other relics; the reverence for the Bodhi Tree, the tree under which he attained enlightenment, points in the same direction, while the tradition that he was protected as he meditated there by the snake king Mucalinda attests the absorption of Nāga worship. The tradition of pilgrimage to the sites associated with the Buddha became established at a very early period – the emperor Aśoka in the middle of the third century B.C. records his own visit to the Buddha's birthplace – and in all probability predates its appearance in Hinduism, where the first evidence for it is from later parts of the *Mahābhārata*.

An almost exact contemporary of the Buddha was Vardhamāna Mahāvīra (probably 540–468 B.C.), who is often too simply called the founder of Jainism, for the Jain belief is that there are 24 Tīrthaṃkaras, 'ford-makers', of whom Mahāvīra is the last. While the details of the earlier figures are purely legendary and linked with the Jain concept of a steady decline of the world in its present phase, the 23rd Tīrthaṃkara, Pārśva, may be an historical figure. He is held to have lived 250 years before Mahāvīra and to have propagated views differing in certain minor particulars from Mahāvīra's. Mahāvīra himself was born into a small clan or tribe north of Magadha (a similar background to the Buddha's); the Jain scriptures stress that all Tīrthaṃkaras are born as *kṣatriyas.* After a similar upbringing to the Buddha's, he too gave up the life of a householder when he was 30, apparently entering the order already established by Pārśva but soon leaving it to pursue more extreme asceticism, and abandoning all ties with the world, including clothing. After years of wandering he achieved enlightenment at the foot of a *sāl* tree (designated in the texts as a *caitya*) and so became the Jina, the one who had conquered. During the remaining 30 years of his life he wandered about and taught in the same Magadha area as the Buddha, claiming the interest and even patronage of the same rulers. Subsequently also the Jains claim the allegiance of the first Mauryan ruler, Candragupta (c.322–298 B.C.), just as the Buddhists do of the third, Aśoka (c.269–32 B.C.). However, they seem to have been less important as rivals of the early Buddhists than a third group, the Ājīvikas, whose leader Maskarin Gosāla is said by the Jain texts to have kept company with Mahāvīra for a time before quarrelling and breaking away, although it is not impossible that the split was the other way round.

Jainism, whose doctrines seem from their archaic cast to

have been preserved with relatively little change from Mahāvīra himself, is both atheistic and materialistic in the sense that it regards all beings, including those termed gods, as part of the cosmic system and subject to transmigration and also considers that the world is composed of six constituent substances, which include selves, *jīva* (literally 'life'). Despite the difference of terminology, its concept of the eternal *jīva*, whose essence is pure intelligence, comes closer to the *ātman* of the Upaniṣads than to Buddhist views of the ultimate unreality of the self. It differs in being regarded as absolutely unique to each individual (in this approximating to the views of Sāṃkhya and Yoga) and in being found not only in animal life from gods to worms but also in plant life and inanimate matter; the latter aspect (which is a sign of the primitive origins of Jainism) is responsible for many of its most characteristic features, leading as it does to an extreme concern for *ahiṃsā*, non-injury to life, expressed in the nose-mask worn by Jain ascetics, the straining of drinking-water and so forth, and in the concentration of Jain laypeople in trade and commerce, away from the risks of harm to plants and living organisms entailed in agriculture and many artisan employments. Those who have entered the Jain Saṅgha are required to devote their whole energies to keeping completely the five vows, including that of *ahiṃsā*, and an extremely strict and detailed regimen is laid down for them. But it was recognised that such strictness was impossible for the lay community, for whom therefore separate provision was made, thereby paradoxically giving them a more assured position in the religion than in early Buddhism, despite their inferior status. The lay community has a greater importance in Jainism and plays its part in the administration of the religion and in the ritual, which is predominantly a lay concern.

Jain doctrines of the nature of the self's bondage to the world and consequently of the method to achieve release are quite distinctive. Whereas Buddhism stresses the importance of attitude or intention as the binding force, Jainism says that the cause of bondage is *karma*, the product of all activity, thought of as a real but subtle substance which builds up layers of matter round the *jīva* to form a special body that weighs the *jīva* down and prevents it resuming its rightful and natural state of free and inactive existence in perpetual isolation, *kaivalya*, the usual Jain term for the state of release. Release can only, therefore, be achieved by dispelling existing *karma*, while preventing as far as possible the acquisition of more; this is achieved by various elaborate penances, culminating in certain circumstances in self-starvation, and modes of conduct. This materialistic and somewhat mechanistic interpretation of *karma* leads therefore to an emphasis on extremes of austerity, which is in marked contrast to the Buddhist emphasis on moderation, a mean between indulgence and masochism conducive to detachment. More generally, the aim of final release from transmigration is to be reached by practice of the 'three jewels' of right faith, right knowledge and right conduct, of which the last consists of observance of the five vows, including *ahiṃsā*; however, the other two reveal the more dogmatic streak in Jainism compared with Buddhism, for right faith means complete confidence in Mahāvīra and his teachings and right knowledge includes acceptance of the Jain philosophical tenets concerning the relativity of knowledge, based on the manifold, multiple nature of everything. These views involve a correspondence theory of truth, whereby judgements are true when they correspond to features of the external world. The Jains also hold certain distinctive views about the nature of language.

Most *jīvas* have no hope of achieving release but will continue to migrate indefinitely, for the number of *jīvas* is infinite and thus, however many pass into isolation (*kaivalya*), an infinite number will remain; there is an infinite number of *jīvas* existing in a purely potential state in readiness to take the place of those which succeed in escaping from the system. Thus the process of transmigration continues for ever and the universe similarly passes through an infinite number of phases of progress and decline. Although the universe is pluralistic and contains an infinite number of *jīvas*, it is a mistake to think that life is either the product or the property of the body, for the principle of life, the *jīva*, is absolutely distinct from the body, though tied to it by its *karma*. In its true nature, to be regained in release, the *jīva* possesses infinite knowledge, insight, bliss and power; knowledge and insight together constitute consciousness, which distinguishes *jīva* from inanimate matter.

Similarly rigid dualism and fundamental atheism are characteristic of the earliest period of the Sāṃkhya system, which bears a general resemblance to Jainism. Although there are elements which may be connected with Sāṃkhya and the related Yoga system in the Upaniṣads, it is significant that a substantial part of the evidence for their early stages in the Hindu tradition is found in the *Mahābhārata*. Furthermore, in both Sāṃkhya and Yoga the aim of release is regularly called *kaivalya*, the isolation as self-contained monads of the selves from matter and from each other. There are differences, however: whereas Jainism considers the connection of the self with non-self as real and defiling, Sāṃkhya views it as illusory. But overall it is plausible to consider that both Sāṃkhya and Yoga originated in some degree in the same milieu as the heterodox faiths.

Sāṃkhya, 'enumeration', may even originally have constituted just a cosmology on purely material lines, attempting to explain the transformation or evolution of matter or nature (*prakṛti*) from subtle into gross forms. For the concept of *puruṣa*, the spiritual entity, is enumerated last in the list of categories of evolution, which probably gave rise to the name of the system, and seems in some respects to be an appendage to the scheme. However, in its oldest extant form the system does include the category of *puruṣa*, 'the person', consisting of an infinite number of selves or spiritual entities, but is still atheistic and has no place for a creator. Ultimately this too is modified, for Sāṃkhya cosmology was frequently made use of by other schools and Vaiṣṇava sects came to incorporate Sāṃkhya ideas, most famously in the *Bhagavadgītā*.

Possibly the germs of Sāṃkhya ideas can be seen in some of the Vedic cosmogonic hymns but more certainly various cosmological speculations in the *Bṛhadāraṇyaka* and *Chāndogya Upaniṣads* can be identified as related to Sāṃkhya views; in particular the notion of *ahaṃkāra*, the principle of individuation, is first mentioned here (Ch.Up.7.25), as is a threefold division associated with the colours red, white and black (Ch.Up.6.3–4). On the other hand the main similarities are in suggestions of a dualism of matter and spirit which is too ancient and widespread a view to point definitely to Sāṃkhya. A little later there occurs a series of categories of evolution similar to that of Sāṃkhya, except for the absence of *ahaṃkāra*, set in a basically Yoga context (Kaṭha Up.3.10–11, 6.7–8). The three colours are linked in the *Śvetāśvatara Upaniṣad* (4.5) with ideas of the one unborn female (=*prakṛti*) and the unborn male (=*puruṣa*) but the terms *sattva, rajas* and *tamas* for the three strands of nature with which these colours are later connected do not occur until the *Maitrī Upaniṣad,* which has a more developed account of the Sāṃkhya system.

Although there are possibly elements of Yoga to be seen in the Vedas in the hymns to the long-haired *muni* (ṚV 10.136) and the Vrātyas (AV 15), the name Yoga first appears in the *Kaṭha Upaniṣad,* where Yoga is likened to a chariot in which the *ātman* sits with reason as the driver while the chariot itself is the body (3.3–6), meaning that mastery of the body is acquired by control of the senses. This method is developed in the *Śvetāśvatara Upaniṣad* which emphasises the connection between breathing and thought (2.8–10). Later still the *Maitrī Upaniṣad* enumerates six stages of Yoga and alludes to definite physical practices.

Much evidence for early Sāṃkhya and Yoga is contained in part of the twelfth book of the *Mahābhārata,* supposedly the homily of the dying Bhīṣma but in fact containing much didactic material from the later stages of the epic's growth. One passage, also marked by the absence of *ahaṃkāra* as early, shows a synthesis between ancient cosmological speculations and yogic theories of evolution (Mbh.12.187=239–40). The *Mahābhārata* also here contains more evidence for a theistic Sāṃkhya than the Upaniṣads; it mentions three types of Sāṃkhya – those who accept 24 categories only, those who accept 25, and those who accept 26, the last being a supreme deity (Mbh.12.306.27–55). However, the clearest theistic emphasis is found in the *Bhagavadgītā* which presents two separate accounts of Sāṃkhyayoga in its seventh and thirteenth chapters. In all the Yoga passages of the *Mahābhārata* there is a strong emphasis on discipline, meditation and control of the senses. Such practices lead to supernatural or magical powers (Mbh.12.232.21–2), which are to be avoided by the true yogin, for the real goal of the discipline is the attainment of the state of Brahman or union with the one. This part of the *Mahābhārata* also contains frequent statements that Sāṃkhya and Yoga are essentially one, as well as the passages dealing with each separately. The two schools in their later stages are complementary but were probably more distinct in their earlier stages. While, outside the orthodox movements, Sāṃkhya has greatest similarities with Jainism in its emphasis on enumeration and a rather dogmatic tendency, Yoga has some analogies with early Buddhism's stress on meditation.

However, neither the emergence of Buddhism and Jainism as ultimately separate religions nor the gradual development of Sāṃkhya and Yoga into orthodox schools of thought exhaust the variety of new movements appearing in this period. As we have already seen, the Ājīvikas under their leader Maskarin Gosāla (also Makkhali or Maṅkhali) were prominent at the time of the Buddha and Mahāvīra, and the Buddhist scriptures mention other unorthodox teachers, some of whose views seem related to the Cārvāka or Lokāyata school of thought. Unfortunately, what is known about the Ājīvikas comes from the polemical literature of Buddhism and Jainism, for the sect's own writings have not been preserved and it finally disappeared around the fourteenth century A.D., despite having been quite influential in the fifth to third centuries B.C. Indeed, the second of the Mauryan emperors had an Ājīvika fortune-teller at his court and Aśoka presented caves as monasteries to them, as did his grandson and successor Daśaratha. There is even one passage in the *Mahābhārata* which seems to reflect Ājīvika teachings, with some admixture of Sāṃkhya elements, and is ascribed to one Maṅki, perhaps a corruption of their leader's name (Mbh.12.171); after suffering catastrophe, this Maṅki declaims on the power of fate and the need to be free of desire, casts off all desires, and attains Brahman or immortality.

The origins of the sect lie in the same groups of wandering ascetics and their name may well be derived from the distinctive 'way of life' (*ājīva*) of those who had abandoned the responsibilities of family and social life for the relative freedom of a wandering existence. The trend to organisation was perhaps more a defensive reaction to the threat of state intervention and less linked to doctrine in the case of the Ājīvikas, among whom were apparently to be found agnostic or sceptical and materialistic views, as well as the determinist views associated with Maskarin Gosāla; the interest of the kings of Magadha in the new groups emerging among the wanderers may not have been exclusively benevolent. On the other hand some references in the Jain scriptures suggest that Maskarin Gosāla considered himself the 24th leader of the group and record, in connection with the split between Mahāvīra and Gosāla, that he held that he was animated by the soul of an earlier figure.

Both Jain and Buddhist sources agree that Maskarin Gosāla was a rigid determinist and record certain stories to illustrate this. Fate (*niyati*) was the sole determinant of every occurrence and the doctrine of *karma* was therefore fallacious; accordingly, there could be no escape from the cycle of rebirths (*saṃsāra*) by eliminating one's *karma* by whatever means. Rather, each individual's passage along the path of transmigration was ordained from the beginning and one achieved release simply by coming to the end of a fixed but extremely large number of lives; the process was likened to that of the ripening of a fruit, proceeding automatically, or to a ball of thread unwinding when thrown. Events must take their course and could not be influenced by man's actions. The deep despondency apparent here seems summed up in the presages of final disaster pronounced by Gosāla in his last illness which in part relate to the demise of the tribal states; the old order was perishing and Gosāla could see only gloom and forces too powerful for an individual to control in the future. Even entry into the Ājīvika community was predetermined – there could after all be no reason for it in terms of acquiring knowledge or merit as a means to release.

Two other figures were important in shaping Ājīvika beliefs. Pūraṇa Kassapa was perhaps an older contemporary of Maskarin Gosāla, holding similar views, but with a pronounced antinomian emphasis. The thief, adulterer or murderer in his view commits no sin and there is no merit to be gained from generosity or self-control. Apart from his habitual nudity – a feature shared in any case with Maskarin Gosāla and Vardhamāna Mahāvīra – the only personal detail recorded of Pūraṇa Kassapa is the manner of his death, suicide by drowning. The other figure, Pakudha Kaccāyana, held a form of atomic theory in which there are seven permanent and unchanging elemental categories: earth, water, fire, air, life, joy and sorrow. These do not alter or develop and thus all change is illusory; in addition, since life or the self is, like the other material elements, unalterable there can be no moral responsibility even for murder. This view was apparently harmonised with Maskarin Gosāla's determinism by the argument that, since future events are already determined, they in some sense already exist and thus time and all temporal change is less than wholly real.

In addition to these figures connected with the Ājīvika movement and the Jain leader, Mahāvīra, Buddhist sources also refer to other unorthodox teachers. One of these, Sañjaya, espouses a thoroughgoing scepticism which repudiates knowledge of the self and regards metaphysical questions as meaningless; it is however hard to ascertain whether such total scepticism was ever widely current. But the distinctly materialist views of Ajita Keśakambalin evidently did attract a certain following for they resemble the doctrines of the later Cārvāka or Lokāyata school of thought. Ajita Keśakambalin held that there was no after-life but that the four elements (earth, water, fire, air) of which man is made disperse at death; thus charity and other forms of morality are pointless. Surprising as it may seem in the Indian context, such views were not unparalleled at this period. The views of the first cause which the *Śvetāśvatara Upaniṣad* rejects in favour of a creator deity include fate (*niyati*) and elements (*bhūta*), the doctrines associated with Maskarin Gosāla and Ajita Keśakambalin; at a later date the Cārvākas cite some of Yājñavalkya's teaching in the *Bṛhadāraṇyaka Upaniṣad* in support of their views. Both epics include some allusion to such views; in the *Mahābhārata* an individual named Cārvāka draws the wrath of other Brāhmans by his words (Mbh.12.39.22–47), while in the *Rāmāyaṇa*, when Rāma is being urged to put aside his scruples and accept the kingdom after his father's death, one of those who urge him is a Brāhman Jābāli who puts forward the same arguments based on self-interest elsewhere ascribed to the Cārvākas. The latter instance suggests a link with politics, which is strengthened by the fact that Bṛhaspati, by now reduced to a divine teacher, is regarded as the founder of politics and the author of a Sūtra which reputedly was the original text of the Cārvākas; at a much later date Bṛhaspati is credited with the maxim 'better a pigeon today than a peacock tomorrow', which fits well with the generally hedonistic approach of the school.

In their heyday, the Cārvākas or Lokāyatas seem to have been regarded as quite a menace by more orthodox schools of thought, who deplore their atheistic outlook and regard with deep suspicion their use of logic to disprove the next world, to deny the efficacy of ritual and to dismiss the authority of the Vedas. They held a form of radical empiricism, declaring that knowledge is acquired only through sense-perceptions and that inference is not a valid method of acquiring knowledge, since it depends on universals which are outside direct experience. From this epistemological position the Cārvākas criticised the entire social, moral and religious framework of orthodox Hinduism, which in response developed various counter arguments. They declare, as did Ajita Keśakambalin, that the body is produced from the four elements and that consciousness comes from their combination; thus the self is not something distinct from the body. They pour particular scorn on the rituals aimed at securing rewards in the next life and ask why, if the offerings of food made to the dead can reach them, the process is not adapted to ensure nourishment for travellers away from home. In common with other heterodox movements, they belittle the status of the Brāhmans, suggesting that their aim is so to manipulate people's religious sensibilities as to produce maximum profit for themselves. Indeed, they seem to have regarded religion as being inconsistent with ethical values, because of the dominance of irrational ritual. Such views can hardly have been popular in religious circles but references to them are found over a very considerable period – the last detailed mention of them comes from the fourteenth century A.D. Their effect, along with the criticisms of the heterodox faiths, must have been considerable in forcing a critical re-examination of their doctrines by more orthodox forms of Hinduism, which nonetheless by adaptation was able to survive and indeed outlast these attacks.

The formative influences on developed Hinduism included, however, not only such heterodox elements generated from within itself or by interaction with non-Aryan groups in India, but also cults entering India from outside during the period of foreign invasions between the second century B.C. and the second century A.D. The figure of Kalki as the future *avatāra* of Viṣṇu may, as we have seen, be owed to such events. One cult which became widespread, especially in north India, was the cult of the sun introduced no later than the first century B.C. by the Magas, who probably arrived with the Śakas. Sun-worship is of course traceable back to the *Ṛgveda* in the hymns to Sūrya but had subsequently tended to decline in significance, apart from the daily invocation of the sun as Savitṛ with the *Gāyatrī* (ṚV 3.62.10) which traditionalists still perform at sunrise.

5. Sūrya, the sun god

The innovation of the Magas was to install a cult image in human form of their solar deity Mihira (=Mithra), identified with Sūrya and surrounded by his divine attendants, in their sanctuaries, thus replacing the daily sun-worship with a full-scale cult. Because of the similarities resulting from a common background between the Iranian cult of Mihira and the Indian worship of Sūrya, the process of fusion was relatively simple and the cult became one of the leading religions of India during the first millennium A.D. The *Mahābhārata* alludes to worship of Sūrya both with invocations and with all the apparatus of a cult and to sun-worshippers as a well-regarded group. Nevertheless, the tradition of its foreign origin was maintained within the cult, for the Purāṇas record the legend that the sun cult was first established in India by Kṛṣṇa's son Sāmba, who was cured of leprosy by the sun-god. In gratitude he built a temple to him but, as there were no competent Brāhmans, the deity himself advised him to go to the mythical 'island of the Śakas' where he was constantly worshipped by the Maga priests, who were his own descendants; Sāmba then returned with eighteen Maga families who settled round Sāmba's temple and established their cult. The naming of Kṛṣṇa's son as the initiator of the cult suggests an initial link with Vaiṣṇavism, which is not implausible in view of Viṣṇu's solar aspect, but at a later period the sun cult was effectively absorbed by Śaivism. Sculptural representations of Sūrya from the Kuṣāṇa period support his foreign origin by showing him in typical Kuṣāṇa costume establishing a continuing iconographic convention; his feet are hidden by his chariot or covered in long boots, for which later a mythological explanation is provided.

Sūrya is regarded as the supreme deity who is willing to bestow favour on his worshippers and grant them freedom from sin and illness, long life and ultimately a state of final release in his world. The Magas who propagated his cult are descended from the Iranian priestly clan of the Magus and it is interesting to note that, as ritual specialists, they were accepted into Indian society at the appropriate level, that of Brāhmans; however, there is ample evidence in the Iranian tradition that the Magus were well used to adapting their particular skills to the prevailing religious climate. They did, however, retain the Iranian name for the sacred thread or girdle, which is part of the common Indo-Iranian tradition. But when much later, probably in the seventh century A.D., another Iranian group, the Bhojakas, arrived, their integration was much less easy, not only because of the greater introspection of Indian society but also because this group were definitely Zoroastrian, not eclectic like the Magas, and so were unwilling to accept the authority of the Vedas. Nevertheless, they are termed Brāhmans in an eighth-century inscription, though generally regarded with contempt by other groups of Brāhmans.

CHAPTER FIVE

The Orthodox Synthesis

The ruling groups among these invading peoples, the Yavanas (=Greeks), Śakas and Pahlavas, are among those to whom a place is assigned in the *Manusmṛti*, in a process of accommodating the new social realities to the theoretical pattern. From the beginning of the Christian era the older Dharmasūtras, which had been closely linked to the ritual schools, were expanded and remodelled in verse form to become the group of texts known as the Dharmaśāstras. No longer tied to a particular Vedic school, the Dharmaśāstras aimed to prescribe rules which were authoritative for all of society with a consequent enlargement in their scope and content. The earliest and most famous of these texts is that of Manu, the *Manusmṛti* or *Mānavadharmaśāstra*, which probably attained its present form around the second century A.D. The work presents itself, not as the work of a named teacher like most of the Dharmasūtras, but as the *dharma* declared by Brahmā to Manu, the first man, and passed on by him through Bhṛgu, one of the ten great sages. This claim to divine origin made by all the Dharmaśāstras is intended to secure their general acceptance.

After an introductory chapter in which Manu at the request of the sages describes the creation of the world by Brahmā and his own birth, the *Manusmṛti* then expounds the sources of *dharma* and enumerates the main ceremonies from birth to the end of the student stage of life in the second chapter, followed by the householder in the next three, and the last two stages of life in the sixth chapter. Here already a development is seen. Although the Dharmasūtras recognise the four styles of life (*āśramas*), they do not make them successive but rather present them as the four possible modes of life open to the student after he has completed his basic education; indeed two of the Dharmasūtras reject the multiplicity of *āśramas*. However, with the growing importance of renunciation, attested to a limited extent in the Upaniṣads and very obvious in the heterodox movements, such rejection was impractical. But so too was the open-ended acceptance of it in other Dharmasūtras. A way was needed of containing this trend towards opting out of society within manageable proportions, and so was evolved the theory here presented in the *Manusmṛti* by which the *āśramas* came to be associated with the ceremonies marking the major events of one's life and so evolved into the concept of the successive stages of life. Thus one could only properly reach the fourth stage, that of one who has totally renounced the world, the *saṃnyāsin*, by passing through the other three; in the long run this meant the virtual elimination of the third stage of the forest-dweller, who still maintained some basic ritual practices, but more immediately had the effect of limiting the numbers of *saṃnyāsins* from within the orthodox tradition.

The next three chapters of *Manusmṛti*, dealing with the duties incumbent on a king and related topics, show the greatest divergence from the older works and in fact have analogies with the oldest textbook of politics known, which is probably contemporary in date. Incidentally, the epics and Purāṇas also contain considerable legal material; there are many parallels to verses of Manu in both epics. While the *Manusmṛti* is still largely a textbook of human conduct, the later Dharmaśāstras approach more and more nearly to purely legal textbooks; important later Dharmaśāstras, such as those of Yājñavalkya and Nārada, date from the Gupta period and later. The king's duties envisaged in the *Manusmṛti* include the administration of justice, which approaches pure law but nevertheless still seeks to impose graded punishment according to the offender's class (*varṇa*). This section concludes with an account of the duties of the third and fourth classes (*vaiśyas* and *śūdras*).

The tenth chapter then deals with the mixed castes, the rules of occupation in relation to caste, and occupation in times of distress. It is here that the greatest degree of accommodation has taken place. In his theory of mixed castes, Manu proposes an elaborate system of marriages between *varṇas* producing in their varying combinations the many castes (*jāti*), which were by then the actual social divisions rather than the four classes (*varṇa*), and which were in many cases occupational groups or guilds that had adopted the closed pattern of endogamy which is the essential mark of a *jāti*; the scheme is artificial but it brings the theory into line with actual practice while appearing to do the opposite. It is in this section that Manu describes the Yavanas, Śakas, Pahlavas and others as lapsed *kṣatriyas*, who have lost their status through neglect of *dharma*, and by this legal fiction opens the possibility of their reception into the orthodox community by adopting the orthodox way of life and performing appropriate expiatory sacrifices; thus, their actual status as rulers can be given religious approval, provided they acknowledge the Brāhmans as religious leaders. The *Manusmṛti* may be a theoretical textbook but the practicalities of life are not overlooked, and this is an attitude which has in fact marked later Indian legal theory as well.

Also from about the beginning of the Christian era, in most cases, there developed out of various earlier speculations the six systems of orthodox Hindu philosophy, which consolidated and formalised trends of thought from the Upaniṣads and from other sources to provide definite schools of thought to counter the doctrines of the heterodox faiths. These six systems are traditionally grouped into three complementary pairs, as they certainly became, although that does not necessarily reflect the original situation. Since they were all coming into existence over basically the same period, it is not surprising that there was considerable mutual influence and so in what follows the distinctive features of each will be highlighted at the expense of the areas of agreement.

The link between the Nyāya and Vaiśeṣika systems seems to have existed from the earliest times and may predate the codification of their views in the form of Sūtras; in these philosophical systems also the fundamental concise texts which form the basis of subsequent elaboration in commentary form are termed Sūtras, 'threads'. Nyāya is primarily a school of logic and epistemology, claiming that knowledge of truth is the means for attaining the goal of release (*mokṣa*). Thus logic is pressed into service in support of orthodoxy by the argument that clear and logical analysis is essential for proper understanding of religious truths. The Nyāya emphasis on the validity of knowledge and its theory of reality are counters to the attacks of the Cārvākas. The proponents of the system are firm realists, believing that every term in their system denotes entities in the real world, a view summed up in one of their frequent phrases that 'to exist is to be knowable and definable'.

The school claims its origin from a teacher, Akṣapāda Gautama, traditionally assigned to the third century B.C., but the

Nyāyasūtra attributed to him is no earlier than the first century A.D. and is later than the *Vaiśeṣikasūtra* of the companion school. Indeed, the *Nyāyasūtra* shows evidence of the combination of a dialectical system, which is basic to the school, with a section on natural philosophy, which was independent until considerably later. The first extant commentary on the *Nyāyasūtra* is that of Vātsyāyana, probably of the fourth century A.D., which explains in detail the Sūtra text and in the process fashions a coherent system out of the rather varied parts of the Sūtra. Almost from its inception the school was in conflict with Buddhist epistemology and many subsequent writers directly attacked and were attacked by Buddhist logicians. Uddyotakara in the late sixth century incorporated the Buddhist Dignāga's logical teachings into the Nyāya system, substantially remodelling them in the process, while refuting Dignāga's theory that words define by excluding unwanted meaning in defence of Nyāya realism. Subsequently, the Buddhist dialectician, Dharmakīrti, in the seventh century launched an attack on the doctrine of Īśvara, the personal deity, of the Nyāya and Vaiśeṣika schools arguing that their proofs for the existence of Īśvara were vitiated by logical fallacies. This had the effect of concentrating their arguments on this point and ultimately in the emergence of the last great exponent of the older Nyāya, Udayana, at the end of the tenth century. One of his works is the first systematic account of Nyāya theism, aimed at vindicating the existence of Īśvara through philosophical reasoning; in it Udayana reveals himself as a worshipper of Śiva. Thus, a school which originally had only tenuous religious interests was turned by outside influences into a champion of orthodoxy.

An important topic in the field of logic, where Nyāya ideas were borrowed by other schools, was that of the 'means of (valid) knowledge', *pramāṇa.* The developed Nyāya system held that there were four: perception, inference, analogy and verbal testimony, in descending order of validity. Perception originally meant just sense perception but was later extended to cover all forms of immediate apprehension, including insight achieved through asceticism; the earlier use fitted in well with the system's realist emphasis on the existence of objects external to the perceiver. Inference rested on a generalisation based on a quality of 'pervasion', analysis of which led to theories of universals and particulars. Three kinds of inference were distinguished and a form of syllogism in five members was evolved to give expression to inferences. The comparative redundancy of the Nyāya syllogism compared with the Aristotelian is occasioned by its use in debate, where repetition helped to reinforce a point. A good deal of the presentation of the *Nyāyasūtra*, as of later texts, is best understood in terms of the formulation of rules and techniques for debate, whether between pupil and teacher or between rival teachers; its polemical background is obviously relevant.

Analogy or comparison is really a weaker form of inference through which we gain knowledge of something from its similarity to another already well-known object. Verbal testimony was originally a recognition that we accept many things outside our own direct experience on the authority of others, although the relation between word and meaning is also discussed here; subsequently, as Nyāya was more fully absorbed by orthodoxy, it covered the authority of scripture (*śruti*), which however ought in theory to be the strongest and not the weakest of the means of knowledge – a clear indication of this later adaptation.

The main proof adduced by the theistic Nyāya for the existence of Īśvara is based on the nature of the world as an effect which demands a first cause; Udayana argues that a non-intelligent cause requires an intelligence to direct it, which must be the eternal and omniscient Īśvara. A second argument is really a development of this: the need for a conscious agent to direct the process of combination which gives rise to the production of an ordered universe and the union of souls with bodies. Udayana compares the way that activity occurs in atoms with the activity of the body under the guidance of the soul and accepts that this implies a kind of body-soul relationship between god and atoms. Incidentally, Udayana gives one of the most explicit formulations of the law of contradiction ('there is no occurrence within a class (of both) when two are mutually opposed'), a law which was widely used in Indian logic despite statements to the contrary.

Whereas Nyāya concentrated on logic, the Vaiśeṣika system was more interested in physics or, to use an older term, natural philosophy. As a result it supplied the ontological structure to the merged system which eventually developed and after the tenth century treatises were written amalgamating the subject-matter of both systems. The earliest text is the *Vaiśeṣikasūtra* of Ulūka Kaṇāda; though older than the *Nyāyasūtra*, the *Vaiśeṣikasūtra* presupposes certain concepts of the Sāṃkhya and Mīmāṃsā systems, but was known to Buddhist writers by the second century A.D., probably therefore originating around the first century A.D. The basic doctrine of the school is that nature is atomic, a view occurring with some variation of detail in Buddhist, Jain and Ājīvika doctrines. An individual atom is devoid of qualities but possesses potentialities, realised when it combines with others of the same type to form molecules of the five elements (earth, water, fire, air, ether). Each element has individual characteristics (*viśeṣas*, hence the name of the school), which distinguish it from the four other non-atomic substances (time, space, soul, mind). The atoms are eternal and indivisible and thus creation or recreation of the world by Brahmā consists in the combination of all the separate atoms into the elements.

The *Vaiśeṣikasūtra* opens with the declaration that exaltation and release depend on a clear knowledge of the six categories within which everything is comprised: substance, quality, action, universal, particularity and inherence. Substance is divided into the nine forms already noted; ether, time and space are unitary but the others are multiple, including *ātman*. The plurality of selves is proved by their difference of status and each *ātman* has its characteristic individuality (*viśeṣa*). There was some dispute whether Īśvara should be classed as an *ātman* or as another (tenth) substance but extant works adopt the view that Īśvara belongs to the *ātman* class, though distinct from ordinary selves. Kaṇāda lists seventeen qualities or attributes, ranging from colour and touch through relationships such as remoteness and proximity to effort and including number, which as quantity would in Western thought usually form a separate category; later writers brought the number up to 24. Both qualities and action belong to substances. Action consists of ascent and descent, contraction and expansion and motion.

The other three categories are logically inferred rather than perceived, and may have been absent from the earliest form of the system. A universal or generic property occurs in individuals by inherence, a unitary relation with manifold realisations, which also serves to connect qualities and motion to substances and bodies to their constituent parts. Inherence also explains how the universal and the individual in which it is realised or the quality and substance can occupy the same space, since they combine to form a structured whole. Particularity (*viśeṣa*) is the ultimate distinction between atoms, independent of any observer, and it reflects the pluralistic nature of the system.

The next major work of the school, Praśastapāda's *Padārthadharmasaṃgraha,* though drawing heavily on the *Vaiśeṣikasūtra,* is not strictly a commentary on it but an independent explanation of the basic views of the system, and its arrangement was followed in later works. Praśastapāda substantially remodelled the system to take account of Buddhist ideas and so, for instance, introduced a refinement to the Vaiśeṣika theory of perception probably under the influence of Dignāga, who had objected that, according to the Vaiśeṣika doctrine of categories, perception was always of an object qualified by its inherent attributes. Praśastapāda therefore elaborates a theory of an initial perception simply of the object in itself (not therefore liable to error) before the emergence of the qualified perception. Certain points of his theory of inference may also reflect the impact of Dignāga's views.

Praśastapāda also elaborated the atomic theory, of which Kaṇāda had really propounded only the basic idea. He postulates that in the creation of the world the atoms must first combine into dyads, which then grouped into triads which were the basic molecules. When two atoms combined in a dyad, the addition of like to like produced only smallness; the smallest substance to possess greatness or size is the triad, in which it is produced by plurality (which to the Indian mind then started at three, since Sanskrit possesses a dual number used for all twos). Like atoms, dyads cannot be perceived by ordinary people, but the triads can just be seen and are identified with the small dust particles that can be seen floating in a shaft of sunlight. In general, however, the Vaiśeṣika position is that the qualities of the components can produce only homogeneous qualities in any compound formed from them. With regard to causation also, they adopt the views that an effect does not pre-exist in its cause but is different from it and that all effects are impermanent and will cease at some time.

In later writers we see an increasing merging of the Vaiśeṣika with the Nyāya system, until Udayana was producing works on both systems combined as well as separately. In the tenth century, as well as admitting the existence of a deity, the system accepts the category of non-existence, a rather superfluous scholastic refinement. Despite some similarities to modern quantum physics, the Vaiśeṣika atomic theory and its related hypotheses, like Greek atomic theories, were never really submitted to experimental verification. Later still there emerged from the thirteenth century the 'New Nyāya' (Navyanyāya) which, while accepting many tenets of the Vaiśeṣika system, goes back to the Nyāya emphasis on logic and, especially in its greatest exponent Raghunātha (fifteenth to sixteenth century), from a realistic standpoint develops a sophisticated formal logic; here alone in India does philosophy break away from religion.

The earliest phases of the Sāṃkhya and Yoga systems have already been examined on the basis of the Upaniṣadic and epic evidence. The earliest surviving text of the Sāṃkhya as a separate school is in fact relatively late and also, exceptionally, is not a Sūtra; this is Īśvarakṛṣṇa's *Sāṃkhyakārikā* of probably the fourth or fifth century A.D. Nevertheless, it is clear from the evidence of the *Mahābhārata* in particular that there was a long line of earlier teachers including the legendary founder Kapila (identi- fied once with Prajāpati), Āsuri, Pañcaśikha, and Vṛṣagaṇa. There is a work attributed to Kapila, the *Sāṃkhyapravacanasūtra,* but it is very late, probably belonging to the fourteenth century. Of course, the didactic parts of the *Mahābhārata* do preserve something similar to the basic texts of other schools and in fact one passage on Sāṃkhya is particularly linked with Pañcaśikha (Mbh.12.211–12).

The *Sāṃkhyakārikā* quickly became popular; the first known commentary on it is Gauḍapāda's of perhaps the fifth century and it was translated into Chinese in the middle of the sixth century by a Buddhist monk. The text takes as its starting point the fact of human suffering, which cannot be removed by perception or by scripture but only by discernment of the manifest, the unmanifest and the knower (SK 1–2); it thus introduces its basic concepts of matter or nature, *prakṛti,* in its evolved and unevolved forms and *puruṣa,* the spiritual principle. It next declares that there are 25 categories, of which the first is *prakṛti*. The evolution of the world is due to the inherent nature of *prakṛti* not to any outside agency. The second category, the first evolute from *prakṛti*, is intelligence, *buddhi*, or in its cosmic aspect 'the great one', *mahat*, recalling the *mahān ātmā* of some Upaniṣads; from this is then produced individuation, *ahaṃkāra*. Next are evolved through individuation the five elements, first in their subtle and then in their gross forms, the five organs of sense and the five organs of action (speech, grasping, walking, excretion and procreation). Finally, individuation produces the twenty-fourth category of mind, *manas*, regarded simply as the co-ordinating faculty which processes our sense impressions.

As thus presented this scheme of cosmic evolution implies that the whole world, including human beings, is evolved through individuation from matter, and consequently that the spiritual is superfluous. However, in classical Sāṃkhya there is a further category, that of *puruṣa*, which should therefore have no connection with the world but yet does in some way become involved. The individual souls of which this category is composed can achieve release by realising their essential difference from matter; in fact, the dichotomy between *prakṛti* and *puruṣa* parallels that between *saṃsāra* and *kaivalya*, the isolation of release. Although the world is in no way derived from *puruṣa*, it is regarded as functioning for the sake of *puruṣa*; the *Sāṃkhyakārikā* illustrates the way in which the inanimate *prakṛti* serves the conscious *puruṣa* by three images: the spontaneous flow of milk to nourish a calf, an individual's response of satisfying a basic need, and a dancer who performs for a spectator.

Despite the warmth of these images, overall the Sāṃkhya metaphysics expresses a negative valuation of the world. Ultimately *prakṛti* is unconscious and, since the system is centred on consciousness, which is the characteristic of *puruṣa*, the world itself is irrelevant apart from acting as a means of escape from itself. The image of the dancer in fact sums up the Sāṃkhya position that the *puruṣa* is simply an inactive spectator; existence is a show where events on stage only acquire meaning by being enjoyed by a spectator, who becomes absorbed in it and so identifies with it, until the spell is broken at the end of the performance – liberation takes place when the false identification ceases. Later this dualism of soul and matter was modified in response to theistic trends, beginning already in the *Mahābhārata* but only really taking hold from about the tenth century, and *puruṣa*, from being a purely inactive spectator, becomes the generator of matter.

Another feature of the Sāṃkhya system, which has achieved wide currency outside it also, is the concept of the three strands (*guṇas*) constituting *prakṛti*: *sattva*, *rajas* and *tamas*. They subsist in the unevolved or unmanifest form of matter and pervade the whole manifest world from *buddhi* downwards. The characterisation of the *guṇas* is primarily in terms of psychic states but extends much more widely, revealing the mingling of macrocosmic and microcosmic dimensions. As the world evolves the previous equilibrium between the three is disrupted and one or another predominates in different entities; after an enormously long period there is a relapse to quiescence, a reabsorption of the universe, until the inherent nature of the *guṇas* breaks the equilibrium and the process starts all over again. The *sattva guṇa* is related to what is good, pleasant and truthful, *rajas* to what is energetic or passionate, and *tamas* to what is dark and inert; broadly speaking there is an opposition between *sattva* and *tamas*, with *rajas* as the active force; they are naturally associated with the colours white, red and black. At times they are brought into a degree of relationship with the concept of the 25 categories, with the *sattva* form of individuation developing into *manas* and the senses and the *tamas* form into the elements in their gross and subtle forms (SK 25). Elsewhere *sattva* is said to predominate in the world of the gods, *tamas* in the lower creation and *rajas* in the middle, the human state. Basically, however, the theories of the categories and of the *guṇas* remain separate explanatory systems.

The Yoga system is first expounded separately in the *Yoga-sūtra* of Patañjali. On the basis of its author's identification with a grammarian of the same name, the work is sometimes assigned to the second century B.C. but in its present form is substantially later. It consists of four chapters, the first on the nature and aim of meditation, the second on the means for achieving the aim, the third on the attainments achieved on the way and the goal, and the fourth on the nature of the detachment from matter reached through Yoga. It has probably been built up into this relatively coherent pattern from several separate texts, which show different starting-points and stages of procedure in the progress from impurity to *kaivalya*, and which presumably originated in separate schools of Yoga. As part of this process of systematisation the school absorbed most of the Sāṃkhya cosmology and thus the yogin was considered to reverse the process of evolution detailed in the Sāṃkhya and to return to the original unevolved, unitary state.

The main section of the text (YS 2.28–3.55) distinguishes eight 'limbs' or stages in the technique of Yoga, of which an older variant is presumably the six-membered Yoga of the *Maitrī Upaniṣad*; the first five concern the training of the body and the last three the perfecting of the self. The first stage is self-control or restraint (*yama*), which regulates the yogin's external activities and consists of the five moral rules of *ahiṃsā*, truthfulness, not stealing, chastity and non-acquisitiveness. The second, observance (*niyama*), consists of five regulations for personal behaviour: purity, contentment, austerity (*tapas*), study of the scriptures and devotion to the Lord. Although devotion to the Lord is developed elsewhere in the *Yogasūtra* (1.23–51), this Īśvara is not active or creative – indeed essentially he is distinct through never having become involved with the ills of the world – and so is not an object of true devotion but an aid to meditation identified and interchangeable with the syllable *oṃ*.

The third stage, which begins the characteristically Yoga practices, is posture (*āsana*), remaining seated in certain positions. It is comparatively little emphasised in the *Yogasūtra*, where it is just a matter of assuming a suitable position, but later texts name many positions (from their names evidently based on methods of identification) which are difficult and can only be assumed after long practice. Next, in breath-control (*prāṇāyāma*), the involuntary process of breathing is brought under the control of the will and artificially regulated, originally perhaps to secure mastery of time, equated with the rhythm of breathing. Then follows withdrawal (*pratyāhāra*) of the senses from their objects, eliminating their contact with the external world which is what binds one to *saṃsāra*; one method is to concentrate on a single point until everything else disappears from consciousness and then to transfer the attention from an object to a mental image. As the mind is freed from its ordinary concerns, so it becomes more open to distraction, to which this method provides the necessary counter and leads into the next stage.

The remaining three stages tend to shade into one another. The sixth is fixing the thoughts (*dhāraṇā*) without the aid of the senses, whose operation has been suspended. The stage of meditation (*dhyāna*) is reached when the *puruṣa* remains stably directed to one point without distraction. The last stage of ecstasy or trance (*samādhi*) is reached when one is no longer conscious even of meditating and arrives at an identification of subject and object; it cannot be described in words but is a state of transcendent bliss, leading to the attainment of *kaivalya.* Thus the inhibition of consciousness proceeds to the point of its elimination and transformation into universal self-awareness.

As the yogin proceeds through the stages, signs of success (*siddhis*) begin to appear. This starts even with the first two stages, so that practice of *ahiṃsā* produces absence of hostility in the yogin's presence and so on (YS 2.35–45). As the later stages are reached, the *siddhis* become various magical feats such as levitation. There is no agreement whether these feats are purely subjective or objective activities. However, they are an integral part of Yoga practice as indicators of successful practice but also function as temptations, into which the yogin may be diverted away from his real goal of achieving release, just as *samādhi* is not an end in itself but must be transcended to reach release.

Commentaries on the *Yogasūtra* still extant belong to the period of the seventh to the eleventh centuries. At the end of that period come Bhoja's *Rājamārtaṇḍa,* which already shows greater concentration on the *siddhis* and the techniques to achieve them. Bhoja lists eight, which become standard: minuteness and greatness (the abilities of shrinking and expanding indefinitely), lightness and heaviness (by which one can levitate and penetrate matter respectively), irresistible will, supremacy, subjection of nature and fulfilment of desires. The emphasis on the acquisition of power or control so often visible in Hinduism is again becoming dominant over the concept of renunciation and detachment. From about the twelfth century Yoga was sometimes developed in ways that increasingly reflect this, with the emergence of the 'Yoga of force' (*haṭhayoga*) and the 'Yoga of spells' (*mantrayoga*), and it tended to become associated with Tantrism.

Whereas the four schools already looked at were only gradually taken into the orthodox synthesis, the remaining two were always orthodox and directly religious. Indeed the Mīmāṃsā system began not as a school leading to release but as a direct successor to the ritual Sūtra literature, whose aim was to ensure the correct interpretation of the Vedas. To this end it formulated general rules of interpretation (*nyāya*, a term later commonly used to denote logic), which were adopted and extended in the schools of Dharmaśāstra. Its basic standpoint is that the Vedas, being eternal and uncreated, possess absolute authority and that the Vedic commands constitute man's entire duty (*dharma*). It is the function of Mīmāṃsā, 'enquiry', to interpret those commands systematically and to deduce logical principles for the consistent application of the apparently unsystematic Vedic texts. Although certain sentences in the Veda appear incoherent or meaningless, this is not really so; it is incorrect to take any Vedic utterance out of context and treat it in isolation.

The earliest text is Jaimini's *Mīmāṃsāsūtra* of about the second century B.C., an earlier date than the basic texts of other schools, but it nevertheless presupposes a long history of Vedic interpretation, for the school is in a real sense a continuation of the Brāhmaṇa traditions. The *Mīmāṃsāsūtra* describes the different sacrifices and their purposes, elaborates the theory of *apūrva* and also discusses some philosophical questions in its first chapter on the sources of knowledge and the validity of the Vedas. The term *apūrva* denotes the mysterious, transcendent power produced by correct performance of a rite (or any component part of it) which subsequently produces the result promised, often after the death of the sacrificer; essentially it is a device to tie firmly together the action and its delayed result, though possibly indebted to the earlier concept of *brahman* as the power inherent in the sacrifice. Jaimini regards deity as a redundant category irrelevant to his central concern, the discussion of *dharma*; belief in the eternality of the Vedas precludes their divine authorship and Jaimini also rejects a deity as the creator of the relation between word and meaning, affirming that the relationship is innate (MS 1.1.5). The first extant commentary on Jaimini's work by Śabara (fifth or sixth century A.D.) develops these arguments, as well as defining *dharma* more exactly as consisting of sacrifice, libation and giving, of which the common factor is the transfer of possession from oneself to another; there is a limited role here for deities as notional recipients of the sacrifice. However, effectively Mīmāṃsā has become atheistic through a fundamentalist concentration on the scriptures themselves.

In order to establish the inerrancy of the Vedic injunctions, the Mīmāṃsā system seeks to prove that words, their meanings, and the relationship of word and meaning are all eternal, while the meaning of the sentence is derived solely from the component words. In the process it distinguishes two methods of interpretation of words, by etymology and by actual usage, affirming that the latter is always to be preferred; this is one of a number of interesting contributions of the Mīmāṃsā to the study of language, which had otherwise become the exclusive preserve of the grammatical schools. Above all, however, Mīmāṃsā is concerned with distinguishing the rules or commands from the explanations, for the rules are intrinsically valid but the auxiliary material (collectively called explanation and consisting of descriptive passages, metaphors, predictions of results and so forth) does not affect the command and must not be construed as the reason for the act.

The Vedas are in theory the sole source of authority and the authority of *smṛti* (all other traditional material) is derived from them on the assumption that there is a corresponding Vedic text to back up the assertion of a *smṛti* text – or was once, for the Mīmāṃsā, with the realism that it often shows, accepts the possibility that Vedic texts may have been lost. In addition, the customary practices of those who regularly perform Vedic sacrifice, unless motivated by self-interest, are to be regarded as authoritative. The existence of the *ātman* is accepted on the grounds that it is required to make sense of Vedic – usually Brāhmaṇa – texts which speak of the performer of a certain ritual going to heaven and so forth. Since the body is cremated after death, there must be some independent entity to enjoy heaven. In fact the Mīmāṃsā system continued to accept the older views of the after-life long after they had been abandoned in other schools, and only tardily and reluctantly admitted the concept of liberation (*mokṣa*), at the period around the seventh century when it was dividing into separate schools.

The founders of these two sub-schools, Kumārila and Prabhākara, each wrote a commentary on Śabara's commentary. Kumārila and his school, unlike Prabhākara, do not restrict verbal testimony to the Vedic commands but classify it as human – all statements of trustworthy individuals (basically the Nyāya view) – and non-human – the Vedas – declaring that Śabara had given a more limited definition only because the Vedas alone are relevant to the subject of enquiry, *dharma*. The two schools also differ in their analysis of the nature of error, although both remain true to the school's strongly realist position, which was clearly put by Śabara who stressed that cognition operated directly on external objects and upheld the intrinsic validity of all cognition. Kumārila also argues forcefully and extensively in his *Ślokavārtika* against the existence of a creator deity; the virtual demise of the Vedic pantheon in popular belief was not unwelcome to Mīmāṃsā but the rise of belief in a supreme deity, with the concurrent shift away from sacrificial ritual, posed a more serious threat to the system, as Kumārila appears to have realised. However, other later Mīmāṃsā writers admit the reality of the supreme deity.

The Vedānta system is regularly coupled with Mīmāṃsā and indeed is sometimes called the 'further Mīmāṃsā', but the relationship is one of succession rather than complementarity, as with the other two pairs, and would probably have been contested at first by the Mīmāṃsā system. Whereas Mīmāṃsā deals with ritual acts and bases itself on the Brāhmaṇas, Vedānta is concerned with knowledge or insight and its doctrines are based on the Upaniṣads. But, since Vedānta also relies on the authority of the Vedas, it must and does accept study of Mīmāṃsā as a necessary preliminary to its own system. Its basic text is Bādarāyaṇas's *Brahmasūtra* or *Vedāntasūtra*, written early in the Christian era as a deliberate synthesis of the Upaniṣadic views, largely in the original wording and sometimes therefore obscure. In the process Bādarāyaṇa places an interpretation on the teachings of the Upaniṣads, while referring occasionally to divergent opinions of other teachers on particular points. However, the *Brahmasūtra* is not the basic text in the same sense as in other systems, for the Upaniṣads themselves provide the basis of the system and furnish the diversity of approach apparently always characteristic of Vedānta, which has probably never been a unitary system.

The first chapter of the *Brahmasūtra* establishes the connection of certain texts with Brahman, which is affirmed as the goal of enquiry and the source of the universe. The second chapter deals with the consistency of the ideas relating to Brahman and *ātman* drawn from the Upaniṣads and refutes the doctrines of other schools. The third chapter expounds the means for the realisation of Brahman through knowledge, worship and disciplined activity. The fourth and last chapter discusses *mokṣa*, giving a detailed account of the successive stages of spiritual ascent until the final merging with Brahman. Among the Upaniṣads quoted to establish this interpretation, the *Chāndogya Upaniṣad* is the most frequent, followed by the *Bṛhadāraṇyaka Upaniṣad* and the *Taittirīya Upaniṣad*, which significantly belong to the oldest, most impersonal Upaniṣads; however Bādarāyaṇa also uses the *Kaṭha* and *Śvetāśvatara Upaniṣads* and possibly the *Bhagavadgītā*.

Between the *Brahmasūtra* and its first extant commentary by Śaṅkara, lies a lengthy period of development which is not fully documented in the surviving texts. Among the figures of this period is the grammarian Bhartṛhari of perhaps the fifth century, who posited a first principle which he called Śabdabrahman, conceiving of Brahman as being essentially word or speech, symbolised by *oṃ*, and regarding all objects as manifestations of and dependent on their names and thus ultimately identical with Brahman, the absolute consciousness and source of naming. This nominalist position marks an important step towards the idealist views of Śaṅkara, for Bhartṛhari held that evolution, though proceeding from and occurring in Brahman, does not involve a change of being in the absolute.

Within the Vedānta system itself the first systematic exponent is Gauḍapāda, the author of the *Māṇḍūkyakārikā* (a commentary on the *Māṇḍūkya Upaniṣad*) and traditionally the teacher of Śaṅkara's teacher but more probably about three centuries earlier than Śaṅkara. Gauḍapāda's main doctrine was that of non-origination, according to which the whole world is merely an appearance; nothing ever really comes into being, since nothing other than Brahman really exists, and the whole world is an illusion like a dream. It is significant that Gauḍapāda chose as the basis of his commentary the *Māṇḍūkya Upaniṣad*, with its exposition of the four states of *ātman* in terms of waking and dreaming, and he goes so far as to declare that there is in principle no difference between waking and dreaming (MK 2.4). Even more significantly the last chapter of the commentary (which is nearly as long as the other three together) draws heavily on Buddhist material, to the extent that its author has sometimes been considered a Buddhist, and presents for the first time – in an even more radical form – several views and arguments later developed by Śaṅkara. In addition, Gauḍapāda establishes the illusory nature of experience by a critique of the concept of causation and an appeal to the doctrine of *māyā*, a term which in Vedic times had meant creative activity and even in the *Brahmasūtra* occurs only once and hardly in the sense which Gauḍapāda now gives it of the inexplicability of the relation between the world and Brahman and the dream-like insubstantiality of the world.

Two approximate contemporaries of Śaṅkara in the seventh century, Bhāskara and Maṇḍanamiśra, also provide some insight into the nature of the Vedānta before Śaṅkara. Although Bhāskara was acquainted with Śaṅkara's work and occasionally quotes him, the views expressed in Bhāskara's work are frequently identical with those that Śaṅkara refutes and obviously therefore derive from an earlier commentator. Bhāskara regards Brahman as having two aspects, one of cause and the other of effect, in which it transforms itself into the world by a process of development characterised by power (*śakti*) and expansion; he bases his views on such texts as the sixth chapter of the *Chāndogya Upaniṣad*. Essentially therefore everything in the world is a unity, Brahman, but equally the plurality of the world is real, the identity in diversity (*bhedābheda*) which summarises Bhāskara's approach. He appeals to everyday experience to show that unity and plurality are not contradictory but complementary and scornfully dismisses Śaṅkara's views as being simply those of Mahāyāna Buddhists.

Maṇḍanamiśra was an exponent of both Mīmāṃsā and Vedānta and so was especially interested in the relationship between ritual action and knowledge of Brahman. He also develops the theory of error propounded by Kumārila into the characteristic doctrine of later Advaita Vedānta that error can be described neither as real nor as unreal. Other features of his views, though absent from Śaṅkara's works, were adopted by Śaṅkara's followers; these include his view that Brahman is linked with the world by the relationship of unreal appearance caused by *avidyā* ('ignorance' or more exactly 'misunderstanding'), which has two aspects – first of concealing Brahman from itself and thus producing selves and then of projecting the illusion that there is an empirical world.

Śaṅkara, traditionally said to have been a Nambūdiri Brāhman from Kerala in south India, is regarded as the founder of the Advaita (non-dual) school of Vedānta which insists on Brahman as the sole reality, denying any duality. In an apparently short lifetime (traditionally 788–820 A.D.), he achieved not only an impressive output of philosophical works but also a remarkable amount of propagation of his views directly and by the institution of an organisational framework. His major work is a commentary on the *Brahmasūtra* (thereby by later standards establishing his status as the founder of a sub-school – innovation validated by tradition), but he also wrote commentaries on the *Bhagavadgītā* and on several Upaniṣads, as well as an independent work the *Upadeśasāhasrī*. It is not certain whether various minor works on Vedānta ascribed to him are really his, but there is no justification for the attribution to him of various Śākta works praising the goddess.

As an orthodox Brāhman, Śaṅkara subscribes to the authority of the Vedas but uses verbal testimony almost exclusively to establish his central doctrine of the identity of *ātman* and Brahman, gleefully quoting scripture (BĀU 4.3.22: 'Then [i.e. in liberation] . . . the Vedas are not Vedas') to prove that scripture ceases to be valid with the arising of knowledge and convicting his opponents of the absence of true knowledge with his customary flair in debate. However, in order to reconcile the contradictions of the Vedas, he adopts an exegetical device already used in Buddhism, the concept of the two levels of truth. On the lower level of conventional reality, the world exists and evolves according to the Sāṃkhya pattern under the creative guidance of Īśvara, the personal deity propounded in some Upaniṣadic texts, but on the higher level of absolute reality the whole world is unreal, an illusion (*māyā*) associated with ignorance (*avidyā*), and Brahman alone really exists.

The multiple and finite entities of the phenomenal world are essentially identical therefore with Brahman, the Absolute. Their multiplicity and individuality lie in their separate identities which *avidyā* superimposes on the absolute. But, just as in ordinary life a man might see a piece of rope coiled up and in poor light mistake it for a cobra coiled ready to strike, thus superimposing an illusory snake on a real rope, so all perception and experience is of something and does not refer to nothing. Whenever we perceive something, it is because there is something. When we perceive the world around us, we do perceive something but our mistake, our *avidyā*, consists in taking it as something other than Brahman. Śaṅkara is here at pains to avoid the negativism of the Mādhyamika school of Buddhism, which declares that everything is a void with no reality underlying it. Śaṅkara also largely avoids defining the nature of *avidyā* or its substratum, unlike some of his followers; but Śaṅkara no doubt was aware of the logical problem involved, whereas his pupil Sureśvara declares that *avidyā* resorts to and belongs to the *ātman*, and the question divides the two sub-schools of Advaita which subsequently emerge. For Śaṅkara himself the nature of *avidyā* was indescribable, since if it were unreal we should not be entrapped by it but if it were real then Brahman would not be the sole reality. Śaṅkara also applies this concept of indescribability or inexplicability to the question of causation, for the effects into which we suppose that causes are transformed are actually superimposed and so neither real nor unreal.

Phenomena are only illusorily independent of Brahman and so the essential unity of Brahman is unaffected by the multiplicity of individual phenomena, just as the waves appear multiple as they rise from the surface of the ocean, into which they subside, and in no way affect its unity. This image of the ocean also illustrates the point that Śaṅkara's thought is not just negative. He denies the absolute reality of the world in order to affirm the sole reality of Brahman, with which in its essential nature *ātman* is identical. However, the individual self, the *jīva*, is a combination of reality and appearance – real in so far as it is *ātman* or Brahman, but illusory in so far as it is limited and finite. In this context Śaṅkara makes use of the Upaniṣadic utterance 'you are that' (*tat tvam asi*), demonstrating that their identity is reached by removing the incompatible elements of individuality and transcendence to reveal the pure consciousness which is the ground of the *ātman* as of Brahman. Śaṅkara is more guarded in his approach to other characterisations of Brahman and is very reluctant to make any positive statements about it which might be regarded as limiting its absoluteness. In his major works at least he avoids using the well-known formulation of later Advaita that Brahman is being, consciousness and bliss (*sat, cit, ānanda*), even when commenting on the

6. Bhū Devī, Earth as Viṣṇu's consort

Upaniṣadic definition of Brahman as truth, knowledge and infinity (Tait.Up.2.1) on which the formula is based; instead he there elaborates a theory of indication whereby such statements point to Brahman rather than define it. Indeed, he is obviously in sympathy with the declaration that Brahman is 'not like this nor like that' (BĀU 2.3.6). The unqualified Brahman is precisely that transcendent state of being about which nothing can be affirmed. However, Brahman is not just an abstract concept but the goal of spiritual quest, *mokṣa*. Release is achieved with the arrival of true knowledge, the intuition that oneself and Brahman are in truth identical. This saving knowledge destroys the *karma* of past lives and a state of embodied release is attained.

Admired as Śaṅkara is as a philosopher, philosophy was not in fact his prime concern but the tool with which to achieve *mokṣa*, for himself and others. His treatment of the problem of where *avidyā* resides illustrates this, for it is philosophically incomplete but psychologically effective. All Śaṅkara's exposition is aimed not so much at logical consistency as at persuasion, although Advaita is indeed consistent, since all relations and contradictions disappear in *mokṣa*. However, his overall religious purpose is most clearly seen in his organisation of an order of *saṃnyāsins* and foundation of teaching institutions (*maṭhas*) at the four corners of India to propagate his doctrine. The order, which may well again reflect Buddhist influence, is now represented by ten groups, three reserved for Brāhmans and the rest open to the four *varṇas*, although Śaṅkara himself affirms that only Brāhmans can become *saṃnyāsins*. These orders are Śaiva in affiliation and Śaṅkara himself is often considered a Śaiva, which seems implausible in view of his low estimate of Īśvara; more probably it is in implicit contrast to the devout Vaiṣṇavism of his later antagonist Rāmānuja. But of his essentially religious stance there can be no doubt.

CHAPTER SIX

Sectarian Developments

With the passage of time the worship of either Viṣṇu or Śiva as supreme deity, the origins of which were traced in the third chapter on the basis of the epic evidence, developed into more fully organised sects. At the same time as the Vaiṣṇava and Śaiva sects were themselves evolving, they were apparently attempting to absorb the parallel emergence of worshippers of the goddess Durgā or Kālī, who is eventually connected more closely with Śaivism, although traces still remain of Vaiṣṇavism's flirtation with her.

Within Vaiṣṇavism the early Bhāgavata movement recedes into the background and the Pāñcarātra sect, already mentioned alongside the Bhāgavatas in some epic passages, develops an elaborate theology, of which the germs are to be seen in the *Nārāyaṇīya* (Mbh.12.321–39) with its doctrine of the fourfold nature of the supreme being. Whereas the Bhāgavatas seem to have accepted the orthodox social order (as the *Bhagavadgītā* undoubtedly does), the Pāñcarātra tradition is placed alongside the Sāṃkhya, Yoga and Pāśupata schools, its doctrine is regarded as esoteric, and its adherents seem to have practised an ascetic way of life according to the *Mahābhārata*, all of which suggests that it stood somewhat outside the main stream of orthodoxy; indeed, as we have already noted, its followers may well have originated among the groups of wandering sages from whom the Buddhists, Jains and Ājīvikas drew their strength. Certainly, despite claiming to derive from a lost school of the *Yajurveda*, the Pāñcarātra movement always allied itself more with popular devotional religion than with traditional ritualism, unlike the Vaikhānasa sect, which forms with it the other main strand of Vaiṣṇavism. There is also evidence of definite tantric leanings, especially in the *Lakṣmī Tantra*.

Of the extensive Pāñcarātra literature, composed mainly between the fifth and tenth centuries, three texts are particularly authoritative and probably also among the oldest: the *Jayākhya*, *Sāttvata* and *Pauṣkara Saṃhitās*. All are cast in the form of a dialogue, narrated at several removes, between the Lord (Bhagavat) and a legendary figure. In the *Jayākhya Saṃhitā* the setting for the dialogue is apparently in Kathiawar and in the *Sāttvata Saṃhitā* it is in the Western Ghats, but both texts are now closely associated with Pāñcarātra faith and worship at specific centres in south India, while the *Pauṣkara Saṃhitā* is associated with the major Vaiṣṇava centre in the south, Śrīraṅgam. Prominent in all three texts is the typical Pāñcarātra doctrine that Viṣṇu manifests himself in the four *vyūhas,* successive emanations from the deity and yet simultaneously part of his essential nature.

The theory of the four *vyūhas* seems to have evolved early in the Christian era, more or less concurrently with the *avatāra* concept, and there are several references to it in at least an embryonic form in the *Mahābhārata.* Since the earliest texts of the school have sometimes been associated with Kashmir, Zoroastrian influence has been suggested for the doctrine, but the evidence is weak. The theory gives a cosmological basis to the legends of Vāsudeva Kṛṣṇa by identifying him and his family with cosmic emanations in a system which has a definite Sāṃkhya background. Vāsudeva, identified with Viṣṇu, is the supreme deity, eternal and infinite, who is pure bliss and consciousness, the ultimate reality. In his transcendental form he creates from himself the emanation Saṃkarṣaṇa (=*jīva*) and matter (*prakṛti*) at the beginning of time; from the association of Saṃkarṣaṇa and *prakṛti* is produced Pradyumna and mind (*manas*); from these come Aniruddha and individuation (*ahaṃkāra*); only then do the three *guṇas* and the gross elements evolve, along with Brahmā who as demiurge fashions the world and living beings from them. Although the Sāṃkhya background is obvious, despite the deviations in order, there is a major difference in that the three emanations are very closely related to Vāsudeva and described as forms of the deity but nevertheless distinct, as the kinship pattern shows. Indeed, presumably a degree of independence between deity and individual soul (*jīva*) was accepted, since Saṃkarṣaṇa is Kṛṣṇa's brother not his son, who is Pradyumna. In the developed system Saṃkarṣaṇa, Pradyumna and Aniruddha are both aspects of the deity and deities in their own right, a paradox which is not resolved in the theology but left to symbolise the situation of the soul after release which retains sufficient individuality to experience the bliss of union with the deity.

From each emanation evolve three sub-emanations named after aspects of Viṣṇu; these become tutelary deities of the twelve months, perhaps an importation from the sun cult where another of Kṛṣṇa's sons, Sāmba, plays an important part. They are also important as objects of meditation in the elaborate diagrams called *yantras*. The emanations and sub-emanations belong to the pure creation, to which also belong the *avatāras* of Viṣṇu or his *vyūhas* (for in adapting its *avatāra* doctrine to the *vyūha* theory, the Pāñcarātra system transferred some incarnations to the *vyūhas*); the significance of these various aspects of the deity consists chiefly of their helpfulness when properly meditated on.

According to the cosmology of the *Lakṣmī Tantra* there are three stages of creation, the pure, the mixed and the impure. The text is notable for its treatment of Lakṣmī as the power (*śakti*) of Viṣṇu – an important innovation since the early Saṃhitās – and its glorification of women in general as created in her form. The pure creation is said to follow from the first phase of her manifestation as both the instrumental and the material cause of the universe; thus Lakṣmī, as Viṣṇu's *śakti*, is creatively active and manifests herself as the *vyūhas*. Hence the world, which Lakṣmī projects in the second and third stages of creation, is a part not of Viṣṇu but of his consort Lakṣmī, who is in reality identical with him and yet distinct as an attribute. This paradox is an attempt to explain the coexistence of an infinite and perfect deity with a limited and transient creation. Viṣṇu transcends temporality and Lakṣmī possesses the distinction of days and nights which corresponds to the periods of emanation and reabsorption in the cosmic cycle.

Traditionally, the Saṃhitās comprised four subjects, from the theology of the *vyūha* doctrine and related knowledge, through Yoga (interpreted very much as in the *Bhagavadgītā* as a means of delivering the soul wholly to the deity) to the construction of temples and images and ritual activity. The texts regularly declare that the adherent should perform the five daily acts of worship which comprise concentration on the deity, gathering materials for worship, worship of the deity, studying the scriptures and performance of Yoga. Everyone who comes for initiation into the sect, even a woman or a child, should be initiated without distinction of descent or class, as the texts expressly state. The Saṃhitās recommend the branding of Viṣṇu's weapons, his discus (*cakra*) and conch, on the arms of the initiate, a practice which appears from independent references to be very early. The sect attached great importance to the discus, as denoting Viṣṇu's will to maintain the universe, and it is identified with the aspect of Lakṣmī as the instrumental cause of the world in later developments.

The pronounced concern for ritual is given its justification in the doctrine of Viṣṇu's five types of self-revelation in his aspects as the supreme, the emanations, the incarnations, the inner controller of all selves, and the image. The greater part of the texts are taken up with the construction of the image, its installation and consecration, and the liturgies offered to it. Here there is evident a belief in the gracious descent of the deity to be present in the world in this form as the focus of image worship. Those who turn to him are saved by their worship of him in the simple ritual of offering (*pūjā*) but those who ignore this chance to receive his grace or are careless in the routine of worship offend his majesty and must make expiation. A worthy response to divine grace is expressed very largely in terms of building a suitable residence for the image and of ensuring the regular performance of worship. The *Ahirbudhnya Saṃhitā*, of about the eighth century, contains elaborate iconographic descriptions of multi-armed images of Viṣṇu with his discus, although in some respects it is more philosophical than other Saṃhitās and contains a particularly full account of the process of evolution of the impure creation.

The Vaikhānasa sect has a genuine connection with Vedic tradition, for in origin the Vaikhānasa school formed part of the Taittirīya school of the *Black Yajurveda*. Subsequently, and by not altogether easily documented stages, the Vaikhānasas transformed themselves into an orthodox Vaiṣṇava sect, distinguished from the Pāñcarātras in particular by their maintenance of Vedic traditions. They claim that their temple worship is simply a continuation of the Vedic sacrifices into the fire, declaring that regular and correct worship of Viṣṇu in a temple brings the same results as the fire oblation even for people who do not maintain their fires. Many Vedic technical terms and names of ritual objects still occur in every work dealing with the conduct of worship. They even claim that worship of the image had not only begun in the Vedic period but is a transformation of the aniconic Vedic ritual, since Viṣṇu's five aspects represent the five sacrificial fires. Altogether the Vaikhānasa sect is marked by extreme conservatism.

The *Vaikhānasasūtra*, of perhaps the third century A.D., reveals already the amalgamation of the cult of the Vedic Viṣṇu with that of Nārāyaṇa, employing to achieve this end a blend of Vedic and non-Vedic *mantras*. One hymn to Viṣṇu, commonly called the *Vaiṣṇavam* (ṚV 1.22.16–21), appears to be developing in it from an invocation of the deity to a type of confession of faith in Viṣṇu. Subsequently, by the end of the first millennium, ritual handbooks or Saṃhitās have evolved, which are attributed to four ancient sages, Atri, Marīci, Bhṛgu and Kāśyapa, who are supposed to have received their knowledge from Vikhanas, the legendary founder. These give a detailed description of the daily worship to be performed by the temple priest based on the earlier *Vaikhānasasūtra*. Despite an overall conservatism, shown for example in the total absence of the idea of mental worship so popular with the Pāñcarātras and others, the handbooks incorporate some more popular aspects of worship, presenting a complete temple and image ritual with various offerings and processions, and stress the typical Vaiṣṇava concerns of attachment and service to the Lord, enumerating also the *avatāras* and their mode of worship. In contrast to the Pāñcarātras, the Vaikhānasas evolved the theory of Viṣṇu's five aspects as Viṣṇu, the all-pervading supreme deity, Puruṣa, the principle of life, Satya, the static aspect of deity, Acyuta, the immutable aspect, and Aniruddha, the irreducible aspect. They also assign a significant role to Śrī as nature (*prakṛti*) and as Viṣṇu's power (*śakti*) who projects the universe. At the same time they distinguish between Viṣṇu in his primeval and transcendent form and Viṣṇu involved with creation and relate this to their cult images, having a large immovable one in the sanctuary for the former and a portable image representing the deity's movable aspect underlying his manifestations. But on the whole Vaikhānasa literature is almost entirely ritual, prescribing their rituals and laying down all the detailed rules for its performance.

From the end of the tenth century Vaikhānasas are prominently mentioned in south Indian inscriptions and were evidently priests of Vaiṣṇava temples, entrusted with the management of the shrines and of their lands. Despite the subsequent rise of the Śrīvaiṣṇava sect, examined in the next chapter, they were not wholly eclipsed in this role and to the present day continue to perform worship in Sanskrit at some temples, especially the Veṅkateśvara temples at Tirupati and Kāñcī. The dominance of Brāhman officiants and the exclusive use of Sanskrit as the ritual language are still prominent features.

Within Śaivism, the earliest sect known, the Pāśupatas, is associated with the name of Lakulīśa, who is regarded as an incarnation of Śiva and as the author of their basic text, the *Pāśupatasūtra*; it is a regular Śaiva belief that Śiva himself was the first teacher of their doctrines. A tradition recorded in several Purāṇas states that Lakulīśa would be the last incarnation of Śiva, who animated a dead body in the cremation ground of a place just north of Baroda in Gujarat, and would have four named pupils, whom a thirteenth-century inscription identifies as founders of the four branches of the Pāśupata sect. This legend may have a historical basis, for a Gupta inscription of the fourth century mentions a Śaiva priest as tenth in descent from Kuśika, the name of one of these disciples; if the identification is valid, then Lakulīśa himself can probably be dated to early in the second century. From the seventh century and probably earlier, there were Pāśupata temples in most of India and allusions to Pāśupata ascetics in secular literature are frequent from the seventh century onwards. Worship of Lakulīśa is attested by a number of post-Gupta statues from north India representing Lakulīśa as a naked yogin with a club or staff (*lakuṭa*) in his left hand and his penis erect; the frequency of such statues drops sharply at the beginning of the eleventh century. This seems to represent a decline in the cult in the north and there is some evidence of migration southwards to Karnataka, where the Kālāmukha sect emerged at about that date.

The *Pāśupatasūtra* is in the usual brief style of Sūtras and gives an authoritative account of the ritual and discipline of the sect, but neither it nor the commentary on it by Kauṇḍinya (probably fourth century) gives any philosophy; indeed, the philosophy appears to be a relatively late adaptation of Sāṃkhya-Yoga and Vaiśeṣika concepts to the sect's religious practices. According to the Pāśupatas, Śiva is absolutely independent, and matter (*prakṛti*) and selves (*ātman*) are dependent on him as effects, not causes as in Sāṃkhya; selves in liberation become eternally associated with Śiva. Kauṇḍinya stresses the *yamas* and *niyamas*, of which the first group is virtually identical with the Yoga list and the second varies somewhat, being defined as non-anger, obedience to the teacher, purity, abstemiousness and carefulness. But, despite its closeness to Sāṃkhya and Yoga – or perhaps because of it, the sect asserted its distinctiveness and Kauṇḍinya especially directs his main criticisms against them. In the Nyāya and Vaiśeṣika systems Uddyotakara (who actually calls himself a Pāśupata teacher), Udayana and Praśastapāda all have definite Śaiva links.

The most obvious feature of the Pāśupata sect is their organised system of training and code of conduct. The purpose of the system is the ending of suffering (PS 5.40, cf. *Yogasūtra* 2.1–3) and the adoption of such actions as lead to union of the individual *ātman* with Śiva. The main topics of their doctrine, found in the *Pāśupatasūtra*, are the annihilation of suffering, the effect (i.e. selves as creatures, *paśu*), the cause (Śiva as Paśupati), the discipline and the practices. The aspirant had to pass through five stages in the progress to union with Śiva. In the first stage he was attached to a temple, went naked or wore one garment and applied the sectarian markings, which consisted mainly of smearing with ashes thrice a day; he should worship Śiva with dancing, roaring like a bull and laughing, thereby gaining various yogic powers. In the second stage he left the temple, abandoned his sectarian markings and invited ridicule by apparently nonsensical or indecent actions. The last three stages consist of a steady progress in asceticism through victory over the senses and the severing of all worldly ties to the total cessation of activity, with the aspirant living successively in an abandoned house or cave, a cremation ground and in Śiva.

Through this regime the Pāśupatas sought purification from past *karma* and acquisition of good *karma*, believing that thereby they could build up a superhuman body which would make them equal to Śiva. The ultimate goal of freedom (*mokṣa*) was interpreted as not just the release from suffering implied in the five aspects of their doctrine but freedom to act at will, meaning effectively omnipotence and the sharing of Śiva's nature. All Pāśupata texts emphasise this unusual conception of the goal, as they term it, this positive aspect of *mokṣa*; it has obvious links with tantric ideas.

The rationale behind the activities appropriate to the various stages lies partly in a concept of imitation and partly in one of appropriation. In the first stage, for example, the aspirant imitates the animal (*paśu*) in his bellowing and Śiva in his wild laughter and dancing; several others of the peculiar activities no doubt originated as imitations of the animal. There are in fact traces outside the Pāśupata tradition of animal vows in Sanskrit literature, which the sect may have adapted to its own ends. The *Pāśupatasūtra* also says that an ascetic will be ignored and insulted by those about him and that their censure cancels his bad *karma* and transfers their merit to him (PS 3.6–10), elsewhere declaring that he should wander among other people like a madman (PS 4.6). At the same time he was directly to eradicate the evils arising from desires through the process of discipline and thus arrive at the conquest of the senses. However, the practices advocated included trembling and sudden falling down which, taken with the animal imitations, probably suggests a background in ideas of possession by the deity among various primitive peoples, the view of the shaman into whom the deity temporarily came.

Accommodation of such archaic practices into a more civilised framework might well have resulted in ideas of deliberately outrageous behaviour. However, there are signs that another explanation is also involved. Both inside and outside the Pāśupata tradition there is evidence that they were divided into Vedic and tantric, orthodox and heterodox groups, between which there was some animosity. This suggests that the orthodox group was an attempt to reform a more heterodox faith and that the *Pāśupatasūtra* is part of this process with its stress on the aspirant only pretending to be drunk, to make indecent gestures to women and so on without actually violating morality. Thus, symbolic gestures were substituted for original actions and suitably rationalised.

The revulsion which orthodoxy felt for the more heterodox form of the Pāśupata system was still more clearly directed against another Śaiva sect, that of the Kāpālikas, with the result that no Kāpālika text is extant. But secular literature from the seventh century onwards contains a number of fairly sensational allusions to them and several Purāṇas refer to them disparagingly. Their basic position was of devotion to Śiva in his horrific Bhairava aspect and worship of him both through imitation and by propitiation. They are consistently associated with a particular vow or penance prescribed as early as the Dharmaśāstras for the accidental killing of a Brāhman, whereby the sinner has to live in the forests, begging his food while announcing his offence and carrying the skull (*kapāla*) of the victim and a staff. The Kāpālikas undoubtedly adopted this vow – hence their name – but the reasons for it are not so clear. Possibly as the most extreme penance it was felt to be the most potent purifier, and thus most efficacious in accumulating merit; possibly it should be linked with the Purāṇic myth of Śiva's beheading of Brahmā as an act of imitation by the worshipper of his deity.

Popular opinion about the sect as reflected in the secular literature accuses them of acts of human sacrifice in propitiation of Śiva; the plot of Bhavabhūti's play, *Mālatīmādhava*, from the late seventh or eighth century hinges on the rescue of the heroine from imminent sacrifice by a Kāpālika and his female disciple. Early in the seventh century a south Indian ruler wrote a short farce in which the characters are a drunken Kāpālika and his female disciple, a Buddhist monk, a Pāśupata ascetic and a madman, and the plot centres on the mishaps occurring to the Kāpālika's skull bowl; here the emphasis is rather on their licentiousness in matters of drink and sex. This and other references suggest that, besides imitating Śiva in performing their characteristic vow, the Kāpālikas also sought to realise in sexual union the divine bliss of Śiva and his consort as part of the whole process of achieving consubstantiality with Śiva.

The literary references and a few inscriptions provide evidence that the sect originated by the sixth century in the Deccan or south India and after the eighth century began to spread to northern India but had virtually died out by the fourteenth century, although Śaṅkara is held, in texts of the fourteenth and fifteenth centuries, to have had an encounter with some Kāpālika ascetics, and Rāmānuja in the early thirteenth century summarises their doctrines and practices along with those of the Kālāmukhas.

The Kālāmukha sect was prevalent in the Karnataka area between the eleventh and thirteenth centuries. The rapid decline of the Pāśupatas in north India and the sudden appearance of the name Lakulīśa in inscriptions in Karnataka during the eleventh century probably point to an actual migration of followers of Lakulīśa southwards; some of the individuals named in the inscriptions are associated with Kashmir. From the rather scanty evidence of Rāmānuja's brief comments and their own inscriptions it appears that their doctrines and beliefs were broadly similar to those of the Pāśupatas. Evidence of temple prostitution and erotic sculpture probably indicate an actual employment of sexual practices similar to the Kāpālikas. Their sudden decline in the thirteenth century is in all probability connected with the rise of the Liṅgāyat movement.

However, Śaivism at this period also had its more intellectual side represented in Kashmir Śaivism or the Trika system, which dates from the beginning of the ninth century at the latest, but on the evidence of lists of teachers should be traced several centuries further back. This school of thought elaborates a monistic viewpoint with some similarities to Sāṃkhya and Advaita Vedānta. Śiva is the *ātman* indwelling all beings and objects individually as well as the universe as a whole; he is the experiencer as distinct from the experienced. The system regards reality as unitary and as being pure and perfect consciousness, conscious of itself through reflection, which is identified with *śakti.* The supreme reality is Śiva as the supreme experiencer, whose essence is pure consciousness, immutable and eternal by his own nature but underlying or pervading the universe as *ātman,* which is essentially pure illumination. Śiva's immanent aspect as *śakti* is not independent but his creative energy is manifested in five aspects of consciousness (*cit*), bliss (*ānanda*), desire, knowledge and activity; these five aspects are Śiva's five faces, the five facets of reality. Creation is basically the self-projection of consciousness which is essentially free but can choose both to limit itself by projecting other entities and to reabsorb them.

By the power of *māyā,* objects which owe their existence to consciousness appear independent of it, thus losing its characteristic omniscience, just as the limitation involved removed the omnipotence. The manifestation of the universe is thus an appearance, not totally unreal as in Advaita Vedānta, but only an aspect of the ultimate reality; however the appearances do not alter their source Śiva, who remains unaffected and complete. Although Śiva is eternal and omnipresent, he conceals himself by his *māyā*; thus the bondage of selves is caused by ignorance of reality, and continuous recognition of reality, of man's identity with Śiva, brings release. This is also interpreted in devotional terms: Śiva in his aspect as Paśupati grants his grace (*prasāda*) producing devotion in the worshipper, so that through their merging the devotee becomes Śiva. Part of the operation of divine grace is to bring an individual to a suitable *guru* who gives him initiation and thus starts the process leading to enlightenment. Thus the devotional pattern of direct approach is combined with the tantric emphasis on the necessity for a *guru*. Other influences on the system come from the philosophy of language and from the Pāñcarātra system; indeed one work by the school's most famous figure, Abhinavagupta, is derived from a similarly named Vaiṣṇava work. Abhinavagupta's position is that all manifestations of phenomena derive from the supreme Śiva from whom all individual selves are illusorily separated and thus *māyā* means, not the total unreality of the world, but its erroneous isolation from Śiva. The spontaneous nature of the illumination revealing Śiva is denoted by the term *spanda*, 'vibration', which perhaps also suggests the understanding of the universe in terms of Śiva's dance.

Alongside the sects worshipping Viṣṇu and Śiva, the cult of the goddess is less easy to define. Not only does the goddess herself often appear under many different names, reflecting in part the amalgamation of many local deities, but she presents two contrasting aspects as benign and horrific, while the relationship between her and Śiva is variously envisaged. Similarly, the cults associated with her, usually termed Śākta or tantric, are not always separable from elements found also in Śaiva, and to a lesser extent in Vaiṣṇava worship. There are of course references to goddesses in Vedic literature but these have no real relation to Devī, the Goddess. One of her specific names, Kālī, is used in the *Mahābhārata* for a minor demoness of destruction; in the latest stage of the *Mahābhārata* another name of her horrific aspect Durgā is praised in two hymns (one of which makes her Kṛṣṇa's sister), and the episode of Dakṣa's sacrifice is narrated, in which Kālī is created from Umā's anger. But these passages say little about Kālī except that she is associated with death and destruction.

On the other hand there is evidence for the worship of the goddess in south India from an early period; the name of Cape

Comorin, more correctly Kanyạ Kumārī, commemorates the worship of a virgin goddess attested since early in the Christian era. The earliest Tamil literature refers to Koṟṟavai as the goddess of the mountains, to whom the tribesmen sacrificed buffaloes as well as other animals, and also as a goddess of war and victory, to whom battle was a kind of sacrifice. The later myth of Durgā slaying the buffalo demon, Mahiṣāsura, looks like the northern adaptation of this goddess. References in the *Harivaṃśa* to the goddess who lives in the Vindhyas may reflect a stage in her penetration northwards. On the other hand cults of mountain goddesses and their consorts were once widespread in the northern mountain ranges of the Hindu Kush and the Himālaya, and involved orgiastic rites and bloody sacrifices. Equally the prominence of worship of Kālī in Bengal derives from local goddess cults there rather than outside influences and the same may well be true of other areas also.

From about the seventh century literary references to the goddess become more frequent, suggesting that her worship became a significant factor in religious life from about that time. Reference is also made to the Seven Mothers (also sometimes eight or nine), who are found however in Tamil literature from the first centuries A.D. The *Devīmāhātmya*, 'glorification of the goddess', inserted into the *Mārkaṇḍeya Purāṇa* possibly by the seventh century, gives a full account of the goddess's birth, appearance and exploits, especially her three defeats of Madhu and Kaiṭabha, of Mahiṣāsura and of Śumbha and Niśumbha; in the last Kālī springs from the forehead of the furious Durgā to give battle to the demons and is withdrawn into her afterwards, an attempt seen also in other myths to integrate or subordinate one form with another. By the eighth century at the latest Durgā and Kālī were being identified with Śiva's consort, Umā or Pārvatī, presumably because of the more malevolent aspects which the goddess and Śiva share. Even so, the process of accommodation may not always have been smooth. In south India, the tradition of a dance contest between Kālī and Śiva won by the god probably reflects Śaiva subjection of an indigenous goddess cult, whereas some later literature, such as the *Devībhāgavata Purāṇa* assigns the goddess the dominant role in the relationship.

As the mythology developed, Devī in her more benign aspects and as Śiva's consort tends to be known by the names

7. Kālī in horrific form playing cymbals

Gaurī, Umā and Pārvatī while her ferocious and terror-inspiring aspect is called Durgā, Kālī or Cāmuṇḍā. Descriptions of the emaciated Kālī, with protruding teeth and tongue and rolling eyes, garlanded in skulls and indulging in cannibalism, are particularly popular. This aspect of Devī becomes particularly prominent in Bengal, though overshadowed until relatively recent times by such goddesses as Manasā, the goddess of snakes, Sītalā, the goddess of smallpox, and Caṇḍī, the goddess of hunters, all very localised deities. In addition to the benevolent and malevolent sides, the goddess also, especially as Tripurasundarī, possesses a voluptuous form representing the bliss (*ānanda*) aspect of Brahman, the absolute. The lack of system in the texts makes it difficult to categorise all the goddess's aspects but among the manifestations of her nature are several groups, such as the ten Mahāvidyās, personifications of her supernatural knowledge, the Seven Mothers, the 64 Yoginīs 'mistresses of Yoga', and Ḍākinīs, a type of fiend.

The worship of the goddess is above all connected with Tantrism, which, as is already apparent however, has a wider distribution in its aspect of a collection of ritualistic and often magical practices and symbols derived from non-Vedic sources. The Tantras ('extension' or 'warp', a metaphor from weaving), from which the term is derived, are handbooks to a particular doctrine, especially but not exclusively the worship of the goddess as the major deity, the Śākta movement. Traditionally there are 64 Śākta Tantras, but Śaiva Tantras are sometimes included in their listing; their dating is complex and uncertain but Tantrism as a movement may originate as early as the fifth century. The development of tantric schools and texts, as well as the penetration of tantric elements into most parts of Indian religious life, reached its peak around the tenth century, from which date also come a number of temples to the 64 Yoginīs; from this period there is also a considerable amount of erotic sculpture, most notably at Khajurāho and Koṇārak, but this is not necessarily directly connected with Tantrism.

Both Śaiva and Śākta Tantras are usually presented as dialogues between Śiva as teacher and his consort, his *śakti*, as pupil, although sometimes the roles are reversed. This is in accordance with the paramount importance of the *guru* in Tantrism. Submission to a *guru* is not, of course, confined to Tantrism – the Vedic lore had to be passed from teacher to pupil and the devotional and Yoga traditions also regard the teacher as important – but in it is made an absolute necessity, and some texts declare that, provided the relationship to the *guru* is right, no matter what else is wrong, success is assured. Thus the first requirement is initiation by a *guru*, during which a *mantra* is communicated to the pupil.

Methods of appropriation are central to the Tantras, with the experience or 'realisation' of the aspirant being vital. Among the methods employed, the recitation of *mantras*, the use of ritual gestures and the yogic identification with the divine are especially prominent. The use of *mantras* is found as early as the Brāhmaṇas to accompany and validate ritual acts, while emphasis on the significance of speech can be traced to the *Ṛgveda* and more immediately to Bhartṛhari's concept of Śabdabrahman; however, the tantric emphasis on them is distinctive. A basic *mantra* is a single syllable, felt to encapsulate some energy or divine power, and more complex *mantras* are built up from series of simple ones. The correct utterance of one evokes the specific power with which it is connected by the elaborate sound symbolism of Tantrism; sound and meaning are felt to be basic to the universe.

Related to *mantra* is *yantra*, functioning analogously in the visual sphere to *mantra* in the audible. Worship and meditation on a *yantra* or the similar *maṇḍala*, geometric diagrams which lead from the exterior to their centre, is a means for the aspirant to participate in the powers of the universe and to fulfil his wishes. The best known *yantra* is probably the Śrīyantra consisting of a square with four entrances, inside which are six concentric circles, enclosing nine intersecting triangles (five female pointing downwards and four male upwards) and at their centre a dot representing the source and base of the universe, the goddess Tripurā.

Symbolic gestures (*mudrās*) are just as effective as *mantras*, which indeed should be accompanied by the appropriate *mudrā* to have their proper effect. They play an important part in the worship (*pūjā*) which is, along with meditation (Yoga), one of the two parts of tantric religious practice. Ritualised worship is obligatory for every tantric, even those who have progressed spiritually beyond the ordinary state. Tantric ritual involves elements drawn from many sources, to a large extent on the additive principle, while aspirants continue to perform the ordinary rituals appropriate to their position in society. There is a daily ritual of worship of the goddess, as well as more elaborate occasional rituals. At the basis of them, as of all tantric teaching, is the realisation of the identity of the deity with the worshipper through the *guru*, who is the deity herself manifest on earth, and the *mantra* imparted by him. After careful purification of everything connected with the rite, the major items are worship of the line of *gurus*, the drawing of a *yantra*, the consecration of the worshipper's own self (by divesting himself of his own body in a reversal of cosmic evolution and investing himself with a pure body into which the goddess descends limb by limb), meditation on the goddess and performance of various *mudrās*, internal worship, the main ceremony of offerings, and circumambulation of the deity.

The internal worship consists basically of the meditative discipline of Yoga, which Tantrism has developed in distinctive ways but which still leads to the goal of merging oneself with the absolute, here the deity. Two forms are particularly characteristic: *mantrayoga*, the meditation on mystical syllables, and *layayoga*, based on an elaborate mystical physiology. The aim of the latter is the dissolution (*laya*) of the world, the macrocosm, within the aspirant's own body viewed as the microcosm and ultimately his dissolution into the deity. The Tantras draw extensive parallels between the human body and the universe, sometimes even locating geographical features within the body. Various *cakras* ('circles' or 'centres') are located in the body along the spine which is assimilated to Mt Meru, the cosmic axis; the body also contains a vast number of channels connecting the senses and the mind, of which the most important, Suṣumnā, runs up the spinal column from the lowest *cakra* to the highest.

The aim of the meditative process is to force Kuṇḍalinī, 'the coiled', representing the limitation of consciousness and energy (*śakti*, the goddess) as the individual and conceived as a snake lying coiled asleep inside the lowest *cakra*, up the Suṣumnā into each of the higher *cakras* in turn until in the highest Sahasrāra *cakra* she merges with the unlimited *śakti* residing there in perpetual union with the transcendent Śiva. The number and description of the *cakras* vary in different texts but usually there are six (with the Sahasrāra lying outside the series) described as lotuses of varying numbers of petals and colours each with its own presiding *śakti* and *mantra*. On either side of the Suṣumnā are the channels Piṅgalā and Iḍā, connected with the polarities of sun and moon, life and death, Agni and Soma. This notion of polarity runs all through tantric thought both in the physical world and the metaphysical, perhaps most frequently expressed in the polarity of male and female, Śiva and Śakti. By the process of breath control, the aspirant awakens Kuṇḍalinī and begins the process of her ascent, at the same time excluding his awareness of the external world. As she ascends, the world is gradually consumed and destroyed and in the final stage the aspirant passes beyond his body to the merging of his individual self with the cosmic energy.

The principal offerings vary according to the school. The best known division of Tantrism is into 'Left' and 'Right' methods, which corresponds to the antithesis between the literal and symbolic enactment of certain ritual details, but parallel to this is the division into Samaya and Kaula, where the Samaya method means the practice of internal worship and the Kaulas perform external worship, including the full set of five offerings. These five are alcohol, meat, fish, parched grain (or 'gestures', *mudrā*) and sexual intercourse, of which the majority are clearly something forbidden in normal worship, although several have always had a place in tribal worship or local cults. But within the tantric context they are definitely envisaged as relating to overcoming the polarities of the ordinary world. Thus the Kaula in his worship identifies his female partner with the goddess and re-enacts with her the unity of unevolved creation in the union of Śiva with his *śakti* (energy or creative power). To further emphasise the polarity a high-caste tantric man might choose as partner a low-caste woman, underlining the male-female opposition by also using the social contrast.

In this context the horrific aspect of the goddess as Kālī has a particular function. Just as the usual taboos of society are not avoided but faced and mastered, so Kālī as the representation of the destructive aspect of reality is confronted and overcome by the aspirant, who thus is identified with Śiva defeating Kālī in the dancing contest. The idea of mastery over oneself and the universe is always there in Tantrism and becomes still more obvious in later groups such as the Nāths.

CHAPTER SEVEN

Bhakti in the South

Irrupting into the pattern of developed theistic sects just outlined, there first appeared in south India a new phenomenon, which was to have a profound effect upon the religious life of the whole country. This was the *bhakti* or devotional movement, which began to blossom in the seventh century, although its roots may be traced back a further two centuries or so. It was characterised by a personal relationship between the deity and the devotee, and worship became a fervent emotional experience in response to divine grace. The movement had two parallel strands, both essentially monotheistic, one centred on Śiva, the other on Viṣṇu. More accurately, the groups worshipped a variety of local deities; Murukaṉ (Murugan), the most prominent, was then identified with Skanda, Śiva's son, and also with Śiva himself in his benign aspects, while others such as Tirumāl were identified with Viṣṇu. In the tenth century, when both branches were codified, 63 Nāyaṉmārs were recognised by the Śaivas as their most important leaders, and their works collected, while the Vaiṣṇavas produced a similar collection attributed to twelve of their most prominent figures, or Āḻvārs.

As early as the fourth or fifth century A.D. the *Tirukkuṟaḷ*, 'Sacred Couplets', reveals the first glimpses of *bhakti* in the stress laid on the importance of selfless love in relations between men and between man and god; such love alone gives meaning and purpose to this life, and release from the sorrow of rebirth by union with the deity. In another work, the sixth-century Tamil *Guide to the Lord Murukaṉ,* the poet Nakkīrar advises devout souls seeking liberation to approach Murukaṉ and obtain his grace:

> He will appear in might and holiness,
> he will tower up to heaven;
> but his harshness will be concealed
> and his form will be revealed
> as a youth of fragrant beauty;
> in loving words of grace

he will say 'Be not afraid!
For I knew that you would come!'

Among the Nāyaṉmārs who firmly established Śaiva *bhakti* between the seventh and ninth centuries, the four most prominent were Campantar (Sambandhar), Cuntarar (Sundarar), Appar and Māṇikkavācakar. Campantar championed the cause of Śaivism against the influential Jain and Buddhist monks of his time, to the extent, it is said, of re-converting the king of Madurai from the Jainism which he and many of his subjects had embraced. In his numerous hymns of praise to Śiva and his great cult centre at Cidambaram, he stresses the necessity of worshipping with the mind; Śiva is said to reside in the hearts of those who fix their minds on him in loving contemplation.

Unusual among the leaders of the *bhakti* movement, Cuntarar was a Brāhman, though his marriage to two low-caste women damaged both his status and his finances. One of the themes of his hymns is the single-minded love of the Deity which makes the simplest offering acceptable and allows the grace of Śiva to reach his devotee. This love is reflected in the worshipper's love for his neighbour, and is expressed in the hymns in imagery of an intimately physical nature.

Tension between Jainism and Hinduism also affected Appar. Though brought up a Śaiva, he briefly became a Jain teacher before reverting to Śaivism and contributing greatly to its revival by going about the temples of south India, singing praises to Śiva and his grace. Like Campantar, a close though older friend, he converted his king from Jainism, and it is largely due to the efforts of this pair that Buddhism and Jainism were virtually eliminated from south India. Appar's poetry is marked by a profound sense of sin and penitence unusual in Hinduism:

> Wicked is my race, and wicked my character and ways; so great is my sin that I sin even in doing good. Wicked am I and foolish not to unite myself with the good. No animal am I, yet I cannot help behaving like an animal. I can preach at men to hate what is wrong, but such a miserable sinner am I that I can only beg and never give.

This feeling of deep humility leads him to beseech with confidence Śiva's forgiveness. Unlike Campantar's works, Appar's poems are almost exclusively emotional; this factor, coupled with their anti-ritualism and autobiographical content, lead to a full transference of worship into the sphere of emotion and mysticism.

The exquisite verses of Māṇikkavācakar's *Tiruvācakam*, which is still sung daily in temples and homes in Tamilnad, form the climax of this outpouring of Tamil mystical poetry. This ninth-century work expresses its author's ecstatic and profound love for Śiva, and his ardent longing for union with the god. It also demonstrates the universality of the appeal of *bhakti*, for Māṇikkavācakar was a man of great intellectual ability, who held the post of prime minister to a Pāṇḍya king before adopting the life of a religious poet, practising austerities at Cidambaram, performing miracles and holding dialogues with Sinhalese Buddhists.

The Vaiṣṇava devotional movement developed along largely parallel lines between the seventh and ninth centuries. It was centred on Śrīraṅgam and also stressed the personal relationship between devotee and deity. Its appeal was also wide-ranging, for the Āḻvārs were drawn from all classes of society and both sexes, and the legends associated with them demonstrate Viṣṇu's loving concern for them in every detail of their lives, though many of these apparently trivial tales should obviously be taken as parables. Under the influence of the *avatāra* stories, several Āḻvārs were considered to be incarnations of Viṣṇu himself, of his wife, or of attributes such as his conch and mace, but this is clearly a method of expressing the immanence of the god rather than a continuance of the old tradition. The first three Āḻvārs, Poykai, Pūtam and Pēy, each produced a century of hymns of divine grace after experiencing Viṣṇu's presence among them while sheltering from a storm. The most celebrated figure is Nammāḻvār, who spent his life in fasting and meditation. Inspired by Viṣṇu, he composed four series of verses to provide the masses with religious poetry now that the Vedas were no longer accessible to them. Though himself a member of the low *śūdra* caste, his works were popularised by his itinerant Brāhman disciple, Maturakavi. Another low-caste Āḻvār, Tiruppāṇ, was a singer and *vīṇā*-player used by Viṣṇu, much against his will, to humble the pride of a group of Brāhman priests and to demonstrate the unacceptability of caste-distinctions. Kulacēkara, by contrast, was a ninth-century king of Kerala who became so rapt in devotion that he was not always able to distinguish fact from fantasy: on one occasion he raised an army to rescue Sītā, heroine of the *Rāmāyaṇa*. Eventually he abdicated and devoted himself to visiting shrines and composing poetry. The inclusiveness of the *bhakti* movement is further demonstrated by the figure of Āṇṭāḷ – a woman. She is said to have been married to Viṣṇu's statue at Śrīraṅgam and thereupon absorbed into it; she thus came to be regarded as an incarnation of Śrī, who was worshipped locally on the same level as Viṣṇu. She composed two poems proclaiming her love for Viṣṇu, describing him in imagery of great beauty; here she entreats him to come, like

> a lion, sleeping the monsoon away in his mountain lair,
> who stirs and opens his fiery eyes,
> shakes himself till his mane bristles,
> drowsily stretches his limbs,
> then leaves his den with a roar.

Viṣṇu's favour towards two other hymn-writers appears rather more eccentric, for he intervenes to help Toṇṭaraṭippoṭi out of an embarrassing difficulty with a courtesan and a golden bowl stolen from his temple, while Tirumaṅkai finances the building of the temple out of the profits of a protection racket.

Whether Śaiva or Vaiṣṇava, these mystics repeatedly stress the same themes in their poems. Religion for them is no longer a matter of contemplation of a transcendent, impersonal Absolute, but of ecstatic response to an intensely personal experience. This leads to a profound sense of the devotee's own shortcomings and to a trustful recourse to the god's forgiveness, with the whole personality being surrendered to the Deity. Since both gods claim whole-hearted devotion, there is no room within the system for a multiplicity of deities, and each cult is effectively monotheistic. This divine love should be expressed in love for one's fellows, and transcends the barriers of caste and sex. Indeed, it is frequently described by means of the symbolism of conjugal love, in poetry of great tenderness and beauty. Bands of devotees travelled the country, singing, dancing, and challenging opponents to public debates, for this movement was not one of passive sentimentality, but a dynamic force which swept the country – eventually including north India – transforming Hinduism and vigorously and successfully confronting Buddhism and Jainism.

With the codification of these poets' works in the tenth century begins the process of transformation of these essentially individual responses into an organised system. Nātamuni, the redactor of the Vaiṣṇava corpus, is regarded as the first of the line of teachers (*ācāryas*) of the Śrīvaiṣṇava sect. Doctrinally however, Yāmuna, traditionally his grandson and direct successor as teacher, is the first notable figure, incorporating a Vedānta outlook into the *bhakti* concept and seeking logically to establish the real existence of the individual and supreme souls (the devotee and the deity) in his writings. He argues for the separate existence of the deity as cause and of the world and souls as effects; the universe is obedient to the deity's will, just as a man's body is to him, and the spiritual beings, souls, perform their tasks under the control of one person, just as the senses depend on the soul. Yāmuna's view of the world as a whole governed by one supreme being on the model of the soul and the body is obviously close to the ideas of the Nyāya writer, Udayana, and equally obviously lays the foundations of Rāmānuja's more developed philosophy. Among Yāmuna's works is also an analysis of the *Bhagavadgītā*, in which he emphasises the way of *bhakti* – giving it its new connotation – at the expense of knowledge and action and propounds a division of its eighteen chapters into three groups of six.

The most important of the Śrīvaiṣṇavas is Rāmānuja, like the previous two the *ācārya*, the authoritative teacher, of the community, and involved in the administration of the Śrīraṅgam temple. He is traditionally said to have lived from 1017 to 1137 A.D., but his birth has probably been artificially brought forward to connect him directly with Yāmuna, who is said to have died in 1038, for the tradition is that Rāmānuja succeeded Yāmuna as a young man to the headship of Śrīraṅgam. The undoubted intellectual link between the two is thus popularly turned into a direct link by succession. Rāmānuja is held to have travelled throughout India to disseminate his system and according to tradition had to retreat from Śrīraṅgam because of the hostility of the ruler and went to Melkote in Karnataka, where he organised a strong centre of Vaiṣṇava learning.

Rāmānuja wrote nine works, all in Sanskrit (a move away from the Āḻvārs' use of Tamil in the interests of a wider and more traditional audience); these consist of three major philosophical works, two briefer commentaries, three devotional works on the theme of surrender to the deity and a manual of daily worship. The first of Rāmānuja's three philosophical works is designed to show that the Upaniṣads do not teach the strict monism propounded by Śaṅkara and strives to integrate a Vedānta position with devotion to a personal deity. Rāmānuja's standpoint is essentially different from both Śaṅkara's and Bhāskara's in assigning a definite and ultimately valid reality to the world and its two components of matter (*prakṛti*) and souls (*ātman*). This is most fully expressed in his doctrine that the deity stands to the world of *ātman* and *prakṛti* in the relation of a soul to the body which forms its attribute. Rāmānuja develops this theme and others in his other two major philosophical works, commentaries on the *Bhagavadgītā* and the *Brahmasūtra*.

Rāmānuja concentrates on the relation of the world to the deity, arguing that the deity is real and independent but that souls are also real but totally dependent on the deity. As the body of god, the world is his instrument and also part of his self-expression, while, just as the soul controls its body, so the deity is the inner controller of individual souls; Rāmānuja necessarily adopts a broad definition of a body as anything which can be controlled by and is subordinate to a conscious *ātman*. The self-body analogy also serves to distinguish the deity, who for Rāmānuja is the fullest expression of the impersonal Absolute, Brahman, from his dependent bodily parts or attributes, and the dependence of an attribute on its substance is compared to the relation of an adjective to the noun it qualifies; Rāmānuja's system as a philosophy is therefore known as the 'qualified Advaita', Viśiṣṭādvaita. Since *ātman* and *prakṛti* constitute the body of the deity, their functioning to further the realisation of Brahman or the deity is easily explicable on this analogy. Similarly Rāmānuja interprets for example the Upaniṣadic saying *tat tvam asi* by declaring that, since all spiritual and material entities constitute the body of Brahman, Brahman thus embodied is denoted by all words and so both pronouns refer to Brahman, *tat* 'that' as the absolute, the first cause, and *tvam* 'you' as the inner controller modified by the embodied soul.

The self-body analogy also emphasises the inseparable and organic relationship between Viṣṇu, or Nārāyaṇa as Rāmānuja more frequently calls him, and the world, as well as indicating the total and eternal dependence of the world on the will of the deity. Rāmānuja also uses it to bring out the all-inclusive nature of the supreme self suggested in the *Bhagavadgītā*. He thus simultaneously affirms the reality of the world and therefore of individual selves and its subservience to the divine purpose, which Rāmānuja explains in terms of *līlā*, literally the deity's 'sport' but better understood as his self-expression, for he is free from any constraint apart from his own spontaneously creative nature. The accessibility of the deity to the world and especially individual souls is also indicated by the analogy, for, as the inner self of everything Nārāyaṇa, the supreme embodiment of all perfection, leads the soul which realises its dependence on him to himself; Rāmānuja even implies that in some sense the deity needs the soul.

This dependence on god was realised through *bhakti*, the intense devotion and submission to Nārāyaṇa in which the devotee realised his total dependence on him. The act of surrender (*prapatti*) is for Rāmānuja both the start and the continuing attitude of devotion to the deity and presupposes acceptance of the soul's subservience; it involves putting oneself completely in the deity's hands, trusting in his will and awaiting his grace (*prasāda*). For Nārāyaṇa, though inaccessible to men in the fullness of his divinity, is full of grace and love for his creation. He has therefore made himself accessible to his worshippers by descending into the world in a form similar to theirs, and has the power to override the workings of *karma*, for he is not in any way subject to *karma*; indeed Rāmānuja vigorously denies any connection of the deity with evil or suffering, which only affect the divine body not the highest self. So too Nārāyaṇa's six beautiful qualities of knowledge, strength, sovereignty, firmness, power and splendour – a grouping taken through Yāmuna from the Pāñcarātras and reflecting the lordship or transcendence of the deity – are balanced by a second group of auspicious qualities, consisting of compassion, graciousness, forgiveness and generosity and indicating his approachability by his worshippers.

Rāmānuja stresses the continued individual existence of souls after liberation; the individual *ātman* at release returns to Nārāyaṇa to dwell in full communion with him, and yet distinct. Everything forms a part of the deity as his body, subservient to him, and so is indissolubly connected to him in a perfect unity. Nevertheless, the *ātman*, always conscious of itself, is both one with Nārāyaṇa and yet separate as the one subject to his commands and call to action in the moral sphere. By contrast with god and selves, *prakṛti* is sometimes termed *avidyā*, in the sense that being unconscious it is naturally opposed to knowledge. But, though called *avidyā* in this sense, *prakṛti* is the material cause of the world, real and eternal but dependent on the deity, in support of which Rāmānuja cites various Upaniṣadic texts. Against Śaṅkara, Rāmānuja argues that it is contrary to the evidence of our senses that there is a cessation of distinction and that, even if some scriptural texts claim that Brahman is one only without a second, there are others which depend on the notion of plurality; Rāmānuja asserts that we have to start with the evidence of our senses as the most basic data that we are given, a distinctly realist and common-sense position in comparison with Śaṅkara's.

Whereas for Śaṅkara the writing of a commentary on the *Bhagavadgītā* was an uncongenial task undertaken as a concession to the work's popularity, for Rāmānuja it was a welcome opportunity to develop his views more fully, after acknowledging his indebtedness to Yāmuna's analysis. It is on the authority of the *Bhagavadgītā* that Rāmānuja propounds the need for ritual action as a first stage in the path of devotion. Though technically not scriptural and thus only valid to support and clarify Vedic statements, in practice the *Bhagavadgītā* is authoritative and often the meaning of scriptural texts is made to agree with it. Rāmānuja's commentary on it is less polemical than his commentary on the *Brahmasūtra* and more devotional. He endeavours to show that its three methods of approach to the deity by action, knowledge and devotion are not separate but successive stages of the same way. In this context Rāmānuja sees surrender (*prapatti*) as a part of the path of *bhakti* and, whenever the grace of Nārāyaṇa is mentioned, the efforts of the worshipper are also stressed.

More of Rāmānuja's understanding of *prapatti* is found in the three devotional works, which are the most popular of his works with modern Śrīvaiṣṇavas. The first, in the form of a dialogue between Rāmānuja and Nārāyaṇa with Śrī, his consort, is seen as the record of Rāmānuja's own taking refuge at the feet of the deity in surrender to his mercy; the second is a briefer prayer of surrender addressed to Raṅganātha (the form of Viṣṇu worshipped at Śrīraṅgam), asking for acceptance as the perpetual servant of the Lord; the third consists mainly of a detailed description of Viṣṇu's heaven, to be regularly meditated on in connection with one's surrender to the deity. Whether or not these more devotional works are by Rāmānuja himself, they present an understanding of the practice of *bhakti* by repeated meditation on the deity's perfections which is in close agreement with his views more concisely expressed elsewhere and which are in fact an echo of the wording used in his other works.

Together with the manual for daily worship, based on the Pāñcarātra tradition, the three devotional works serve to emphasise the devotional element of Rāmānuja's religion; his philosophical views are clearly dictated by his personal faith. Even more than Śaṅkara, he endeavoured to give an organisational expression to his beliefs and traditionally also engaged in the same lengthy tours to propagate his ideas. His position as not only the *ācārya* of the Śrīvaiṣṇava community but also the superintendent or general manager of the Śrīraṅgam temple gave him unrivalled influence; indeed the temple chronicles, supported by general Vaiṣṇava tradition, declare that Rāmānuja was the first great organiser of the temple administration. He replaced the Vaikhānasa pattern of worship with the more liberal Pāñcarātra pattern, and expanded the fivefold division of temple servants, which had existed from the time of Tirumaṅkai Āḻvār or before, into a tenfold one, with in addition ten groups of *śūdra* servants; an important ritual role was assigned to a group of *śūdra* ascetics. This code for the ritual and management of the temple was in force until the temple was desecrated by the Muslims in A.D. 1323 and thus the important ritual roles of *śūdras* were maintained throughout that period. The increased participation of worshippers from all social levels with the establishment of the more liberal Pāñcarātra tradition spread from Śrīraṅgam to other Vaiṣṇava centres and is one of Rāmānuja's main legacies to the Vaiṣṇava faith as a whole, giving ritualised expression to the Āḻvārs' disregard of and even opposition to caste restrictions, arising from the equality of all men before the deity.

Rāmānuja's ritual handbook lays down the daily routine for an orthodox Śrīvaiṣṇava in the five daily acts of the Pāñcarātra tradition, while the five sacraments of the sect begin with the branding of Viṣṇu's symbols or weapons and also include the application of the sectarian mark on the forehead, the taking of a religious name, receiving a *mantra* and presenting an image for worship; among the *mantras* of the sect is one drawn from the conclusion of the *Bhagavadgītā*. The images of the deity are important in the cult, although Rāmānuja places more stress on the inner aspect, making it clear that the worshipper must continue to keep in mind a mental picture of the deity and his activities.

By the fourteenth century the Śrīvaiṣṇava sect had split into two subsects, each tracing a different line of teachers back to Rāmānuja. The schism centred on a difference in interpretation of *prapatti*, with both schools appealing to Rāmānuja's writings in support of their view; the dispute was over the question of human effort versus divine grace in achieving salvation, a controversy often and not unreasonably compared to the Arminian and Calvinist standpoints within Protestantism. The Northern school held that the worshipper had to make some effort to win the grace of the Lord and emphasised the performance of *karma*, a position commonly summed up as being 'on the analogy of the monkey and its young', for as the monkey carries her young which cling to her body so Viṣṇu saves the worshipper who himself makes an effort. The Southern school held that the Lord's grace itself conferred salvation, a position 'on the analogy of the cat and its kittens', for just as the cat picks up her kittens in her mouth and carries them off willy-nilly, so Viṣṇu saves whom he wills, without effort on their part.

There are in fact other issues which are probably just as basic as this doctrinal point. In general the Southern school is more liberal than the Northern, having a definite preference for the use of Tamil (whereas the Northern school reverted to the more traditional Sanskrit) and teaching the same *mantra* to all castes (whereas the Northern school distinguished between Brāhmans and others). In addition the Northern school believes that Lakṣmī, as well as Viṣṇu, is capable of granting liberation, a somewhat tantric view owed to the Pāñcarātra tradition; in contrast the Southern school considered her to be always subordinate to Viṣṇu, the first of dependent beings but nevertheless dependent. The more traditional attitudes of the Northern school are apparent in the writings of Vedāntadeśika (traditionally 1268–1367), with their many references to caste and caste duty; there is obvious concern that the egalitarianism of the Āḻvārs, reinforced by Rāmānuja's introduction of the Pāñcarātra ritual, was undermining the social order. Both he and the contemporary leader of the Southern school were forced to flee by the Muslim sack of the temple and are commemorated by shrines in the eventually restored temple (although Rāmānuja's reforms were abandoned after its restoration).

Parallel with the emergence of the Śrīvaiṣṇava movement as the theological expression of the mystical insights of the Āḻvārs was the development of the Śaiva Siddhānta system out of the poetry of the Nāyaṉmārs, begun in the tenth century with the compilation of their poetry in the twelve Tirumuṟai. The Śaiva Siddhānta recognises four classes of text as authoritative: the Vedic literature, the 28 Śaiva Āgamas, the twelve Tirumuṟai and the fourteen Śaiva Siddhānta Śāstras. However, it is held that the Vedas are a general revelation, whereas the Śaiva Āgamas are more specific, being revealed by Śiva himself to his devotees, as well as containing the essential truths of the Vedas; in practice therefore the Āgamas supersede the Vedas and in fact the Śaiva Siddhānta Śāstras are more important to the sect than the Āgamas, although the poems of the Nāyaṉmārs remain significant devotionally. The fourteen Śāstras were written by a succession of teachers, six in all, who were mainly of non-Brāhman, usually *śūdra* origin; the last of them, Umāpati, was a Brāhman supposedly outcasted because of his association with the *śūdra* teachers of the movement.

The earliest of these Śāstras, said to have been composed in 1147 by the first Uyyavantar, presents a brief but vivid summary of Śaiva Siddhānta doctrine in 45 triplets of verses. It is less systematic than the later texts but highlights the mystical experience of the communion with Śiva and stresses that the soul, sunk in evil, cannot attain release except through knowledge of Śiva granted by his grace and the soul's love for him. Śiva's grace is always present, though dormant, in every soul, by which is implied that souls are divine or share Śiva's nature. But the soul, forgetting its true nature because of its egoism, thinks itself self-sufficient and so cuts itself off from Śiva. However, Śiva appears in the form of the *guru* to instruct the soul, then bestows his grace and enables the soul to see its true nature, and finally takes possession of the soul, which becomes like Śiva himself. This union is so intimate that all conscious duality between Śiva and the soul is abolished; the author explicitly declares that the soul in this state ought not even to know that it knows Śiva as a distinct reality. Nevertheless, such an intimate union with Śiva does not mean the annihilation of the self, a possibility always strenuously denied throughout the *bhakti* tradition. About thirty years later the second Uyyavantar, who was traditionally a disciple of the first, composed a work which in many respects is a commentary on the previous work.

The most important of these texts is the *Civañāṉapōtam* (*Śivajñānabodha*) of Meykaṇṭar, written around 1221 and containing the first systematic theology of the movement. In form it consists of twelve statements, said to be drawn from one of the Āgamas, and a full commentary on them. The nature of the self is that of the animal (*paśu*), when it is bound by impurity and subject to phenomenal experience; its nature when illuminated by grace is that of Śiva, for it realises its relationship of union with the deity. Meykaṇṭar emphasises, however, that even in liberation souls remain subject to Śiva as his servants. Detachment from the world and attachment to Śiva are complementary. Śiva is perpetually immanent in the individual as the soul of his soul, but yet is other than souls in his transcendence. Through the *guru* Śiva reveals the mystery of his divine immanence by the practice of *tapas*, interpreted within the system to mean the three stages in the progressive practice of *bhakti*, by which the soul is equipped to receive the knowledge of Śiva through his grace.

Almost as important as Meykaṇṭar's work is one by his pupil Aruḷnanti which is partly a commentary on it and partly a refutation of other religious systems; Aruḷnanti also wrote a eulogy of his *guru*, which develops the theme of divine immanence. Both works belong to the middle of the thirteenth century. Following Meykaṇṭar, Aruḷnanti adopts a basically Sāṃkhya theory of reality with Śiva as the efficient cause and *māyā* as the material cause. However, the relationship of unity and yet difference between Śiva and the world is termed by them *advaita*, understood in the sense of non-difference and suggesting that Śiva is united with the individual soul as the soul with the body. Aruḷnanti repeatedly declares that Śiva is actively present in souls and that this immanence reaches its peak in the mystical experience that the soul is united with Śiva in such a way that he is said to be more intimate than the soul itself.

The works of the last of the six teachers, Umāpati, were written early in the fourteenth century. Their author was traditionally a prominent Vaiṣṇava Brāhman at Cidambaram who one day, as he was being transported in a palanquin, heard the words, 'There goes a man blind by day', and discovered that they were spoken by another of Meykaṇṭar's pupils, the author of another Śāstra; as a result he became a convert to Śaiva Siddhānta. Another tradition holds that one of Umāpati's works was sung at a flag-hoisting festival in honour of Śiva Naṭarāja at Cidambaram. Umāpati's major work, the *Civappirakācam* (*Śivaprakāśa*), is designed to serve as an introduction to the Śaiva Siddhānta and so is marked by clarity of presentation. Its most distinctive feature is the stress laid on the concept that Śiva is inaccessible to human understanding and can only be known by divine wisdom.

The Śaiva Siddhānta assigns definite purpose to Śiva's activity, unlike most Hindu traditions, which tend to see the supreme deity's activity in terms of sport or spontaneous, causeless action; his aspect as Lord of the dance, Naṭarāja, symbolises his activity for the liberation of souls. His threefold activity in creation, preservation and dissolution has the purpose of granting his grace, which enables souls to advance spiritually along the way to liberation and to enter finally into union with Śiva. As Meykaṇṭar makes clear, *bhakti* produces in the individual the attitude necessary to receive Śiva's grace in order to love him more perfectly. He and later writers make use of the traditional four types or stages of *bhakti*. The first stage, expressed in tending the sanctuary and service to other devotees, consists of the attitude of a servant towards his master and leads to attainment of the sphere of Śiva. The second, expressed in offerings to the deity and so forth, is like the affection of a child for its parents and results in proximity to the deity. The third stage of loving meditation on Śiva as intelligence is likened to the relationship of friends and enables the devotee to attain the form of Śiva. The fourth stage, knowledge or direct intuition of Śiva, brings union with Śiva comparable to that of lovers. Umāpati, in his explanation of these four stages of *bhakti*, emphasises the common element of love for Śiva and

8. Śiva Naṭarāja (lord of the dance)

participation of the soul in him. When knowledge of Śiva in the form of grace enters the soul, it breaks free from its impurity and realises Śiva within as the inner principle of consciousness. The immanence of Śiva is stressed in the mystical union of the soul with him, but his transcendence is also retained in the soul's realisation of its total dependence on Śiva and surrender to him.

Śiva is the supreme deity, stainless and pure; as the supreme Lord of all things he is one. So the first Uyyavantar sums up and expresses theologically the monotheistic and personal experience of Śiva by the Nāyaṉmārs. He also declares that, because Śiva transcends all conceptualisation, he is unknowable except through his grace and inexpressible by any image or symbol. Nevertheless, he possesses the personal qualities of knowledge, love and graciousness. Meykaṇṭar declares that Śiva is the supreme being, to whom Brahmā and Viṣṇu are subordinate, since all created things dissolve in the one who transcends them and is other than them. Brahmā as creator and Viṣṇu as preserver can only perform their functions by means of Śiva's power or *śakti*, through which Śiva operates in the world, not participating himself in any of the changes to which all other beings are subject.

The Śaiva Siddhānta thus maintains that Śiva is both immanent and transcendent, immanent as his *śakti* but transcendent as Śiva. He is the material cause of the universe through his *śakti*, while as Śiva he is the efficient cause, but ultimately there is no distinction between Śiva and his *śakti*. In the elaborate cosmogony developed by the system on the basis of the Sāṃkhya system, there are no fewer than 36 categories (*tattvas*); indeed, the Śaiva Siddhānta claims superiority on just this point on the basis that the enumeration of more categories is the knowledge of more truths, denigrating the value of other systems as limited to knowledge of no more than 25 categories. Above the usual 24 it elaborates five Śivatattvas or pure principles (Śiva, Śakti, Sadāśiva, Īśvara and Śuddhavidyā) and seven Vidyātattvas or categories of knowledge, which operate basically in the moral sphere. The Śivatattvas, even the first, are not identical with Śiva, who is not directly the cause of any categories since he is not in any way liable to transformation; rather, it is through them that the transcendent Śiva controls the universe.

The Śaiva Siddhānta established teaching centres, modelled on Brāhman *maṭhas*, under the guidance of non-Brāhman *gurus* and a developed system of organisation had evolved by the thirteenth century. The strength of *śūdras* in this area as well as other aspects of the movement reflects both its popular origin and the tradition derived from the Nāyaṉmārs of deprecating caste distinctions. Just as the system gave nominal allegiance to the Vedas but regarded the Āgamas as a superior spiritual authority, so too they do not directly reject the caste system but stress that the Āgamas are open to all four classes and tend to speak of a class of 'First Śaivas', which is sometimes equated with Brāhmans and sometimes placed above them but clearly corresponds in some sense with the adherents of the sect.

From the Tamil-speaking area the *bhakti* movement spread into the adjacent linguistic areas of south India quite rapidly and gave rise there to groups of devotional poets analogous to the Nāyaṉmārs and Āḻvārs, as well as to formal theological systems. In the Kannaḍa-speaking area, roughly modern Karnataka, the order of events is reversed with the emergence in the middle of the twelfth century of Basava as a major reformer and the founder of the Liṅgāyat or Vīraśaiva movement, within which appeared a number of mystics expounding their faith in popular form as *vacanas*, sayings. The background to the rise of Basava was the strength in the area of the Kālāmukha sect, which had brought about a resurgence of the Śaiva faith in the previous couple of centuries; their numbers and influence are clearly attested by several inscriptions.

Basava himself was born in a Śaiva Brāhman family and traditionally his parents were devout Śaivas, but as he grew up Basava became increasingly revolted by traditional religious and social practices, beginning with the investiture with the sacred thread forced on him at the age of eight. At sixteen he is said to have discarded his sacred thread, being thrown out of his home as a result. He went to the town of Saṃgama, a pilgrimage centre with a major temple to Śiva Saṃgameśvara 'Lord of the Confluence', where he received a divine commission to work for the renewal of Śaivism. Subsequently he took service in the administration of a local ruler and apparently made use of his influential position in the state to promote the conversion of a large number of Jains. He had abandoned his traditional creed and now set up a new faith, in which he abolished all distinction of caste or sex; he thus championed the lower, under-privileged classes despite his own Brāhman origin. Naturally, such developments led to tensions in the court and Basava was apparently accused of embezzlement by some officials whom he had dismissed for dishonesty. The final crisis seems to have been the marriage by a Brāhman of his daughter to an untouchable, both fathers being followers of Basava; the king, as the upholder of traditional morality, ordered their punishment, and armed rebellion by some at least of Basava's followers ensued. Basava himself died at this point, around 1167, but there are conflicting accounts of his death. Basava's movement itself was persecuted for a period but survived to become in more recent times the dominant religious community in some parts of Karnataka.

Both Basava and a contemporary, Allamā Prabhu, who played almost as significant a role in the development of the movement, were among the two hundred or more composers of *vacanas*, which became the main vehicle for the propagation of the new faith among the common people. In form these sayings were brief, prose invocations of Śiva under one of his many local names, often epigrammatic in style and dwelling on the uselessness of ritual, learning or wealth and the need to turn to Śiva. They often present a trenchant critique of established values. At an early stage a 'Spiritual Academy' was established, at which both spiritual and social matters were discussed, and gradually a complete organisational pattern was evolved.

The Liṅgāyat sect is better known for its practices and its social doctrines than its theology. It holds that the only real and eternal entity is Śiva, in whom the world exists and to whom it will finally return. The individual soul, as in Kashmir Śaivism, is the limitation of the supreme Śiva through *avidyā* or *māyā*, which can be removed either by knowledge or by proper observance of prescribed rules, formulated in three groups. Among these are the *liṅga* as the symbol of Śiva, which each devotee is given at initiation and always wears thereafter, suspended in a kind of amulet round the neck, and worshipped daily; this individual *liṅga* is the main object of worship, replacing largely the worship of *liṅgas* installed in temples, and in fact Basava opposed image worship in general. The initiation, which replaces the Brāhman investiture, is open to, and indeed compulsory for, every member of the sect and in more recent times is performed soon after birth, thus substituting for all the traditional Hindu ceremonials of childhood and youth.

The *liṅga* is the symbol of Śiva and, in its constant wearing, of the fact that no intermediary is required between Śiva and the worshipper. In consequence, there is no need for priests, sacrifices, pilgrimages, penances or fasts. Basava totally rejected the authority of the Vedas and of the Brāhman caste, although he does quote from the Upaniṣads; but it is repeatedly declared that the Vedas and other sacred texts, including the *Bhagavadgītā*, are of no value unless they lead to personal experience of Śiva. Nevertheless Basava inaugurated what is in effect a new priesthood, the *jaṅgamas* (interpreted as '*liṅgas* in motion'), which was subsequently divided into an ascetic order and the married householders; each Liṅgāyat has his hereditary *guru* from among the *jaṅgamas*, who are organised around a number of *maṭhas*, traditionally founded by five teachers supposed to have preceded Basava. In fact the *jaṅgamas* themselves may provide evidence that some features do antedate Basava, for the term is applied in some inscriptions to Kālāmukha priests and a large group of them were in existence very early in Basava's career.

All wearers of the *liṅga* are equal and, in striking contrast to orthodox Hinduism, there are no ritual expressions of female inferiority and the usual concepts of pollution by menstruation have been abolished. Liṅgāyat women have equality with men, marry only at maturity and have a say in the choice of husband, and are permitted to remarry on the death of their husbands. Another orthodox practice condemned by Basava was cremation, on the grounds that the believer goes straight to union with Śiva and needs no funeral rites to assist his passage, and Liṅgāyats are still usually buried. He also condemned astrology for the similar reason that Śiva was the sufficient guardian of the Liṅgāyat who needed no other protection, but here the surrounding influence has largely negated his efforts. So too Basava's rejection of the caste system has not been entirely effective, for in modern times three main social levels can be distinguished among the Liṅgāyats, which have links with groups outside especially among the Jains. Indeed in some respects – most notably in the adoption of strict vegetarianism –

they seem to be closer to Jains than Hindus and probably many Liṅgāyats were converts from the then declining Jainism. Yet, despite Basava's rejection of the Vedas and the caste system, along with so many other characteristic features of Hinduism, the Liṅgāyat movement has remained a part, though admittedly an unorthodox part, of Hinduism.

Also in the Kannaḍa-speaking area there came the next major figure in the Vaiṣṇava tradition, Madhva, in the thirteenth century. Following the precedent established by Rāmānuja, which became standard in the Vaiṣṇava tradition, he both established a religious system and formulated a distinct philosophical position through a commentary on the *Brahmasūtra*. Indeed, the necessary requirement for the founding of a new Vaiṣṇava sect comes to be the writing of such a commentary – the typically Indian paradox that a claim to innovation in founding a new school can only be validated by mastery of tradition exemplified in the commentary form. In the case of Madhva this is the more piquant in that he makes no reference at the beginning of his works to any line of *gurus*. We know the name of the person who initiated him but we also know that he rapidly rejected his *guru*'s Advaita Vedānta and began a commentary on the *Bhagavadgītā* in order to controvert his views. Traditionally, after various adventures and mishaps, Madhva went into retreat in the Himālaya where, in the presence of Viṣṇu in the form of Vyāsa (an oblique claim to divine inspiration), he composed his commentary on the *Brahmasūtra*. His triumphant return with this began his career as a religious leader; he settled at Udipi, and built a temple to Kṛṣṇa.

Madhva was a prolific author, writing, in addition to the two commentaries already mentioned, some 35 works including several intended to explain his doctrines to his disciples. Madhva signs his works with the name Ānandatīrtha, indicating the equivalence of this with the name Madhva on the basis of a hymn from the *Ṛgveda*, which according to him mentions three incarnations of Vāyu, the wind god, in the three ages as attendants of the incarnations of Viṣṇu. Thus, Madhva himself is the attendant of Vyāsa and has come to re-establish the true worship of Viṣṇu. The focus of his faith is devotion to Kṛṣṇa as propounded in the *Bhāgavata Purāṇa*, a south Indian Vaiṣṇava Purāṇa of the ninth or tenth century, but Viṣṇu's other *avatāras* are venerated and Śiva and the five gods of traditional orthodoxy are recognised. This is in part the result of Madhva's view that the entire Vedic literature reveals Viṣṇu's nature, for he has to accept that other deities are mentioned and accommodates the fact by suggesting that they are suffused with Viṣṇu's essence and therefore worthy of subsidiary worship; however he also propounds the view that some texts which are inconsistent with Viṣṇu's supremacy are lacking in authority and were declared by Śiva in order to confuse the wicked, another form of the same approach which makes the Buddha an incarnation of Viṣṇu.

Madhva accepts the absolute authority of the Vedas and regards them as inherently valid and eternal in the same way as the Mīmāṃsā system. The purpose of the Vedas is to make men know Brahman, that is the deity, who being beyond the reach of the senses cannot be grasped by any other means of knowledge (*pramāṇa*). The Vedas describe for us with perfect accuracy the absolute as full of infinite perfections, according to Madhva, who dismisses monistic passages from the Upaniṣads as purely figurative. He regards Viṣṇu, individual souls and matter as eternally and totally separate; Viṣṇu has complete power over souls and matter, saving souls by his grace. Madhva is thus totally opposed to Advaita Vedānta with its affirmation of the essential unity of existence and it is not surprising that as a system of thought his views are termed Dvaita ('dualist') Vedānta. There are strong religious reasons behind Madhva's opposition, as he makes clear in declaring that the Advaita view destroys the purpose of the scriptures by setting a goal in which everything disappears and arguing that a god who must be surpassed is no god and a spiritual life that subordinates devotion and the grace of the deity makes no sense.

Madhva rejects attempts to make the world a mere illusion or emanation of the deity and puts forward an absolute dualism, making frequent appeal to common sense, the experience of ordinary people. He insists on the absolute difference between inert matter and conscious spirit; matter perpetually undergoes new transformations, whereas spirit is unchanging and self-luminant. The dependence of matter and souls on Viṣṇu does not detract from their separateness, for they exist eternally and their existence is as real as Viṣṇu's. Madhva indeed presents a doctrine of a fivefold difference: between Viṣṇu and souls,

Viṣṇu and matter, souls and matter, one soul and another, and one thing and another. These are ultimate differences which are not abolished even in liberation (*mokṣa*).

Viṣṇu's relationship to the world is one of grace. Madhva claims that the Vedas show that the Lord can turn towards us and more pertinently cites the *Bhagavadgītā* to show that he manifests himself to us. His grace (*prasāda*) can free us finally from the cycle of rebirth (*saṃsāra*) when we recognise his nature and our utter dependence on him through *bhakti.* Since we can only know as much of the Lord as he chooses to manifest, the growth of *bhakti* depends on divine grace but in turn prompts it. Madhva applies to the spiritual world the concept of the capability of each soul which will be fully realised in liberation, introducing a principle of hierarchisation which is in marked contrast to the egalitarian trend of the *bhakti* movement generally. Selves belong to five graded categories from the gods down to men; even the gods are divided into castes. Even in *mokṣa* distinctions remain and those released have a spiritual body corresponding to their capability, by which they can know the entirely spiritual form of Viṣṇu and attain the four types of association with him by entering his world, his presence, his form or his body. Men are further divided into three kinds: those chosen for eventual liberation, those doomed to eternal damnation and those destined to perpetual rebirth .

Madhva also has a different approach to the nature of dreaming, which for him is real, except that in dreams men do not distinguish past and present as memory enables them to do when awake. In dreams men undergo the consequences of past actions as a result of the divine will and are thereby enabled to purge themselves of past evil *karma*; this is why men must believe in the reality of the events taking place in dream for the purification to be effective. This is certainly a novel feature with no apparent external source. However, some features of Madhva's theology – especially the role of Vāyu as Viṣṇu's agent – have been attributed to Christian influence, perhaps through the Syrian Christians of Malabar. Certainly elements of the legends later clustered round Madhva are owed to that source. Nevertheless, in its totality Madhva's system is entirely Hindu and in some respects a reversion to more orthodox values than those expressed in much of the *bhakti* movement.

CHAPTER EIGHT

Bhakti in the North

The spread of the *bhakti* movement northwards took place in two ways, either by the migration of individuals over long distances or by steady diffusion at a popular level. In the first, the usual tendency was the establishment of a definite sect, while the second saw the appearance of popular poets in the same style as the Nāyaṉmārs and Āḻvārs. The earliest example of the first is the relatively minor figure of Nimbārka, a Brāhman from Andhra Pradesh who migrated to Vṛndāvana in northern India. Possibly a younger contemporary of Rāmānuja, he adopted a similar philosophical outlook, declaring that the deity, souls and the world are identical yet distinct, from which his system is called Bhedābheda or Dvaitādvaita Vedānta; religiously, he accepted the doctrine of surrender (*prapatti*) to the deity who for him was Kṛṣṇa and his consort or *śakti*, Rādhā. The sect founded by him, the Nimāvats, is still significant in the Mathurā area.

In the second process of diffusion a key role was naturally played by Maharashtra, which belongs geographically to the south but linguistically and therefore culturally to the north. With the rise to prominence in the thirteenth century of the cult of Viṭṭhala, the *bhakti* movement really becomes established in northern culture. The cult of Viṭṭhala, the Vārkarī Panth 'pilgrims' path', is centred on Pandharpur in the extreme south of Maharashtra and the deity seems to have originated as a Kannaḍa hero, whose memorial stone there became the focus of a local cult, and who because of certain pastoral features was assimilated to Kṛṣṇa and thus to Viṣṇu. The political events towards the end of the twelfth century, which transferred the area from a Kannaḍa-speaking state to a Marāṭhī-speaking one, were no doubt an important factor, but another was the life of an ascetic, Puṇḍalīka, who was noted for devotion to his parents and according to legend drew the deity to this place as a result. The earliest author connected with the cult, Jñāneśvara, whose major work in addition to many devotional hymns is a commentary on the *Bhagavadgītā* completed in A.D. 1290, had a somewhat different background in the Nāth tradition (to be treated below) and was also a Brāhman, though apparently outcasted. But the movement soon passed into the hands of lower caste preachers and poets such as Nāmdev, Janābāī, Sena and Tukārām (respectively tailor, maid-servant, barber and grain trader), who composed their poems in Marāṭhī and inaugurated a more or less consciously nationalistic movement.

Nāmdev (c.1270–1350) according to tradition spent some twenty years in the Panjab where, as well as absorbing some other influences, he played a part in the spread of *bhakti*, for a number of his verses are preserved in the Sikh scriptures. The theme of all his poetry is that the deity is everywhere and accessible to all, so that austerities and pilgrimages, renunciation and contemplation of the absolute are all superfluous, since the one necessity is to love the deity and sing his name. He declares the transcendence of Viṭṭhala, whom even the Vedas cannot understand, and identifies him with the supreme Brahman but only to magnify the deity who is everything to him.

The significance of Eknāth (traditionally 1533–99) lies in his having produced a reliable edition of Jñāneśvara's commentary, as well as the first Marāṭhī version of the *Rāmāyaṇa* and several hymns. His family home was in Paithan and he spent practically all his life there, remaining among his family though living an ascetic life. His example gave the Vārkarī Panth a characteristic emphasis in the view that sanctity was not the prerogative of *saṃnyāsins* alone but could be attained by anyone in the course of his daily life.

In the first half of the seventeenth century Tukārām did much in spreading this faith among the village people and is still the most popular and revered of the Marāṭhī *bhakti* poets. He belonged to a poor *śūdra* family at Dehu, where he spent his life; he too, though married and with a family, felt a longing for the ascetic life. He claims that devotion to Viṭṭhala alone sanctifies, not the accident of caste or even the experience of liberation, and thus places the love of god before everything, declaring that without love, which is impossible without duality, there can be no real spiritual growth. Around Nāmdev and Tukārām clustered a whole group of minor poets; subsequently a major figure is that of Rāmdās (1608–81) the *guru* of the leader of Marāṭhā resistance to the Mughals, Śivājī, and himself militantly nationalistic.

9. Kṛṣṇa with his beloved Rādhā

The cohesive feature of the movement is the annual pilgrimage to Pandharpur (and for the more devout on up to two further occasions annually) in which groups from all over Maharashtra converge on Pandharpur, nowadays starting from the places associated with the great poets of the past but already in existence in their day; for instance, Tukārām asks the pilgrims on their way to intercede for him with the deity. As the group associated with each such figure makes its way towards the destination, they sing his hymns and those of the other poets, thus keeping them alive in a continuing, largely oral tradition, and develop the mood of expectant devotion, while sharing together to a large extent in the common life of the group. Caste distinctions are not entirely obliterated but are certainly minimised, in a way not uncommon in the *bhakti* tradition and here given effective expression. It represents a unique adaptation of the otherwise more traditionalist feature of pilgrimage to the *bhakti* ethos.

After Rāmānuja and Madhva, the next major figure in the history of sectarian Vaiṣṇavism is Rāmānanda, who is nevertheless a somewhat enigmatic figure. He is generally said to have been a follower of Rāmānuja (and fifth in descent from him) but to have fallen out with his *guru* over failure to observe rules of purity during pilgrimage. He subsequently founded a sect of his own, the Rāmāvat or Rāmānandī, with Rāma and Sītā as its combined supreme deity. Rāmānanda himself was a north Indian, born according to one text in 1299, and lived in Varanasi, but he obviously owed his inspiration to the south, although both he and his *guru* seem to have been inclined to tantric practices, probably through contact with the Nāth cult. Indeed the link with the Śrīvaiṣṇava movement may not be as close as is claimed but may be an attempt to establish a line of descent to compensate for the absence of any written works by Rāmānanda. Though not associated with any particular doctrines, Rāmānanda is significant as marking the start in the heart of north India of a popular religious movement using the vernaculars for instruction instead of Sanskrit and disregarding caste by admitting as equals all worshippers of the true god; thus traditionally, among Rāmānanda's close followers were a Brāhman, a barber, a leather-worker, a Rājput and a woman. His followers worship Rāma as the visible form of the supreme deity, Īśvara, together with Sītā as his *māyā*; they also worship the monkey Hanumān both as a great devotee of Rāma and as a great magician.

The Nāth cult, which may well have influenced Rāmānanda, is also somewhat obscure in its origins but there can be no doubt that its development owed much to Śaiva and tantric beliefs and that it has analogies with late tantric Buddhism. The Nāths or yogic 'Masters' are nine great adepts, of whom Śiva himself is the first, parallel to the eighty-four immortal Siddhas of tantric Buddhism, while there is a tradition that Gorakhnāth was a Buddhist turned Śaiva. This tradition links it with the Muslim conquest of Bengal at the end of the twelfth century, but this is almost the only evidence for the dating of these largely legendary figures. Nevertheless it was through the Nāth Yogins that tantric ideas and vocabulary became current among the masses between about the twelfth and fifteenth centuries.

Most of the Nāths were probably historical characters but a mass of legend now surrounds them. The second Nāth is supposed to be Matsyendranāth, the *guru* of Gorakhnāth. Part of the legend about him is that he was thrown into the sea by his parents, because he was born on an unlucky day, and swallowed by a fish; this is obviously an aetiological legend to explain his name. Equally the next element reproduces a common motif, for, while inside the fish, he overhears a secret conversation between Śiva and his consort on spiritual matters but is cursed by the goddess to forget it all in the land of women, from which his disciple Gorakhnāth rescues him. Gorakhnāth is however the most famous Nāth *guru* (and has become virtually the patron deity of the Gurkhas of Nepal) and all later Indian traditions make him the incarnation of Śiva, but his place of origin and date are both uncertain.

The literature of the sect, composed partly in Sanskrit and partly in an old form of Hindi, aims to teach the illiterate masses the rudiments of its particular method; it is purely didactic in character and prosaic in style, even when presented in verse form. The main aim of Nāth yogic techniques was the perfection of the body. What distinguishes Nāths from ordinary men (as is abundantly clear also from the mythology surrounding them) is their power of control over death and decay: Yama has no hold over Nāth *siddhas* (successful ones, possessors of *siddhis*) and if he attempts to lay hands on them is severely chastised. Whereas for other schools freedom from the body is indispensable for final liberation, the Nāths sought liberation in a transformed or remade body, the perfect body. The body is therefore no longer a hindrance in the quest for *mokṣa* but the main instrument for it and so must be preserved as long as possible and in perfect condition, with its aging prevented. This is achieved through the techniques of the 'Yoga of force' (*haṭhayoga*), which modifies the Kuṇḍalinī Yoga of Tantrism by asserting that in the topmost *cakra* lies the quintessence of the body in the form of *soma* or *amṛta* (nectar of immortality). From there the *soma* ordinarily drips away to be burnt up in the fire of the sun located in the lowest *cakra*, which is also the fire of destruction. However, if this outflow can be checked and reversed, by methods similar to the ascent of Kuṇḍalinī, then the yogin can burn away the ordinary body, and with the *amṛta* build a perfect, immortal body. Through this perfect body he can then attain a divine body, leading to the state of Śivahood. This inward discipline of *haṭhayoga* is the only means to attain immortality and accordingly all other religious practices are useless; thus, external rituals, caste distinctions, sacred languages and scriptures are all alike rejected.

However, to judge by the mass of legend circulating about them, the Nāths laid claim to extensive occult powers (*siddhis*) and gained great prestige as wonder-workers. The Nāth Yogins are now a type of Śaiva ascetic, with some resemblance to the Kāpālikas, and are also known as Gorakhnāthīs and as Kānphaṭa Yogins, from the split ear-lobes which, with the attendant large earrings, are a distinctive mark of the sect. Traditionally there are twelve subsects and there are a large number of monasteries, one of the most prominent being that at Gorakhpur.

The Nāth cult is one of two outside influences which modified the Vaiṣṇava *bhakti* movement into what is termed the *sant* tradition. The other was the presence of Islam which, in its Sūfī orders, did have some contact with popular Hinduism, serving in considerable measure to reinforce existing *bhakti* emphases on the irrelevance of caste and the worship of one god but also adding a rejection of image worship, which had hitherto been little present in Hinduism. The *sants*, holy men, were not an organised group or sect but loose gatherings of pious individuals, mostly from the lower castes, and some from Muslim backgrounds. They differed from Vaiṣṇava *bhakti* in emphasising worship of the supreme deity directly (although this is a not uncommon attitude among later Vaiṣṇavas) and in holding that the path of spiritual progress was demanding and difficult, not the easy path of ordinary *bhakti*. Nevertheless, Nāmdev is sometimes considered a *sant*, although as a member of the Vārkarī Panth he clearly belongs within the Vaiṣṇava tradition.

Kabīr, however, is clearly a major figure among the *sants*. Traditionally he is regarded as the disciple of Rāmānanda, but in the literature of his sect and elsewhere his dates are given as 1398–1518; the most probable period for his career is the first half of the fifteenth century. He was born into a Muslim weaver community in Varanasi or a nearby village; in the recent past this group had converted to Islam *en masse* and rather superficially, retaining a large proportion of their former customs and beliefs. Certainly, although Kabīr's own name is a Muslim one, it is obvious that his knowledge of Islam was relatively slight. The major influence on his thought came in fact from the Nāth tradition, with some contribution from Vaiṣṇava *bhakti*, but the whole was shaped by Kabīr's individuality.

His verses have proved popular over the centuries and several different collections of them exist, both inside his own sect and in others, but their transmission and authenticity are not always satisfactory. His sayings were composed in an old form of Hindi and in a vigorous and abrasive style, well suited to his message. His outspokenness and use of irony reflect his ardent desire to awaken men to their desperate religious state. His approach to the deity is as much through the way of knowledge as that of devotion, for his deity is an absolute being without a personal form, still less an earthly incarnation, despite the use of Rām as his usual name. Yet his approach to this attributeless Brahman was filled with a very real sense of love in the *bhakti* style, though blended with the idea of such love as a way of suffering which may owe something to the Sūfīs.

The striving of the soul to reach the hidden deity (hidden far away and deep within one's own heart), the difficulties and dangers of the search and the loneliness of separation from the deity come out very clearly in his verses, as well as the inexpressible bliss of the union and merging with the One in which all duality is abolished. Kabīr rejects everything that is external or mechanical in religion and lays exclusive stress on inner experience, where through his grace the deity may reveal himself within one's soul. The individual must first, however, prepare himself by the path of love, a devotion addressed directly to the supreme deity and involving anguish such that few will commence and fewer still complete the journey. But suddenly revelation occurs and the True Guru, the deity, looses the arrow of his word to pierce the soul and bring it the true life of mystical union. While Kabīr describes the goal in monistic terms ultimately derived from Śaṅkara, his thought seems nonetheless monotheistic though highly abstract.

His rejection of externals was applied to both Hindu and Muslim practices, in both of which he sees a hindrance to the expression of true religion as a matter of personal experience. Thus he rejects both the Muslim prayer ritual and Hindu image worship, the Muslim pilgrimage to Mecca and the Hindu pilgrimage to various sites (including his native Varanasi), the Muslim practice of circumcision and the Brāhman wearing of the sacred thread (on the grounds that they are not applicable to women), and so on. His rejections are often buttressed by appeal to common sense and couched in ironical and incisive expressions, in a way which certainly did not endear him to either religious establishment.

Nevertheless, there is no doubt that Kabīr attracted a large following among both Hindus and Muslims. In a late tradition the two groups wrangled over the disposal of his body, but when they came to it found instead a spray of flowers, which they divided and dealt with according to their respective rituals. His disciples then developed into a sect, despite Kabīr's own opposition to sectarianism and traditionally his son's refusal therefore to lead them. The modern sect, who regard themselves as Hindu, still maintain their monotheism, a strong ethical code, and opposition to caste and image worship.

Somewhat later than Kabīr and in the Panjab, Nānak (1469–1539), the first Sikh Guru, preached a broadly similar message, commonly claimed as a synthesis of Hinduism and Islam, but in fact sharing the same *sant* background as Kabīr; however, Nānak shows much more of Vaiṣṇava *bhakti* than the Nāth *haṭhayoga* in his synthesis. Muslim influence on Nānak prob-

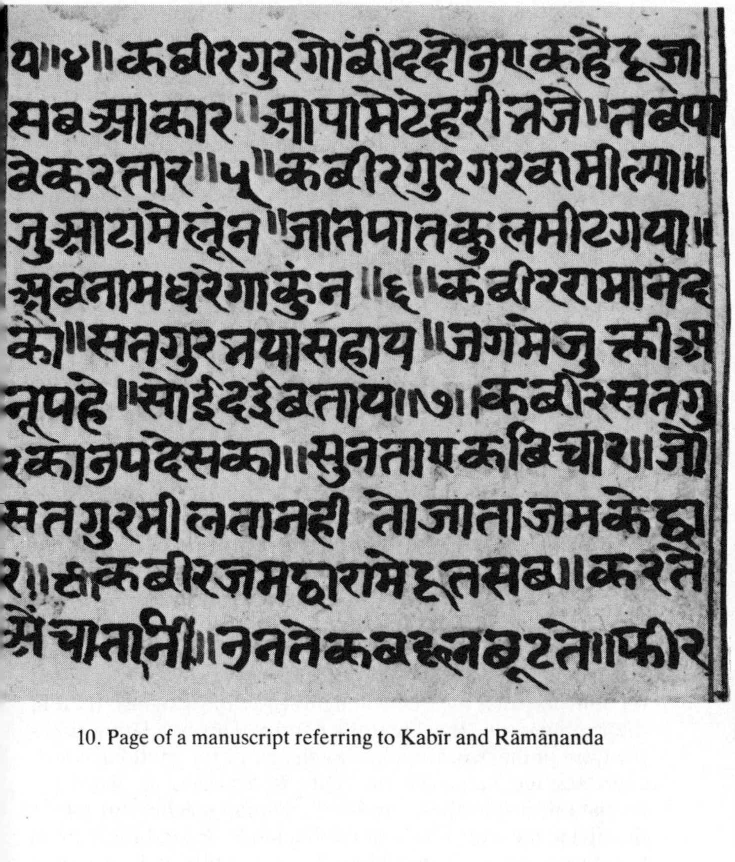
य॥४॥कबीरगुरगोबींददोनुएकहैदूजा
सबआकार॥आपामेटेहरीभजे॥तबपा
वेकरतार॥५॥कबीरगुरगरवामील्या॥
जुआयामेलूंन॥जातपातकुलमीटगया॥
अबनामधरेगाकुंन॥६॥कबीररामानंद
को॥सतगुरभयासहाय॥जगमेजुक्तीअ
नूपहे॥सोईदईबताय॥७॥कबीरसतगु
रकाउपदेसका॥सुनतापरकबिचार॥जो
सतगुरमीलतानहीतोजाताजमकेद्वा
र॥८॥कबीरजमद्वारामेदूतसब॥करते
सैंचाताणी॥उनतेकबछूटनदूटता॥फीर

10. Page of a manuscript referring to Kabīr and Rāmānanda

ably also came mainly through this background; but he was directly involved in the political aspects of Muslim domination, for he worked in the town of Sultanpur for a time, probably employed by the regional governor, and witnessed the invasion of the first Mughal ruler, Bābur. While at Sultanpur Nānak received a divine inspiration, which was followed by a period of travel around India (and even in some legendary versions as far as Mecca). Subsequently, by 1520, he established the village of Kartarpur near Lahore on some land donated by a follower and settled there for the remainder of his life.

Nānak was a strict monotheist and a determined opponent of caste, preaching the equality of all men and declaring that all can attain liberation by response to the deity through devotion and meditation on the divine Name. Nānak uses many different names for his deity – Hari, Rām and Gopāl from the Vaiṣṇava tradition, Allah and others from Islam – but these are just names; his deity is above Brahmā, Viṣṇu and Śiva. More significantly he uses as names terms which describe the deity as eternal, inexpressible and formless and so lays considerable stress on his transcendence. Above all he uses the concept of the Name, as the expression of the full nature of the deity, which is Truth; meditation on the Name is therefore not just the mechanical repetition of some particular name but a systematic exploration of the nature and essence of the deity.

The deity is not only transcendent, however, but also gracious. By his divine Order he has so created and regulated the universe that anyone willing to see can recognise therein the expression of the Creator's nature. This revelation takes the form of the 'word' spoken by the *guru*, for anything which expresses the nature of the deity is regarded as 'word' or revelation, just as the *guru* is not a human teacher but rather the divine message reaching the human heart and there awakening a response. Nānak himself clearly never had a personal *guru* but nevertheless refers in several of his poems to the True Guru, who is for him as for Kabīr the deity himself. For later Sikhism, of course, the concept of the *guru* and his role as the communicator of the divine Truth is interpreted through their understanding of Nānak and his successors as the ten personal Gurus of their faith.

Both Word and Name are expressions of divine Truth, as also is the divine Order. Truth as the nature of the deity sets him apart from the *māyā*, the falsity of the world's values and men's attitudes. For men wilfully remain blind to the divine revelation; they are not irreligious but seek liberation in ways which are basically self-centred and thus reinforce the pride and greed that bind men to the endless cycle of rebirth. All the externals of religion, Hindu worship at the temple and Muslim worship at the mosque, are rejected as worse than useless if the inner attitudes are wrong; Nānak's polemics against them are as cutting as Kabīr's. These are still the values of the world and must be set aside in favour of cleansing the mind and heart by loving devotion and humble submission to the formless, supreme Lord.

While Nānak rejects the Vaiṣṇava concept of *avatāras*, he retains the concept of divine grace, using it especially to explain the problem that, although the divine Order is present for all to see, only some men respond to it. Only by the imparting of divine grace can the *guru*'s voice be heard, but it is not just a capricious divine initiative, for a response is still required from men and indeed this is only the beginning of the process of spiritual discipline leading to liberation. That discipline consists of the cultivation of the attitude of devotion and the profound meditation on the Name, by which men draw nearer to the deity in awe, in five stages of spiritual ascent, and put themselves more and more in harmony with the divine nature. Finally the cycle of rebirth is ended and the soul merges in a condition of supreme bliss with the deity.

Nānak had gathered a band of followers around him and before his death nominated a successor. Subsequently, the institution of a common eating place and an initiation ritual also involving eating together gave expression to Nānak's hostility to caste and served to separate the community of his disciples (the literal meaning of the term Sikh) from the surrounding Hindu community. At the same time political developments brought the community to the suspicious eye of the Mughal rulers and led to mutual and self-reinforcing hostility, until in the time of the tenth Guru Gobind Singh (1675–1708) the trend culminated in open warfare. Thus a pietistic group turned into a militantly separate religious community, distinguished externally by the reforms introduced by Gobind Singh, which included uncut hair (usually kept under control by a turban and beard-net). Nonetheless, in the next century or so, Sikhism was well on the way to being reabsorbed by Hinduism until political events connected with the British conquest of the Panjab reversed the process.

Contemporaneous with Nānak but representing a more traditional *bhakti* approach, Caitanya (1486–1533) is the most significant figure in Bengal Vaiṣṇavism. However, the Vaiṣṇava movement in Bengal probably originated in the eleventh or twelfth century. The famous late Sanskrit poet, Jayadeva, wrote his *Gītagovinda* in 1170, a lyrical poem dealing with the separation and reconciliation of Kṛṣṇa and his beloved Rādhā, who is now as usually his mistress. The first poetic treatment of Rādhā as Kṛṣṇa's favourite, it became the model for all this class of Kṛṣṇa literature, so that the predominant mood of nearly all later devotees of Kṛṣṇa is the erotic. In the adjacent region of Bihar, the Maithilī poet Vidyāpati at the end of the fourteenth century produced a series of songs about Rādhā and Kṛṣṇa which, despite being more in the tradition of Sanskrit erotic poetry than vernacular devotional poems, had a considerable vogue and influence in Bengal. Vidyāpati presents especially the feelings of Rādhā in the relationship, her awakening passion and longing for Kṛṣṇa and her anguish when he neglects her.

The best known composer of Vaiṣṇava devotional songs in Bengali is Caṇḍīdās, a name which may conceal more than one poet of the fourteenth and fifteenth centuries; here too the erotic element is strong and may in part have an autobiographical element. Caitanya himself is said to have known and loved the poetry of Jayadeva, Vidyāpati and Caṇḍīdās. Also, just before Caitanya's birth, Mālādhar Basu adapted the *Bhāgavata Purāṇa*, with its rich development of Kṛṣṇa's amours with the cowgirls (*gopīs*), into Bengali in his *Śrīkṛṣṇavijay* (composed 1473–80); Mālādhar emphasises Kṛṣṇa the lover even more than his original and introduces the figure of Rādhā from other sources.

Another element in the formation of Caitanya's thought was the Sahajiyā movement, which consists of a tantric approach probably derived from late tantric Buddhism allied with an erotic Vaiṣṇavism. From the tantric background come the Sahajiyā beliefs that man is a microcosm, that all duality is false and cosmic unity is regained, or represented, by man and woman in sexual union, and that certain forms of mental and physical control are necessary. As ways to overcome the dualities or opposites of the ordinary social order the union of Brāhman and untouchable, of male and female, and the breaking of food taboos were all undertaken. The relationship of Rādhā and Kṛṣṇa was taken as their model in the relationship of men and women, with the fact that Rādhā was married to another used to emphasise the intensity of the affair and the depth of feeling involved in a relationship that goes against conventional values. In more recent times the Bāuls, though claiming to have been founded by Caitanya, represent more nearly this approach; the Bāuls are wandering religious singers and poets, living by begging and both rejecting and being rejected by society.

Caitanya grew up in the town of Nadiya, a noted centre of learning, especially of the 'New Nyāya' philosophy. He was the ninth or tenth child of Vaiṣṇava Brāhman parents, but only he and one older brother survived, and this brother became a *saṃnyāsin* and in effect dead to the family, while Caitanya was young. Caitanya grew up to be proficient in the traditional, Sanskrit-based learning and even somewhat contemptuous of the popular *bhakti* movement. However, this changed abruptly when in 1508 he went to Gaya to perform memorial rituals for his father; there he met again an ascetic with south Indian connections, whom previously he had scorned, but who now induced in him a powerful religious experience and initiated him into the worship of Kṛṣṇa.

On his return to Nadiya, Caitanya joined a group of *bhakti* devotees who used to meet nightly to sing songs of praise to Kṛṣṇa and began to have the periods of ecstasy and possession by the deity, which were to mark the rest of his life and to mark him out as a charismatic figure. He thus became acquainted with the chanting of songs and invocations, which was to develop into such a feature of his sect and to become familiar on the streets of European and American towns through the activities of an offshoot from it, the Hare Krishna movement. After a while as a lay devotee, Caitanya received initiation as a *saṃnyāsin* in 1510 and adopted the name by which he is generally known (in full Śrīkṛṣṇacaitanya); this was not so much a renunciation of the world as a total commitment to the worship of Kṛṣṇa.

Caitanya soon settled at the Vaiṣṇava pilgrimage centre of Puri in Orissa (according to tradition yielding to his mother's wishes in not settling in the even more distant Vṛndāvana), and, apart from extensive tours of south India (including four months at Śrīraṅgam) and of Vṛndāvana, remained there until his death. He was prominent as a leader of the singers and dancers who accompanied the great car of Jagannāth in the annual festival, and generally displayed an emotional approach to religion, meeting his death probably in one of his fits of ecstasy.

Caitanya was not strictly the founder of a new sect, since he did not comment on the *Brahmasūtra*, but the movement centring on him has in effect become one and subsequently developed a claim to descent from the school of Madhva, which was not otherwise represented in north India. In fact, Caitanya's only known composition is a poem of eight verses in Sanskrit expressing his rapture at the deity's embrace. Nor did he apparently seek to establish a sect round himself, being absorbed in his own devotional ecstasies, but the influence of his personality and evident devotion drew others to him. Six of these, the so-called Gosvāmins, were particularly prominent and became the recognised theologians of the sect; the tradition within the movement is that Caitanya himself sent them to restore the sacred sites at Mathurā and Vṛndāvana and to compose the theological works necessary for a new sect. The tradition of the disappearance of the ancient Kṛṣṇa sites in the Mathurā area and their rediscovery by the Gosvāmins is a similar pious rewriting of history.

All but one of the six Gosvāmins were Brāhmans, although the first three, the brothers Rūpa and Sanātana and their nephew Jīva, may well have lost status through employment at the court of the local Muslim ruler. But the Caitanya movement does not show the anti-caste feeling apparent in much of the *bhakti* movement and, apart from the ecstatic approach to religion, has been rather conservative. Thus, for example, the six Gosvāmins elaborated in over 200 works between them, written significantly in Sanskrit, a theology which virtually ignored the popular beliefs about Caitanya. Jīva Gosvāmin accepts unreservedly the traditional view of the absolute authority of revelation (even to rejecting the other *pramāṇas*, means of knowledge) but widens the category to include the

Purāṇas (regarded by an artificial play on their name as the completion of the Vedas), of which the most important is the *Bhāgavata Purāṇa*.

Jīva declares that there are three aspects of ultimate reality: Brahman, the Supreme Self, and Bhagavat. Brahman is the undifferentiated absolute of the philosophers and regarded as only a partial manifestation of the infinitely qualified Bhagavat, the highest and personal expression of deity; the Supreme Self is that aspect of the deity which enters into relationship with *jīvas*, living selves, and with nature (*prakṛti*) or *māyā*. The Bhagavat, who is Kṛṣṇa, possesses infinite *śaktis*, described in the texts as his consorts, which bring about a real world but are always dependent on him. Thus Kṛṣṇa alone is to be worshipped, not as an *avatāra* but as the supreme deity.

However, the position of the sect as a whole, expressed clearly in the Bengali poetry and biographies of Caitanya, is that Caitanya is an *avatāra* of Kṛṣṇa or even Kṛṣṇa himself. The most developed view is that Kṛṣṇa became incarnate in the form of Caitanya and assumed the fair complexion as well as the emotions of Rādhā in order to experience within one body the bliss of union with his *śakti*. This erotic aspect is present also in the worship of the devotee, who becomes a *gopī* in his relationship with Kṛṣṇa, feminising himself and in a sense allowing himself to be seduced by Kṛṣṇa. The fact that Rādhā is married to another is used to suggest that love for the deity should triumph over all obstacles of convention; there may well be an element of sublimation of illicit emotions. These were the beliefs of Caitanya's ordinary followers in Bengal, far from the Gosvāmins' theorising in Vṛndāvana; lacking clear leadership the movement there split in two but even so spread rapidly in the sixteenth and seventeenth centuries.

The movement founded by Vallabha (1479–1531) – another contemporary of Nānak and Caitanya in the troubled period of the breakdown of the Delhi Sultanate and the establishment of Mughal rule – conforms more nearly to the standard pattern of a Vaiṣṇava sect but shares with Bengal Vaiṣṇavism a strong erotic flavour. According to Vaiṣṇava theologians, Vallabha's followers are a branch of the sect established early in the fifteenth century by Viṣṇusvāmi, a migrant to Gujarat from south India (and sometimes named as the *guru* of the Marāṭhī poet Jñāneśvara). Vallabha's own parents came from Andhra Pradesh to settle in Varanasi, but he was born near Raipur in Madhya Pradesh while they had fled south to escape a Muslim raid on the city's temples.

After his father's death when he was eleven, Vallabha appears soon to have begun the first of three protracted pilgrimages all over India. During them he is said to have received instructions from Kṛṣṇa to go to the Mathurā area and reveal the identity of an image that had mysteriously appeared on Mt Govardhana; while there he received in 1494 a vision of Kṛṣṇa, who revealed to him the means to liberation by complete submission to Kṛṣṇa. Subsequently, in his second pilgrimage, he received from Kṛṣṇa in his form as Viṭṭhala at Pandharpur a command to marry – an anomaly for a spiritual leader and explained as the deity's plan to ensure a line of teachers. His marriage took place almost immediately and he had two sons, the second and more important being Viṭṭhalnāth. At the same period Vallabha also composed commentaries on the *Brahmasūtra* (completed by Viṭṭhalnāth) and the *Bhāgavata Purāṇa*.

According to his sect's beliefs, Vallabha's teachings were divine and came directly from Kṛṣṇa through the mouth of his *avatāra* Vallabha. In practice, Vallabha's doctrines are based on the *Bhāgavata Purāṇa*, which he declares to be the final scriptural authority (a position similar to the Gosvāmins), and justified philosophically as Śuddhādvaita Vedānta. Vallabha holds that there are three attitudes to the world, corresponding to the three stages in his religion: the first is initiation into the sect, the second the study of his philosophy and the third is the Puṣṭimārga ('way of well-being'), the perfect service of the deity.

Vallabha's Śuddhādvaita ('pure non-dualism') is a rather unsophisticated attempt to go one better than Śaṅkara, whose Advaita he declares to be tainted by the concept of *māyā* as a second to Brahman, whereas his own view is that the whole world is real and is Brahman, which is another name for Kṛṣṇa. Individual souls and matter are one with Brahman and have no separate existence. Vallabha describes Brahman as being, consciousness and bliss (*sat, cit, ānanda*), which are not just qualities of Brahman but are Brahman. Creation occurs by Brahman concealing part of himself by his power of *māyā* (present after all) to become the physical universe, which consists only of the *sat*, being, part of Brahman; however, he holds, nothing has changed in Brahman, the eternal and immutable. Similarly, the individual souls are the manifestation also of the *cit*, consciousness, of Brahman but with the *ānanda*, bliss, still concealed. The individual souls are thus just parts of Brahman but in the process of manifestation are filled with ignorance (*avidyā*), which causes them to forget both their true nature as Brahman and the proper duty of any part to its whole, that of service. This state of ignorance is *saṃsāra*, the cycle of rebirth, and the re-establishment of right understanding can only come by the replacement of worldly attitudes by non-worldly through the grace of Kṛṣṇa.

Individuals differ in spirituality and thus fall into three categories, corresponding to the three ways, of which the first two consist of continuous activity and ritual action and the third is the 'way of well-being', Puṣṭimārga, with which alone Vallabha is concerned. This is the path of devotion from its first seeds of affection implanted by Kṛṣṇa's grace through seven ascending stages to the overwhelming passion which cannot do without him, when by the grace of Kṛṣṇa one can become part of the eternal sport (*līlā*). The individual must abandon his self- centredness and concentrate entirely on the service of Kṛṣṇa, which is especially interpreted as the congregational worship of Kṛṣṇa in the sect's own shrines. The image is regarded as Kṛṣṇa himself and worshipped in accordance with the pattern of Kṛṣṇa's life, in eight stages throughout the day from the *levée* onwards. Dressing and ornamenting the image appropriately, the provision of flowers for the room, the performance of music and singing, and on special occasions of dancing, combine to make of the worship an aesthetic experience. For this purpose Vallabha and his son Viṭṭhalnāth patronised a group of poets known as the 'Eight Seals', among whom were traditionally Sūrdās and Nanddās.

Whether Sūrdās, the blind poet of Agra, was in reality an adherent of the Vallabha sect is doubtful but his poetry, though following the wider tradition of Kṛṣṇa *bhakti*, was in sympathy with its approach and he was a close contemporary of Vallabha. He composed a number of Hindi works on the theme of *bhakti*, especially to the child Kṛṣṇa. His main work, the *Sūrsāgar*, is based, apart from its first chapter, on the *Bhāgavata Purāṇa*; its tenth chapter (more than twice as long as all the rest) amplifies the theme of the tenth chapter of his original, Kṛṣṇa's childhood and youth, and adds to it much that is original in Kṛṣṇa's sporting with the *gopīs*, and the circular dance with them and Rādhā, innovating also in form in his bee songs and flute poems (recording the response of the *gopīs* to Kṛṣṇa's flute).

Vallabha recognises four main types of devotion, the attitudes of the servant, companion, parent and lover. The type which Vallabha himself favoured, like Sūrdās, was that of parental affection. The other main type is the erotic, in which the devotee imagines himself one of the *gopīs* enjoying Kṛṣṇa's nightly *līlā* in Vṛndāvana. The other two were not frequent, although some of the Eight Seals imagine themselves in their poetry as Kṛṣṇa's companions. A fifth type of devotion sometimes propounded, of devotion practised in peaceful contemplation, runs counter to Vallabha's strong emphasis on emotional involvement and affection (*preman*, a favourite term also of the Divine Light master, Guru Maharaj Ji). However, Vallabha's second son Viṭṭhalnāth, who succeeded his elder brother to lead the community between 1543 and 1586, greatly increased the importance of Kṛṣṇa's beloved, called here Svāminījī, and of the erotic devotion, probably through influence from Caitanya's followers. His seven sons then divided the leadership, each having a specially consecrated statue as his symbol of authority, of which the most esteemed is that identified by Vallabha through divine guidance. Later leaders of these sub-sects adopted the title Maharaja and took to comparably ostentatious living, as well as allegedly taking their claim to be living embodiments of Kṛṣṇa literally in their relations with female disciples; the culmination of this trend was a case in which the Bombay Supreme Court in 1862 found one of the Maharajas guilty of gross profligacy.

Although Sūrdās is the great poet of Kṛṣṇa in Hindi, the *bhakti* movement began in Hindi-speaking areas, as we have seen, with Rāmānanda, whose devotion was directed to Rāma, and its greatest figure is Tulsīdās (probably 1543–1623). His major work, the *Rāmcaritmānas* 'Lake of the Deeds of Rāma' (begun in 1574 at Ayodhyā and finished after several years at Varanasi), is the best known, though not the first, adaptation of the *Rāmāyaṇa* into Hindi or indeed into any modern Indian language, its nearest rival probably being Kampaṉ's (Kamban's)

Tamil version made between the ninth and twelfth centuries at the height of the *bhakti* movement there. Tulsī's version is not directly based on the original of Vālmīki but rather on two later Sanskrit versions, the *Adhyātma* and *Bhuśuṇḍi Rāmāyaṇas*, as well as a number of other sources. The *Adhyātma Rāmāyaṇa* was probably a product of Rāmānanda's school and shows the same monistic trend. Tulsī himself seems to have been a Rāmānandin but does not display so consistent a theology, though often indebted to the *Adhyātma Rāmāyaṇa* in which the emphasis on the name of Rāma so prominent in Tulsī is already present.

Tulsīdās tends to distinguish Rāma from Viṣṇu (though not going as far as Kabīr and the *sants*) and to elevate him to the status of supreme deity, as an incarnation of the absolute and even directly the unqualified, formless Brahman. Indeed, Tulsī declares that his unqualified form is more intelligible than his qualified, since the reasons for his incarnation are too mysterious and wonderful to be comprehended. Thus, while there is some leaning towards monism, Tulsī's prime concern is with devotion to the incarnate and gracious deity, but not narrowly so. In addition to his major work and another, more episodic treatment of the Rāma story in the *Kavitāvalī*, he composed several other slighter works which include a poem on the marriage of Śiva and Pārvatī and a collection of songs to Kṛṣṇa, who is seen as a form of Rāma, while the framework of the *Rāmcaritmānas* itself is a dialogue between Śiva and Pārvatī. Even so, in the final analysis all other deities are so far subordinate to Rāma that he alone is truly god; Tulsī is simply more generous in the veneration that he gives them.

Tulsī's own attitude to Rāma is mainly the devotion of a servant for his loving master, although the attitude of parental affection is also present. He quite naturally therefore has a special place for Hanumān, the monkey helper of Rāma who already in Vālmīki's poem shows outstanding devotion to his master but now becomes the pattern of such service rendered wholeheartedly, despite his very human failings. His catholicity may also be seen perhaps in his stress on the name of Rāma, for, while in Vaiṣṇava theory all Viṣṇu's names are equally beneficent, the name Rāma seems to have assumed particular value for Vaiṣṇavas and even to have spread to certain Śaiva groups, such as the Nāths, and reformers like Kabīr and Nānak.

Certainly no other Vaiṣṇava poet seems to have gone as far in the exaltation of the divine Name or justified it so carefully as Tulsīdās does in the prologue to his *Rāmcaritmānas*. For Tulsī the Name is indeed the essence of the supreme deity and its saving power is infinite. He even affirms that the Name is superior to Rāma himself, who cannot comprehend the greatness of his Name, for Rāma in person saved only a few but his Name continues to bring salvation: all who chant it or listen to it will be saved, and Tulsī by composing in their own language his poem, which is full of the Name, is bringing salvation within the reach of all.

Another interesting work is Tulsī's *Vinayapatrikā*, 'Letter of Petition', written in the latter part of his life, after the pestilence which devastated Varanasi in 1616, and showing a deeper introspection which marks also his *Kavitāvalī*. This takes the form of a letter of supplication which Tulsī himself has to deliver at Rāma's court. After a prologue invoking the aid of various deities including first of all Gaṇeśa (Śiva's elephant-headed son, who is the lord of obstacles and so invoked at the commencement of any enterprise), and after appeals to Hanumān to act as intermediary, Tulsī enters Rāma's court and reverently salutes all his family before presenting his petition that he may be filled exclusively with devotion for Rāma's feet and may no longer be subject to the troubles of this evil age. Thus even in this more directly devotional poem Tulsī maintains both his own attitude as the humble servant and his understanding of Rāma as the gracious ruler.

The whole Rāma story develops of course a strong moral element, as already noted, with the tendency to stress Rāma as the upholder of *dharma*. Sītā's purity too must be preserved and so, borrowing from the *Adhyātma Rāmāyaṇa*, Tulsī narrates in his main work that on Rāma's instructions the real Sītā enters the fire just before Rāvaṇa's arrival to remain with unassailable chastity, until after the conquest of Laṅkā the illusory Sītā who has replaced her enters the fire in the ordeal and the real Sītā emerges. Thus Tulsī, expressing the already present tendency, produces works with a real ethical concern very different from the eroticism of much of the Kṛṣṇa cult. Such eroticism is not universal, as shown by the poetry of Mīrābāī (1403–70 or a century later), a Rājput princess who became a fervent devotee of Kṛṣṇa and, largely ignoring the mythology, presents her longing for him to come as her husband to be the lord of her heart, in poems of deep pathos in their telling of her pining in separation from him.

Tulsī's strong moral emphasis is a conservative element by comparison with the often radical anti-caste position of some *bhakti* trends, including that of Rāmānanda to which he himself probably belonged. It would have tended to the encouragement of social stability and cohesion in the face of Muslim pressures which at this period included the more sympathetic but syncretising interest of the Mughal emperor Akbar (1556–1605). Nevertheless his success in opening the story of Rāma to the masses was not without opposition from the most orthodox of the Brāhmans, while it led his contemporary Nābhādās, the great chronicler of the *bhakti* movement, to call him an incarnation of Vālmīki.

An index of Tulsī's popularity – and a factor in it – is provided by the Rāmlīlā, literally 'Rāma's sport', a continuing popular religious institution of north India. The Rāma story is enacted in dramatic form in a series of performances lasting several days at the annual Daśahrā festival, employing an unusual stage technique combining simultaneous acting and dialogue with the recitation of the text, which is based on Tulsīdās' *Rāmcaritmānas*. Traditionally the Rāmlīlā was established around 1625 by a follower of Tulsīdās, which may be true of its present form. However, there is some evidence that popular Rāma plays were in evidence in Tulsī's day and one of Caitanya's biographies refers to Caitanya being quite carried away when acting the part of Hanumān in a similar type of performance at Puri.

The actors in these performances are drawn from the local community, which organises and finances the whole effort. The actors who play Rāma, his brothers and Sītā are young Brāhman boys, since they are regarded as embodiments of the deities, worshipped as such by the audience, and so must be completely pure. The whole thing is as much a religious ceremony as a dramatic performance, as well as having a significant role in the transmission of faith in Rāma among the illiterate masses, a function similar to that of the mediaeval European mystery plays.

The recitation of the text takes priority and carries the thread of the story, while in essence the acting and dialogue give dramatic expression to particular episodes. The use of several locations over the several days of performance serves to emphasise the setting of the story in the community concerned. Altogether, the Rāmlīlā seems a successful method for communicating the mythology and moral teaching of the Rāma tradition, the more so as neither Tulsīdās nor the Rāmlīlā have any strong sectarian connections and so are open to all Hindus. The popularity of the Rāma story and people's familiarity with it must be largely due to the Rāmlīlā, while the vision of Rāma's righteous rule as a goal may well have helped to keep alive Hindu political aspirations under Muslim rule. Certainly, the pilgrimages of the Vārkarī Panth, in some ways analogous, helped to foster the rise of Marāṭhā resistance to the Mughals.

CHAPTER NINE

Revival and Reform

Despite the stimulating effects of Tulsīdās, the Vārkarī Panth and the like, the vitality of Hinduism seems to have sunk rather low by the end of Mughal rule. The impact of British rule was therefore all the more traumatic, but it led in due course to the appearance of a series of religious and social reform movements, of which a new feature (though anticipated by Rāmdās' role as Śivājī's *guru*) was its political aspect; social reform became less connected with religious attitudes and tended to generate political pressure groups, while religious reform took on a nationalist tone which in turn led to political involvement. This is in spite of the differing types of response involved, from frank Westernisation, through various types of revivalist and reactionary movement, to a syncretistic self-assertiveness.

The Brāhmo Samāj, the first of these reform movements, was founded by Rājā Rām Mohan Roy (1772–1833), whose writings and oratory exercised a profound influence on Indian intellectual life in the nineteenth century. He was born into the highest rank of society, as a Kulīn Brāhman, the son of a landowner, and destined himself to become a wealthy property owner in Calcutta; the title Rājā was not hereditary but conferred on him by the Mughal emperor, as whose envoy he died on a visit to Britain. His personal experience provided the stimulus for one of his lifelong campaigns, that against the compulsory self-immolation of a widow (*satī*) on her husband's funeral pyre; this issue in the case of one of his own relatives, together with a dispute over his rightful share of his patrimony, caused him to become estranged from his family.

His intellectual experience was broad. He received a traditional education in a family belonging to the devotional Caitanya movement, but he was brought up in Patna, a centre of Muslim learning, and the main influence of his first work – a treatise against idolatry published in Persian – is undoubtedly Islamic. Subsequently, while in the service of the East India Company, he learnt English from his superior (and friend, John Digby), which enabled him to absorb much from Western culture, including a belief in modern science and elements of Christian ethics imparted to him by William Carey and other Baptist missionaries, with whom for a time he enjoyed a mutually stimulating relationship. He was thus uniquely equipped by birth, education and circumstances for the role of social and religious reformer that he was to play.

After a thorough study of the Upaniṣads and Vedānta, he concluded that reason as expressed in the Upaniṣads was the basis of Hinduism and that all social institutions should be judged from that standpoint. He held that the Upaniṣads taught a pure theism and did not countenance image worship (the theme of his *Abridgement of the Vedānta*, published in 1816), declaring that the recognition of human rights was consistent with basic Hindu thought, as with that of other religions once the dogma and superstition were removed, instanced in his *The Precepts of Jesus* (published in 1820 and consisting of ethical extracts from the New Testament). Meanwhile, in the social field, he had mounted a long campaign against the custom of *satī*, successfully creating a climate of opinion which enabled Lord William Bentinck to make it illegal in 1829, and campaigned against child marriage. He also worked for the establishment of English-speaking schools and newspapers, as well as founding the first Bengali newspaper. He was well aware of the value of propaganda on behalf of his social causes and of education (for women as much as men) as an agent of change. Nevertheless, he was careful to appeal to the past, and in the social sphere announced his intention of restoring to India her ancient tradition of *dharma* by removing the senseless accretions of later times, and in the fight against *satī* and other evils quoted Manu and other writers on Dharmaśāstra to prove his points.

In 1828 Rām Mohan Roy founded the Brāhmo Samāj (initially called the Brāhmo Sabhā) 'to teach and to practise the worship of the one, supreme, undivided eternal God'. It adopted a deistic type of theism, much influenced by European deism and by the Unitarians, with whom Roy had been associated after 1821; at the same time it rejected Brāhman claims to mediation, idolatry, sacrifice and caste and adopted a congregational form of worship similar to Unitarian services. The trust deed of the Samāj's first building opened in 1830 sets out Rām Mohan Roy's basic religious ideas, declaring that it was

11. Indian stamps depicting religious leaders

कम्बर KAMBAR
9TH CENTURY A.D.
0.15
भारत INDIA

1.00
1479-1531
भारत
INDIA

नै.पै. 15 nP
INDIA
1772-1833
RAJA RAMMOHUN ROY
राजा राममोहन राय
भारत

1824 1883
15 नै.पै. nP
दयानन्द सरस्वती
INDIA POSTAGE

भारत INDIA
20 पै. P.
1836
1886
श्री रामकृष्ण परमहंस
SRI RAMAKRISHNA PARAMAHAMSA

भारत-INDIA
नै.पै.
15
nP
विवेकानन्द
1863-1902

SRI AUROBINDO
श्री अरविन्द
INDIA
0.15
1872-1950
भारत

भारत
INDIA
25
गांधीजी GANDHIJI

to be 'a place of public meeting . . . for the worship and adoration of the Eternal Unsearchable and Immutable Being who is the Author and Preserver of the Universe' and banning any image or other representation of the deity within the building, while also laying down that no object of worship for anyone was to be reviled or spoken of contemptuously; the overall pattern is of the rather remote praise and adoration of a transcendent deity, lacking any intercessory or mystical element. The doctrine of transmigration (*saṃsāra*) was rejected, along with *karma*, no doubt because of their intimate connection with caste, which was in theory repudiated.

The Brāhmo Samāj was supported by a number of wealthy men, particularly Dwarkanath Tagore, one of India's first Western-style capitalists, whose patronage was a crucial factor in its survival during the troubled decade after Rām Mohan Roy's death. Roy's vision of reform from within the Hindu community (from which he never parted) was being strongly challenged at this period both by extreme young radicals who totally rejected the traditional pattern, throwing away their sacred threads and eating beef, and by the ultra orthodox, who under the leadership of Rādhākānta Deb (1794–1876) formed the Dharma Sabhā in 1830. In 1843, however, the Brāhmo Samāj began to revive under the new leadership of Dwarkanath's son, Debendranath Tagore (1817–1905).

Debendranath Tagore had undergone a profound religious experience five years previously, after which he founded a group for religious discussion and prayer, which he now merged with the Brāhmo Samāj. This religious, even mystical, tendency persisted into the third generation: Debendranath's son, Rabindranath Tagore (1861–1941), the winner of a Nobel Prize for Literature, became fascinated by the poetry of the Bāuls. In an attempt to set monotheism firmly within the framework of classical Hinduism, Debendranath tried to find authority in the Vedas but became disillusioned with further study and decided that reason and conscience should be the test of the authority of any scriptural text. Accordingly he compiled a selection of texts from various sources for liturgical use. Later he also produced a set of ceremonies to replace the traditional Hindu rituals, changing the Samāj from an informal grouping into an organisation whose members were formally initiated. With these changes and the sending out of the first Brāhmo missionaries, the Samāj grew quickly in numbers and began to take a prominent place in the life of Bengal.

Under the contemplative Debendranath, the main preoccupation of the Samāj was religious, but concern for widow remarrriage and other social reforms increased after Keshab Chandra Sen (1838–84) joined the Samāj in 1857 (the year of the Indian Mutiny, a basically political event with substantial religious overtones). Within five years Sen had joined Tagore in the leadership of the Samāj, despite the contrast between Tagore's quietism and Sen's energetic approach, with its rejection of caste, advocacy of various social reforms, and ultimately acknowledgement of the truth of Christ's teaching. But a clash of wills was inevitable and came over Sen's insistence and Tagore's refusal that Brāhmos, most of whom were Brāhmans, should abandon their sacred threads; in 1866 the Samāj split into the conservative Original Brāhmo Samāj and the new Brāhmo Samāj of India. The Original Samāj soon lost popularity and became virtually the responsibility of the Tagore family alone.

The Brāhmo Samāj of India was more popular. After the split Sen became further engrossed in Christianity and at the same time introduced the practice of singing chants in the style of the Caitanya cult. Then after about 1875 he came under the influence of Rāmakrishna, a then almost unknown devotee of Kālī, and his views became increasingly mystical, combining simultaneously Christianity and Goddess-worship, causing serious tensions within the movement. Meanwhile, his social reform concerns had met with some success in the passage of the Native Marriage Act III in 1872, legalising Brāhmo marriages and imposing minimum age limits for those married under its provisions. Sen's blatant disregard of this in the marriage of his daughter to a young maharaja in 1878 was the final straw for many, who seceded to form the Sādhāran ('general') Brāhmo Samāj, while Sen formed his Church of the New Dispensation, supposedly a synthesis of Hinduism, Islam and Christianity but with the last the dominant influence. Sen's death in 1884 left his group completely disoriented and it broke up still further. The Sādhāran Brāhmo Samāj persisted but turned increasingly to social work, remaining small but influential among the intellectuals.

Meanwhile in Maharashtra the Prārthana Samāj emerged

from an earlier body founded in 1867 as the equivalent in that area of the Brāhmo Samāj, with which it shared some links. In doctrine it was broadly similar to the Brāhmo Samāj but sought deliberately to base its worship on the devotional poems of the Vārkarī Panth, especially Tukārām. However, under its chief leader, Justice M.G. Ranade (1842–1901), it devoted itself more to social reform, particularly in the elimination of caste restrictions and the improvement of the status of women and untouchables. Stress was always laid on the link between reverence for the deity and respect for men, and with the passage of time the movement's religious basis was increasingly submerged by its social aims.

Whereas the Brāhmo Samāj and to a lesser extent the Prārthana Samāj typify the Westernising response, the Ārya Samāj, founded in 1875, represented initially a return to the past along orthodox lines, though developing into something rather different. The aim of its founder, Svāmī Dayānanda Sarasvatī (1824–83), was to restore Indian culture to its pristine dignity, rejecting everything subsequent to the Vedas as superstition. Dayānanda was born into a Gujarati Brāhman family in a minor princely state in Kathiawar and had a wholly orthodox upbringing without any contact with Western intellectual influences, but developed a strong aversion to contemporary practices. He tells in his autobiography the story of how one Śivarātri (an all-night vigil in honour of Śiva still celebrated in January-February each year, when Śiva's image or *liṅga* is garlanded with flowers) when he was fourteen, his father introduced him to the ritual; Dayānanda alone of those present remained awake to see mice in search of food running about over the image and woke his father to ask how the omnipotent deity could allow mice to pollute his body without the slightest protest, but his father's reply failed to answer his problem of reconciling the deity with the image.

Efforts by his family to get him married when he was in his early twenties led to his leaving home to wander about India in search of a *guru*. In 1860 he found a blind scholar of the Vedas, Svāmī Virajānanda, who advised him to study and interpret the Vedas, rejecting the falsehoods of Purāṇic Hinduism.

From the beginning of the 1870s he began to formulate his beliefs systematically and started his career of religious and social reform. At first he dressed as a *saṃnyāsin* and propagated the Vedic faith, as he called it, by oral teaching in Sanskrit but later, after contacts with the Brāhmo Samāj, he dressed more conventionally and used Hindī in preaching and debate, as well as adopting the organisational approach to religious and social reform which was an innovation derived from the West. In 1875 he published the most important of his many works, the *Satyārth Prakāś* ('Light of Truth') and, after meeting leaders of the Prārthana Samāj in Bombay, founded the Ārya Samāj. In 1877, on the establishment of a Samāj at Lahore in the Panjab, he revised the principles of the organisation and so gave it its definitive form; before long the movement began to spread rapidly in the Panjab, which proved particularly receptive to it and became its heartland.

Though borrowing from the Brāhmo Samāj organisationally, Dayānanda rejected its adherents as being ignorant of their own culture and traditions. He claimed to go back to the Vedas, meaning by this only the hymns, which he proceeded to interpret in a 'yogic' manner, claiming that this alone was valid. He denied that the Vedas were polytheistic and held that Agni, Indra, Varuṇa and the others were merely names for the one supreme deity; he rightly claimed that they had nothing to say on image-worship, caste, polygamy, child marriage and the seclusion of widows. On the other hand his acceptance of *karma* and *saṃsāra* cannot be justified from them, any more than his monotheistic position (very clearly stated in the first two of the Ten Principles of the Ārya Samāj), and his allegiance to the orthodox six systems is also anachronistic; however both these and especially his belief in the Vedas made him respectable to the orthodox, who were not too disturbed by his rather cautious and ambivalent attitude to caste, denying that it was a religious institution but accepting it as a purely social institution. The system of the four classes (*varṇa*), to which he advocated a return, was after all an ancient institution.

Although the Ārya Samāj was hesitant in advocating reform of the caste system, being anxious to remain within the mainstream of Hinduism, it was on this issue that its characteristic development hinged. For another of Dayānanda's prime concerns was to counter what he saw as a menacing stream of conversions to Islam and Christianity, especially among low-caste Hindus. The rite of purification (*śuddhi*) for the readmission of such converts to Hinduism was a major weapon in this field, an innovation but designed to placate orthodox opinion (and not so different from the procedure envisaged in the law-book of Manu). However, for many such converts from low-caste or untouchable backgrounds, conversion had been a way of escape from their social degradation, such as Buddhism had once provided and was to do again in the 1950s as a result of Dr B. R. Ambedkar's lead. Thus out of the *śuddhi* movement there logically developed about the beginning of the twentieth century a campaign to recruit low castes and untouchables, with a ceremony evolved to invest the new recruits with the sacred thread and to take water from wells reserved for high castes, thus making them the equals of caste Hindus, but significantly not abolishing their group identity (for there has always been an element of social mobility for groups but not for individuals, though never before on this scale).

Nevertheless, the success enjoyed by this new campaign gradually involved the Ārya Samāj more and more in communal agitation and into alliance with the Hindu Mahāsabhā, an ultra-orthodox political group, despite Ārya Samāj claims that it did not take part in politics. There were indeed internal tensions over this and related matters which produced a split in 1893 between the more liberal or progressive element, who argued for modern education, freedom of diet and the Samāj as the nucleus of a world religion, while the conservative wing favoured traditional Hindu modes of education, vegetarianism and a place for the Samāj within Hinduism; each wing founded its own educational institutions, which were a considerable factor in the rapid growth of the movement. In general, however, the progressives prevailed and as a result the Ārya Samāj tended to become an intolerant and aggressive body, which encouraged a new self-respect that too often turned into militancy.

The rise to prominence of Lala Lajpat Rai (1865–1928) exemplifies this political trend, for he became a noted Congress leader (breaking away, however, in 1925 to found his Nationalist Party) as well as working as a lecturer in the Dayanand Anglo-Vedic College, and his key ideas are essentially those of the Ārya Samāj. It is perhaps only historic justice that the Ārya Samāj, which had done so much to fan the flames of communal suspicion in the Panjab, suffered severely in the partition of the sub-continent in 1947, with their headquarters at Lahore being confiscated by Pakistan and many of their members killed in the disturbances, in which another Panjab-based community, the Sikhs, also played a significant role.

The Rāmakrishna Mission was established somewhat later than the other movements so far mentioned, after the death of the figure from whom it takes its name, but in some respects is the most traditional while in others the most modern and certainly the most widely influential intellectually. The paradox is implicit in the contrast between the simple and traditional figure of Rāmakrishna (1834–86) and his greatest disciple and propagandist, Vivekānanda (1863–1902). Rāmakrishna was born in a poor Brāhman family near Calcutta and began his career as a temple priest at an early age. Then, when he was eighteen, he and his elder brother became the officiants at a temple of Kālī at Dakshineshwar built by a wealthy Bengali lady. From this point Rāmakrishna began to experience a strong attachment to the goddess and to have visions of her, which became steadily more intense. He also began to have visions of Kṛṣṇa and others and the varieties of his mystical experience convinced him that all religions must be true, leading him to worship each manifestation in the fashion he conceived to be appropriate. His contention therefore was that all religions are true and there is no need for synthesis, but rather each individual should follow his own chosen path.

Sometime during this period Rāmakrishna was instructed in the Tantras by a female Bhairavī ascetic and then in Advaita Vedānta by an Advaitin *saṃnyāsin*, who initiated him into his order under the name by which he is generally known. He was always essentially a mystic and apparently never completely reconciled his belief in Advaita and experience of unity in meditative trance (*samādhi*) with the duality implicit in his devotion to the goddess. He had married as a young man a girl of six, but by the time she joined him he had become a *saṃnyāsin* and so the marriage was never consummated; instead he saw in her the representation of the goddess and called her the 'Holy Mother' (a different type of expression of the tantric worship of the female principle). His appeal lay in his personality and power of attracting others, for there was nothing especially new in his teaching, which was however presented in a spontaneous and attractive manner and included a message of service. His first influence was on Keshab Chandra Sen of the Brāhmo Samāj, through whom his reputation as a mystic began to spread. In many respects he appears a typical mediaeval religious figure in the tradition of Caitanya.

However, he inspired Vivekānanda (one of a number of young educated Bengalis who flocked round him at the end of his life) to found the Rāmakrishna Mission, which has become a major force for the propagation of Hinduism beyond India and the promotion of its self-respect internally. Narendranath Datta (1863–1902), who took the name Vivekānanda after his initiation by Rāmakrishna, was a typical product of the Western-educated middle class and had for a time been attracted to the Brāhmo Samāj but was captivated by Rāmakrishna on meeting him. After their second meeting Vivekānanda devoted himself to spreading Rāmakrishna's ideas and became the leader of the group round him. After Rāmakrishna's death he started a period of wandering around the whole of India terminating at Madras where he raised funds to attend the World Parliament of Religions at Chicago in 1893, where he enjoyed a considerable success and for the first time presented Hinduism to the world at large as a major religion, emphasising its antiquity. Indeed, here and later he developed the theme of Hinduism as the 'mother of religions'.

A similar standpoint had already been taken by an organisation which began outside India. The Theosophical Society, founded in 1875 by Madame H.P. Blavatsky and Colonel Olcott in New York, transferred itself before long to India, where it became a fervent admirer of Hinduism as not only the oldest religion but the source of all others. A subsequent convert to Theosophy, Mrs Annie Besant, also became an enthusiast for Hindu tradition and played a major part in mitigating the feelings of inferiority suffered by many Hindus with regard to their religion. While Mme Blavatsky had considerable influence on W. B. Yeats, the Vedānta Society, which Vivekānanda established in 1894 in New York, attracted writers like Aldous Huxley and Christopher Isherwood.

On his return to India Vivekānanda founded the Rāmakrishna Mission in 1897 and later the Order, defining their complementary religious and social objectives. His basic idea, derived from Keshab Chandra Sen, was that India could learn materially from the West but that India had much to offer the West spiritually. He emphasised Rāmakrishna's view that all religions were equally true but went beyond that to suggest that Hinduism had more to offer than other religions. He thus utilised its attitude of inclusiveness or tolerance to imply the superiority of Hinduism; his position in this regard is basically that of Advaita Vedānta that all religions are true on the relative plane, but only Advaita can achieve the highest stages of spiritual progress. This is really Hinduism's age-old syncretistic absorptiveness reasserting itself under the guise of tolerance.

At the same time Vivekānanda stressed that spiritual renewal should be allied with practical service to the poor and needy, using the Western technology that made it practicable. He preached energetically against some of the social abuses of his time but defended the basic concepts of, for example, the caste system and image worship as each appropriate in their place. He condemned the more radical reformers for having fallen entirely under the influence of the West and for breaking with the past, never acknowledging how far his own and other reformers' concern with social evils was owed to the activities of Christian missionaries. The accent in Vivekānanda's call for social service was indeed to a considerable extent chauvinistic, leading to the type of mystical patriotism exemplified in Aurobindo Ghose.

After a second extended visit to America in 1899–1900, Vivekānanda died at the age of 39, having made a remarkable impact at home and abroad in less than a decade. In India itself the Rāmakrishna Mission concentrated on social service with considerable effect, especially in Bengal. Abroad it concentrated on spreading Neo-Vedānta, developing an extensive publishing operation and doing much to enhance the prestige of Hinduism. However, it has never become a really mass movement, perhaps because of this distinctly intellectual approach which inevitably has limited its appeal.

There is a dramatic contrast between the earlier and later life of Aurobindo Ghose (1872–1950), a shift from politics to religion which reverses the trend of the Ārya Samāj. Leaving Calcutta as a child, he was educated for fourteen years in England gaining much success. On his return to India in 1893 he entered the State Service of Baroda and began to broaden his education with more intensive study of Indian languages and culture and to practise Yoga; he also became involved in the current political and social turmoil. The partition of his native Bengal in 1905 drew him into the nationalist movement to become the leader of the so-called Bengal terrorists. Settling in Calcutta in 1906, for four years he led his Nationalist party against the moderates of the Indian Congress. He was much influenced by the ideas of the religious nationalist novelist Bankim Chandra Chatterjee (1838–94), whose major novel, *Ānanda Maṭh*, contains the poem *Bande Mataram*, 'I praise the Mother', which in its context is a hymn to Kālī as Bengal personified but has since been appropriated by India as a while for a national anthem. Bankim's novels imparted a distinct element of religious revival to the nationalist movement in Bengal. The seeds of the abrupt change in Aurobindo's life were therefore already sown.

In 1908 Aurobindo was arrested on suspicion of involvement in a bomb plot and jailed for sedition. While in Alipur jail he underwent a religious experience which completely reshaped his life, reaching a state of *samādhi* through Yoga. After his release he abandoned politics and in 1910 travelled secretly to Pondicherry, a French settlement south of Madras, where he established an *āśram*, wrote many works and developed his own philosophy, the Integral Yoga. Aurobindo was the focus and spiritual head of this community, assisted by 'the Mother', a French lady whom he met in 1914 and who stayed permanently at the *āśram* from 1920, continuing to run it after Aurobindo's death.

Aurobindo claims that his philosophy stems from the *Ṛgveda*, the Upaniṣads and the *Bhagavadgītā* and actually wrote two substantial works of Vedic interpretation. He shares a return to the Vedic hymns with Dayānanda Sarasvatī, whom he admired for his attempt 'to re-establish the Veda as a living religious Scripture', though rejecting the detail of Dayānanda's interpretation equally with the attempt by B. G. Tilak (1857–1920) to establish an impossibly ancient date for the Vedas. Incidentally, Tilak is usually thought of primarily as a politician and nationalist, but to promote Indians' pride in themselves he published works stressing the antiquity of Hinduism (another version of Vivekānanda's argument that older is better), preached activism on the basis of the *Bhagavadgītā*, and inaugurated new Hindu festivals, such as that in honour of Śivājī,

12. Apsarases (celestial nymphs) from Khajurāho

the champion of Marāṭhā nationalism against the Mughals. The connection between religion and nationalism was often close.

In reality, however, Aurobindo's thought was basically another Yoga system, though incorporating elements of terminology from other systems. Indeed, his major innovation is in addressing an English-speaking readership directly; his major works were conceived and written in English, the best known being *The Life Divine*. However, his system does give a more definite place to the world, which possesses real value, and Aurobindo believed firmly in evolution, seeing its goal as the divinisation of man, an extension or transference to the human race as a whole of tantric ideas about perfecting the body. Indeed he explains the title of Integral Yoga which he gave to his system as expressing the blending of the different Yoga systems each with its own approach through body, mind and so on. As he puts it in one of his tracts for disciples, 'Yoga means union with the Divine – a union either transcendental (above the universe) or cosmic (universal) or individual or, as in our Yoga, all three together'. The tantric element in his views is always strong, as in another definition from the same booklet: 'The whole principle of this Yoga is to give oneself entirely to the Divine alone . . . and to bring down into ourselves by union with the Divine Mother all the transcendent light, power, wideness, peace, purity, truth-consciousness and Ananda of the Supramental Divine.'

Aurobindo's whole scheme of concepts, as in traditional Yoga, refers both to the evolution of the universe as macrocosm and to the structure of the individual as microcosm. His first three concepts, Pure Existence (also Ultimate Reality or Absolute Spirit), Consciousness-Force (also Shakti) and Bliss represent the Vedāntın *sat, cit* and *ānanda* and are grouped together as 'the supreme planes of Infinite Consciousness'. They are related to the lower planes of ordinary existence, Mind, Psyche or Soul, Life and Matter, by the Supermind or Gnosis (=*jñāna*), a level of higher consciousness through which his goal will be realised for 'Now Supermind is to descend so as to create a supramental race'. Since everything is interwoven dynamically, Aurobindo tends to introduce other concepts aimed at clarifying its inner dynamics, such as the concept of Overmind intervening between Supermind and ordinary

Mind. This tendency towards excessive conceptualisation, combined with its expression in English, makes his system perhaps more involved than necessary but equally he seems to have realised the need to amplify for the sake of his larger non-Indian audience. However his appeal has been limited by his remaining exclusively at Pondicherry, where certainly a group of disciples has been built up, without any significant impact on India at large.

It is one of the many paradoxes about Mahatma Gandhi that, despite his undoubted mass appeal, the greater part of his writings are also in English. But then this mild little man, who, for all his reforming zeal, has become in many ways the symbol of traditional Indian values, had more contact with European culture and gained more through it than is commonly realised. Mohandas Karamchand Gandhi (1869–1948) had a relatively traditional upbringing – his father was prime minister of several petty states in Kathiawar successively – and was married at the age of thirteen. But when he was eighteen he left for London to train as a barrister, being called to the Bar in 1891; during this period he first became familiar with the *Bhagavadgītā* which, with the *Rāmcaritmānas* of Tulsīdās, was to become his favourite religious reading, as well as with the Sermon on the Mount. After a short period in India, in 1893 Gandhi went to South Africa, where he was to stay for over twenty years; there he saw the effects of incipient *apartheid* and organised Indian opposition to certain measures. In the process he formulated his policy of *satyāgraha*, 'adherence to truth', on the basis of non-violence, which owed much to the influence of Leo Tolstoy, with whom he corresponded at this period, as well as to the Jain concept of *ahiṃsā* so prominent in his native Gujarat.

In 1915 Gandhi returned to India, immediately starting an *āśram* near Ahmedabad and soon becoming involved in the activities of the Indian National Congress; his first major involvement was a successful campaign in 1917 on behalf of the peasants of Champaran in Bihar against their employers, the indigo planters. He joined in the general boycott of British goods and institutions in 1919, coining for it the name 'non-cooperation', and soon began to advocate civil disobedience. Soon after his release from prison early in 1924, after a sentence for writing seditious articles in his newspaper *Young India*,

Gandhi embarked on a three-week fast in the cause of communal harmony and in atonement for some recent riots. Efforts to ease communal tension were to be a significant part of Gandhi's activities, culminating in his well-known exertions in the wake of partition in 1947.

Also in the 1920s he developed his campaigns for the removal of untouchability and the use of indigenous materials, especially hand-woven cloth, in both cases making use of personal example. Indeed his first efforts at integrating untouchables on a personal basis go back to his South African days. While defending the traditional theory of the classes (*varṇas*), Gandhi spoke and acted resolutely against the evils of untouchability, calling it quite unequivocally 'a curse' and appealing to the social conscience of all Hindus to rid their religion of this blot. His ideas were not of course entirely novel – many other reformers had said the same over the last century – and indeed may well have been able to evoke some sympathy precisely because they were expressed in ways not so different from the *bhakti* tradition (Gandhi himself came from a Vaiṣṇava family) in the stress on religious and not just social principles, characterised in his renaming them Harijans, 'the people of Viṣṇu'. His programmes for the uplift of the Harijans in fact had a forerunner in the Depressed Classes Mission founded in 1906 as an offshoot of the Prārthana Samāj.

The campaign for indigenous products and institutions, symbolised by his adoption of the loin-cloth in 1921 and later by the traditional spinning-wheel, had the definite purpose of emphasising the dignity of labour and forcing the middle class élite, among whom lay the greatest political awareness, to identify with the poorer village people. Nevertheless it later drew from his younger, secularist colleague in the national movement, Jawaharlal Nehru, the comments that it was 'a throw-back to the preindustrial age' and 'As a solution of any vital present-day problem it cannot be taken seriously'. It is doubtful whether Gandhi's efforts on behalf of the untouchables have in the long term been any more successful than those of earlier reformers, but the success of his propaganda efforts have meant that no-one can any longer be unaware of the problem.

His flair for presentation is seen particularly clearly in one of his next causes, undertaken while political progress was stalemated; this was the campaign of civil disobedience against the salt laws and taxes which placed a severe financial burden on the peasants. In 1930 he led a well publicised march from his *āśram* 241 miles to the sea at Dandi, where he made salt from sea water, symbolically infringing the government monopoly; his subsequent arrest was in a real sense a propaganda victory. His release from prison was followed by talks and a pact with the Viceroy, Lord Irwin, which among other things permitted salt manufacture on the coast, a triumph for Gandhi's methods.

Much of Gandhi's life thereafter was taken up with politics, where his influence was immense, but he never lost sight of his religious principles and indeed was recurrently threatening to withdraw from public life to concentrate on his *āśram*. Some of his views there may have been idiosyncratic, such as his methods of testing his own celibacy and his denial of the pleasures of eating, but it is in this more traditional style of religious life that he was really most at home and from which he was able to make the impact that he did on national life. Indeed, it is not unfair to say that Gandhi was primarily a religious figure, who felt that nothing could really be achieved while a foreign power ruled India and believed that the British could be shamed into leaving India; to a surprising extent he was proved right, but the most significant reason for that was precisely Gandhi's own moral stature.

Yet his championship of the untouchables and perhaps still more his efforts at calming communal tensions made him an object of suspicion to some orthodox Hindus. His message of reconciliation, preached so tirelessly and fearlessly at the time of partition incurred the anger of militant Hindus. A bomb exploded at one of his prayer meetings and a few days later, on 30 January 1948, he was assassinated by a Brāhman member of the Hindu Mahāsabhā, dying with an invocation to Rāma on his lips. The fanatic need not have worried about Gandhi's ideals destroying Hinduism; they have been admired but not put into practice. In so far as they survive – apart from emulation of them by many Western protest movements – their main effect has indeed been to preserve orthodox Hinduism by endowing it with a social conscience while retaining most of its traditional values.

CHAPTER TEN

Tradition Triumphant

Gandhi's dying invocation of Rāma, whether meant as a general or a specific designation of the deity, illustrates the enormous hold of the Rāma story on Hindus, a hold all the stronger in that it has never been wholly appropriated by sectarian interests. The way that the Hindi version of Tulsīdās has become an integral part of the whole culture is echoed in other areas of north India. In the south the Rāma story is just as popular; in Tamilnad daily ritual reading from Vālmīki's *Rāmāyaṇa* in temples is complemented by expository recitations from Kampaṉ's Tamil version and by more devotional narration accompanied by songs in a style derived from Maharashtra. The staging of the Rāmlīlā is still an annual feature of local life across most of north India, the audience identifying with the joyful citizens who welcome Rāma's triumphant return (popular instinct with sound taste reverting to the original ending), and many Rajputs claim descent from Rāma.

Hinduism has always been broader than its sects, a fact perhaps obscured by the concentration on sectarian developments in recent chapters. The relationship between the adherents of a particular group or sect and the bulk of Hindus, who may be called 'traditional' (*smārta*, following the traditional *smṛti* literature), is not always easily definable. While most Hindus above the very simplest levels are either Vaiṣṇava or Śaiva, this does not necessarily imply allegiance to a particular sect, with its more exclusive patterns of belief. In certain respects the sects can be regarded as something added on to ordinary Hindu practice, a particular set of doctrines and practices which supplement the basic pattern of rituals and beliefs (although in many cases specific beliefs replace and even oppose the general pattern). The sects also regularly develop their own definite hierarchy of authority as a mark of their separation from the relatively unstructured mass of Hinduism, where Brāhmans as a class exercise a leadership by
rather than a dictatorial control. Thus, the group ca
Smārta Brāhmans tend to advocate rituals directed to t

13. Śikhara (spire) of the Vārāhī temple, Caurasi

of five gods (Viṣṇu, Śiva, Devī, Sūrya and Gaṇeśa) which has in more recent times largely replaced the older *trimūrti* of Brahmā, Viṣṇu and Śiva as the vehicle for the orthodox synthesis; while worshipping these deities impartially, they also lay claim to adherence to Śaṅkara's Advaita, as a mark of intellectual orthodoxy. However, the Smārta Brāhmans are for example usually called on, in the absence of Śrīvaiṣṇava priests, by members of that sect to perform the various rituals of day-to-day life. They play a similar role in relation to other sects and cults, thus mediating between the various separate backgrounds and the broader current of Hindu tradition.

The earlier *trimūrti* concept first comes to the fore in the Purāṇas, a class of text which itself is largely dedicated to this task of synthesis (not only between differing religious trends but also between religious and more secular aspects of tradition) as well as of establishing a religion more accessible and less hieratic than that which prevailed in the Vedic schools. Composed and edited by Brāhmans, the Purāṇas are nevertheless very much a manifestation of popular religion; they bear witness to the fact that the Brāhmans have maintained their position as guardians and transmitters of the religious tradition only by being receptive, albeit often reluctantly, to any innovations which achieve a real popular following. So much is this the case, that the more popular form of Hinduism from the Gupta period onwards has often been called Purāṇic Hinduism, while equally they reflect the growing strength of the sects, since most Purāṇas now have a definite Vaiṣṇava or Śaiva orientation. Thus, though often relevant to sectarian developments (and so frequently mentioned in previous chapters), they constitute the first expression of the more synthesising strand, concentrating on simple rituals rather than exact doctrines, which is characteristic of mediaeval and modern Hinduism.

Nonetheless, the origins of the Purāṇas are very early; the term first appears in the *Atharvaveda* and thereafter is often linked with the stories elaborated to form the epics as the 'ancient' material which, with the Vedas, constitutes the traditional learning. The extant Purāṇas, compiled between the fourth and twelfth centuries, are based on collations of much older material, revealed most clearly in the king-lists which form one of their topics. These fall essentially into two groups, of which the first series of genealogies runs from Manu, the mythical ancestor of the human race, to the immediate descendants of the heroes of the *Mahābhārata* (named in the frame story and to be assigned probably to early in the first millennium B.C.), while the second series, presented as prophecies (which may reflect their addition to established texts) but undoubtedly like all the best prophecies written *ex post facto*, ends with the Guptas or another dynasty of that period (fourth to sixth centuries A.D.).

Traditionally, each Purāṇa covers five topics: the emanation of the universe, its destruction and re-emanation, the reigns and periods of the Manus, the genealogies of the gods and sages, and the genealogy of the solar and lunar dynasties (to which all dynasties of kings trace their ancestry). As part of their popularisation other related topics were added, such as instruction on the duties of class and stage of life (*varṇāśrama-dharma*), sacred sites and pilgrimage, worship of images and construction of temples; among their characteristic themes are the greatness of the rewards which can be secured by little effort and their accessibility to women and *śūdras*, an obvious parallel to the emphases of the *bhakti* movement, in this more activity-related type of religion.

There are theoretically eighteen major Purāṇas and the same number of minor ones, but this is just a conventional enumeration (the significance of the number eighteen being apparent also in the eighteen books of the *Mahābhārata* and the eighteen chapters of the *Bhagavadgītā*, *Nārāyaṇiya* and so on). An attempt to link a third of the number with each deity of the *trimūrti* is rather artificial, but a religious evolution is visible similar to that seen in the epics, with which the Purāṇas share a number of similarities of background, indicating for them too perhaps a less strictly religious inspiration than their present form suggests. After the eclipse of Brahmā, Viṣṇu as a rule is pre-eminent in the earlier texts, whereas Śiva comes to the fore in their later stages.

The first three of the traditional topics for the Purāṇas amount to a full presentation of the developed Hindu cosmology, which probably reached its final form later than the Buddhist and Jain cosmologies, although all three are interrelated. In their original relationship to the other two topics of genealogies, these topics represent a transition from the universal to the more particular and a balance between them. But the full elaboration of their cosmology, with its immense cycles of time repeating themselves indefinitely, has inevitably reduced for Hindus the significance of the particular event, often castigated as lack of a historical sense (which it certainly was not in origin and probably, except in a limited sense, never has been). The world perpetually undergoes a cycle of emanation from a state of non-differentiation through a series of ages to its dissolution (*pralaya*) back into the unevolved state, from which the whole cycle starts again. The time-scales and other details vary but in each case work down from an astronomical figure.

Most commonly, the major unit is the aeon equal to a day of Brahmā (who has a life of 100 years made up of 360 such days and nights of equal length, before he is replaced by another creator deity), which is equal to 1000 years of the gods, each day of which constitutes a human year. In each day of Brahmā the universe is created and in each night it is reabsorbed; within each day are fourteen subsidiary periods of the Manus, in which also the world is emanated and reabsorbed according to older traditions (younger texts minimise these transitions). So far as these major divisions are concerned, the world is now in the period of the seventh Manu in a day of a Brahmā in his 51st year, poised therefore in the middle of time. In similar fashion the world is set well away from the edges of the Egg of Brahmā within which the universe is contained. This egg is held to contain 21 regions, of which the earth is the seventh from the top, being surmounted by six heavens, while below are seven levels of the underworld (the abode of Nāgas and other semi-divine beings) and below that again seven levels of hell.

However, each period of Manu is divided into the great ages, each of which is divided in turn into four periods of decreasing duration, marked by progressive moral and physical deterioration; within this system the world is now in the middle of the last and worst of these ages, the Kaliyuga, popularly held to have begun with the *Mahābhārata* war, just as Viṣṇu's tenth *avatāra*, Kalki, will according to some Purāṇas bring it to an end by overthrowing the foreign, heretic and *śūdra* rulers of the time and inaugurating a new great age, beginning with its first, golden age.

This idea that the current age is one of degeneracy seems to have evolved concurrently with the whole cyclical theory of time-reckoning. There is a progressive decay of all that gives value to life and a continuing decline in moral standards, given expression in the theory of actions to be avoided in this present Kaliyuga, built on certain older texts, especially one from the first chapter of the *Manusmṛti,* where the theory of the four ages is expounded. This theory has been used by later legal theorists, particularly since the twelfth century, to justify the abolition of certain customs which had become repugnant. The rules of conduct laid down in the Dharmaśāstras remain valid but are no longer good to follow, because of man's growing weakness and the decline in his moral sense; laid down for the golden age, they are no longer all effective for man in the Kaliyuga. Thus the theory of the four ages offered the legal theorists a more orthodox means to bring the rules of the Dharmaśāstras up to date, by suggesting that the prohibition of certain practices was due not to popular aversion to them but to the degeneracy of the age. Yet again theory was brought into line with practice, while the impression given is of the opposite taking place.

The Purāṇas are even better known as the great storehouses of Hindu mythology, from which are derived other narrations of the luxuriant myths that form so large a part of traditional Hinduism. In this too they have played a synthesising role, bringing into relationship with the two major deities, Viṣṇu and Śiva, many local deities and cults by means of a particular myth. One major element of this which has not so far been mentioned is the provision of the deities with their individual mounts (*vāhanas*), thus bringing into relationship with each deity an appropriate animal symbol of his particular nature or activity. Thus Brahmā is provided with a goose (because of its lofty migration to remote distances, a symbol to Hindus of the soul's quest for release), Viṣṇu rides on Garuḍa (the mythical bird who in Vedic literature is entirely independent of Viṣṇu) and during the dissolution of the universe reclines on the cosmic serpent Śeṣa or Ananta ('remainder' and 'infinite'), and Śiva has his bull, Nandin. Of course, deities in animal form have been taken directly into the developed pantheon, in particular the monkey Hanumān (who has a wider significance than just his aid to Rāma) and Śiva's elephant-headed son, Gaṇeśa. Interestingly, Gaṇeśa himself is furnished with a mount, the apparently incongruous rat which in reality symbolises another aspect of Gaṇeśa's ability to overcome obstacles.

This system of the deities' mounts represents, therefore, another mechanism, alongside the proliferation of Viṣṇu's *avatāras* and Śiva's ever enlarging family circle, by which the Purāṇas and the traditional Hinduism derived from them have contrived to assimilate the multiplicity of local cults, which have always been a feature of Indian religion, into the framework of a developed religion. Undoubtedly in this there has been an element of deliberate manipulation of the material to achieve the desired end. But another significant feature of the use of myth is its employment as a kind of meta-language, a method of presenting religious concepts in a symbolic form which is open-ended. A myth can be endlessly reinterpreted to suit the needs of the individual or the period in a way that is impossible to achieve with doctrinal formulations. The Purāṇas themselves provide countless examples of the narration of essentially the same myth from a Vaiṣṇava or a Śaiva angle and, in the case of Śaiva mythology, with unlimited scope for exploiting the ambivalence inherent in the nature of a deity who represents in so striking a fashion the totality of the universe.

Pilgrimage is one of the topics included by the Purāṇas from a popular background; such a cult of localities is at variance with the mobile character of Vedic ritual. Early attested in Buddhism, it is also attested within Hinduism in a passage inserted into the *Mahābhārata* on the tour of the sacred sites (Mbh.3. 80–8); this interestingly starts with the one still extant cult spot of Brahmā, a sign of its relatively early date. The cult of pilgrimage to sacred places, *tīrthas* (literally 'fords'), became fairly widespread by the mediaeval period and was a popular way to remove sins and accumulate merit; the merit acquired in visiting them was commonly reckoned in terms of the performance of so many Vedic rituals, but, unlike the sacrifices that they thereby replace, the sacred sites were open to all. Sometimes pilgrimages were undertaken for the performance of a memorial ritual in honour of deceased relatives (especially to Gaya), for the recovery of a sick person, or to consign the ashes of a dead relative to a river, especially the Gaṅgā (Ganges).

As their name *tīrtha* suggests, such pilgrimage centres are usually (though not invariably) associated with rivers, which in Hindu thought are all invested with a measure of sanctity,

14. Nandin (Śiva's mount), a nāga, Kṛṣṇa as a playful child

although much the most sacred river is the Gaṅgā, especially at its confluence with the Yamunā (Jumna) and by legend the Sarasvatī at Prayāga (modern Allahabad). However, the city of Varanasi on its banks is a particularly sacred city, while its source at Gangotri and certain other places in its upper reaches are also esteemed places of pilgrimage. The Purāṇas elaborate the myth of the heavenly Gaṅgā who, as the result of lengthy austerities by the sage Bhagīratha, descends to earth, her fall being broken in Śiva's matted hair to prevent her waters flooding the earth. Everywhere along her banks is to some degree sacred and according to popular belief those who bathe in the Gaṅgā and more particularly those who die in Varanasi gain heaven (a view denounced by Kabīr but just as strong as ever).

Gradually other rivers and other sites came to be centres of pilgrimage, or in several cases no doubt older traditions of pilgrimage associated with local, tribal cults were granted orthodox recognition. To mark this, passages eulogising these *tīrthas* were inserted in one or another of the Purāṇas. Such pilgrimages are not in general the group affairs that the Vārkarī Panth undertakes in its pilgrimages to Pandharpur. In most cases the pilgrimage is an individual affair, with the pilgrim sometimes undertaking all kinds of austerities in his solitary travel. But at some places particular occasions are especially favoured and, for instance, at Hardwar and Prayāga, where the most favoured occasion comes round once in twelve years, there are massive gatherings of pilgrims, among whom wandering *saṃnyāsins* are particularly prominent. Some *tīrthas* are especially revered by worshippers of one deity but the more major ones are respected by all Hindus.

The importance of rivers and of bathing in them is just one manifestation of the universal Hindu concern with purity and the avoidance of pollution. Much of traditional Hinduism is intimately bound up with the observance of the rules of purity or, which usually amounts to the same thing, to preservation of caste status. Bathing in the Gaṅgā washes away sins, basically conceived of as bodily impurities. Many causes of ritual impurity are identical to the taboos of primitive societies, menstruating women, blood in general, excreta and more generally anything removed from the body, and dead bodies; the barber is therefore, for example, a person in an ambiguous and even dangerous position. The uncleanness resulting from contact with these may be removed by various penances, but invariably bathing is included in the ritual. As part of the general abhorrence for anything that has been removed from the body, the left-overs from anyone's meal are regarded as strictly forbidden in normal circumstances. Yet paradoxically in another sense such remnants are the only proper food according to the Dharmaśāstras which declare that the only legitimate food consists of what is left over from the sacrifice; in practice what this means is that a token portion of each meal should be offered to the gods. However it serves to underline the point that what is always in question is the relative status of those involved. If one party is of sufficiently high status, then anything connected with him will be sanctifying, even if normally regarded as polluting. Thus, still more literally, in some sects the food offerings made to the deity are later distributed among his worshippers as a mark of his grace (*prasāda*, the term therefore also denoting these distributed left-overs). So too the feet are impure and the head pure, which makes it a mark of particular respect for a pupil to place his *guru*'s feet on his own head.

The question of purity and pollution is intimately bound up with the caste system. While the origin of castes (*jāti*) is complex, involving the development of guilds or occupational groups into closed communities and the assimilation of tribal groups as separate units into traditional society, the basic factors which affect their ranking are almost entirely connected with their orthodoxy or otherwise in matters of ritual purity. Indeed, castes as a whole can over a period of time alter their ranking by closer approximation to the customs of the Brāhmans. Brāhmans, as the group from which alone priests and ritual specialists can be drawn, have to guard themselves most rigidly against pollution and observe caste restrictions as a matter of religious and moral duty, marrying only within the caste and eating only with caste equals. Such rules have become increasingly strict over the centuries – it is clear for instance that the *Manusmṛti*, though providing the framework to integrate *jāti* with the older *varṇa* system of classes, did permit a degree of intermarriage and was far less restrictive in matters of diet than more recent custom. There are nowadays many detailed restrictions about the types of food that may be accepted from others, but in general the rule is that one may accept cooked food only from someone of equal or higher status. The result has been that some Brāhmans have become cooks, since anyone can receive food from them; such deviation from their proper duties would be justified by appeal to the provisions in the Dharmaśāstras about permissible occupations in time of distress, which in practice is any time in this degenerate Kali-yuga. Thus, especially in south India, one might see a tea-stall or station buffet manned by Brāhmans, stripped to the waist to display their sacred threads almost as a guarantee of the purity of their wares.

The ceremony of investiture with the sacred thread was originally open to all males of the three upper classes (Brāhman, *kṣatriya* and *vaiśya*) and marked their admission into adult society. The boy became the pupil of a teacher who, in a ceremony which included also the imparting of the *Gāyatrī*, placed the sacred thread (a cord of three threads, each of nine strands twisted together) over his left shoulder to hang under his right arm; there then traditionally followed the period of studentship and celibacy, during which the initiate learnt the Vedas and related material, but more usually now this is reduced to a token. Nevertheless, the significance of the ceremony as marking the continuity of the religious tradition is still apparent. Probably from quite early times the custom fell into desuetude for most *kṣatriyas* and *vaiśyas* with the result that the term 'twice-born', denoting those who had undergone the ceremony (marking a second birth into the life of the full community), came to be applied almost exclusively to Brāhmans. However, a few non-Brāhman castes still perform the ceremony to the present day and it is still general among more orthodox Brāhmans.

In order to preserve their ritual purity, Brāhmans had to avoid contact with pollution and with those themselves in contact with it. Thus, groups who handled particularly defiling material were untouchable, or more exactly unapproachable; such groups included those who handled soiled clothes, washermen, or the bodies of dead cattle, scavengers and leatherworkers, or who cleaned latrines, sweepers. And groups whose customs are too aberrant are similarly defiling, if for instance they eat beef or practise marriage customs that offend the norm. Despite the efforts of Gandhi and so many reformers before him, and despite the efforts by the Government of India to reserve educational opportunities and administrative posts for them, untouchability is still very much a fact of Indian life. The worst abuses probably have gone, at least in the towns, although the mass conversions to Buddhism under the leadership of Dr Ambedkar serve to underline the point that the abolition of untouchability by the government immediately after independence eliminated the more obvious external features but did not change people's basic attitudes. In the villages, where after all the vast majority of India's population still live, things change much more slowly.

No doubt in time the abuses connected with untouchability will be moderated, but the caste system will survive. One of its most basic features, that of endogamy, has been virtually unaffected by the attempts of a few reformers to encourage intercaste marriages and of a few Westernised Indians to show their emancipation in this way. The reaction is still as shocked as when Basava attempted it in the twelfth century, while the fate of the Liṅgāyats itself illustrates the strength of the caste system, since they have in effect been turned into a caste by external pressures, though themselves rejecting caste. Other reformist sects have in the same way been turned into quasi-castes and the same process has affected in some degree other religions present in India, which have sometimes evolved internal divisions analogous to castes, and function in regard to the surrounding community like a caste grouping.

While the Purāṇas added instruction on the duties of class and stage of life to their original five topics, their major innovation, alongside the development of pilgrimage to sacred sites, was the inclusion of material on the worship of images and construction of temples. Here again they provide evidence of a trend which has become characteristic of Hinduism in more modern times. In fact, the first extant examples of Hindu temple architecture come from the Gupta period and thus are more or less contemporary with the compilation of the earlier Purāṇas, except for a very few shrines connected perhaps significantly with popular cults such as that of the Nāgas. The earliest shrines consisted just of a foursquare cell but very soon this was regularly raised on a plinth and surmounted by a spire (*śikhara*), whose name identifies it with the sacrificial flame and the mountain peak. For, although temples and image worship were to displace the Vedic ritual, their earliest symbolism was derived from that. The cell set on its plinth was equivalent to the Vedic altar and its pile of firewood from which the flames leapt up or was identified with Mt Meru, the *axis mundi*, while the carefully delimited area of the sacrifice persists in the succeessive courtyards characteristic of south Indian temples. Gradually various elements were added to the basic ones (and regional styles of architecture emerged) as the ritual developed, but the symbolic continuity is maintained and still the temple is the channel of the deity's descent to earth.

The Purāṇas give the first clear prescription of the cult of images, beginning with methods of manufacture, then their installation in the temple, followed by the bathing, perfuming, adorning and consecrating of the statue. Although canons of proportions are given, the concern is not artistic but purely iconographic: the correct representation of Viṣṇu, Śiva or whatever deity it is, including the appropriate attributes, motifs and attendant deities. The opening of the eyes, which as it were animates the figure, is performed in a special ceremony when the image is consecrated in the interior of the sanctuary where it is to be installed.

The liturgy performed in the majority of temples essentially conceives of the deity as a great potentate holding court. Thus the daily routine commences with the god in the form of his image being awakened with music, bathed and dressed; then come meals, audiences and periods of entertainment in royal fashion. The deity is honoured with flowers and garlands and surrounded by incense and lamps, while his worshippers come to do him homage. Worship in the major temples is not normally the aesthetic experience made of it by the Vallabha movement in its private shrines, but the general approach is identical in its view of the deity as a ruler to be ministered to. A difference is that there is no element of congregational worship. A worshipper would go to the temple alone or with his family to make his own particular act of homage, just as pilgrimage is essentially an individual activity, even if at times large numbers congregate. The regular acts of worship carried out by the officiants might well be observed by many in the larger temples but as an audience rather than as direct participants.

However, the service of the deity in this fashion has encouraged the development of temples, especially in south

India, into centres of cultural activity. From the tenth century rulers in Tamilnad were providing endowments for recitations and devotional singing at temples, which both encouraged the singing of the hymns of the *bhakti* poets and provided employment for professional performers. In effect major temples came to include halls for concerts and lectures, which had as much of a cultural as a religious value, and were also an art gallery in the form of the images and religious paintings they contained; even now, annually during its particular festival, the walls of many south Indian temples are painted with religious scenes. On such festive occasions, the deity may go out for an excursion or on a visit, touring the city in a huge, wooden car drawn by his devotees and followed by a procession, which includes lesser deities in their cars, musicians, dancers and attendants; perhaps the best known of these car festivals is that at Puri for Jagannāth (from which has come the term juggernaut). The layout of temples is regularly completed either by steps down to a river or a large tank (artificial pool), to cater for the ritual ablution which is so central to all Hindu religious observance.

Worship (*pūjā*) is not always on such a grand scale, however, and indeed temple worship is still to a large extent optional, though relatively popular. The ceremonies which take place within the home, with or without the aid of a Brāhman officiant, are still the essential ones; these range from the daily ritual to be performed on waking to the ceremonies connected with birth, marriage and death. Worship at shrines also ranges from the elaborate temple worship just described to very simple offerings made at a wayside shrine consisting of a crude image protected by a tiny cell or just a shapeless lump of rock daubed with vermilion. The offerings made at such simpler local shrines will be a ball of rice, or a few flowers or even a handful of leaves.

As this suggests, the form by which a deity is represented is also variable. Normally in temples Viṣṇu or his *avatāras* (mostly Kṛṣṇa) are represented anthropomorphically, although for instance at the famous Jagannāth temple at Puri Kṛṣṇa and his brother and sister are represented by roughly carved wooden statues lacking limbs. The most frequent representation of Śiva, however, is in the form of a *liṅga* (literally 'mark' or 'symbol', as indeed the *liṅga* worn by Liṅgāyats is), a phallic symbol in the form usually of a short cylindrical pillar with a rounded top set in a ring stone (*yoni*) representing the female genitalia. While the *liṅga* may incorporate aspects of ancient cults of the pillar or the sacred tree (stylised to a simple pole), there is no doubt that many are realistic representations of the penis and directly reflect the sexuality which is such a strong current in Śaiva mythology. In some the *liṅga* itself is combined with a sculptural representation of Śiva, and among south Indian bronzes produced as portable images from about the twelfth century there are many elaborate and often beautiful depictions of Śiva in his various forms, especially as Naṭarāja 'Lord of the Dance'. Even so, the most frequent image in temples is the *liṅga* in the *yoni*, symbolising the union of Śiva with his *śakti* as the supreme expression of creative power. As the whole mythology of Śiva makes clear, the world is in a continuous process of production and destruction and it is this that is expressed also in the *liṅga*.

Some of the most prized *liṅgas* are in fact natural, appropriately shaped pebbles occurring in a suitable sacred location. Similarly for Vaiṣṇavas their deity is represented in mineral form by the *śālagrāma*, a specimen of which is kept in almost every Vaiṣṇava household; these are in fact fossil ammonites found especially in the Gandak river and held to be pervaded by Viṣṇu's presence. But Hinduism is ready to see the divine very widely. The *vāhanas* as animal expressions of the deities' nature have already been mentioned. Various plants are also regarded as sacred. The *pīpal* tree (*Ficus religiosa* L.) is revered in Buddhism as the Bodhi Tree but it is also sacred to Hindus as the tree of life rooted in heaven in the ancient texts and so later regarded as occupied by Brahmā; occasionally it is even therefore invested with the sacred thread. Another fig, the *banyan* (*Ficus bengalensis* L.) with its aerial roots which extend its stranglehold all around, has a particular cult at Prayāga (Allahabad) and more generally is regarded as sacred to Time. The most widely revered is the *tulsī* plant (*Ocimum sanctum* L.), sacred to Viṣṇu and sometimes identified with Lakṣmī. The list is seemingly endless.

Another continuing aspect of Hindu religious life has been the seasonal festivals. A particularly well-known ancient festival, known at least since the time of the Gṛhyasūtras, has persisted in some places up to the present day; this is the festival of Indra's banner, celebrated at the end of the monsoon when a tree trunk (or a bamboo) is brought from the forest, set up in the town and decorated with garlands, bells and other ornaments, after which dances and games are performed in its – or Indra's – presence, until on the final day it is lowered and thrown into the river. Yet elements of many other festivals may well be just as ancient. The spring festival of Holī is also attested in literature from quite an early date and is one of the most widespread of north Indian festivals, extending also into the south. Its most distinctive feature is the squirting or throwing of coloured water or powder over passers-by in a kind of Saturnalia, which also includes abuse and suggestive songs in what is basically a fertility ritual; other important elements are the bonfire lit and danced around and the collection of its ashes.

In the south, in the festival of Pongal (in January; its northern equivalent is Makarasaṃkrānti) cattle are decorated with garlands and led about in procession but exempted from work. This veneration of cattle is also an element in several other festivals and pays tribute to their great importance in the average Indian's life, for cattle are directly employed in agricultural production as draught animals, as well as providing important products. Although India has a high density of cattle, its population is also high and in fact it has a lower ratio of cattle to people than for example the United States. But the value of the cow in providing protein through its milk is greater than as a producer of meat, especially when a substantial part of the population is vegetarian in diet; nor is the beef of dead cattle left to rot, for many untouchables eat it. Again the importance of cow-dung as fuel should not be underestimated, even if a higher proportion than at present would be better used as fertiliser. The cow is venerated as the great provider and is naturally therefore identified with the earth and regarded as too sacred to be killed.

Dīvālī, 'the festival of lamps', in October or November, is associated especially with Lakṣmī, the goddess of wealth and prosperity, although Kṛṣṇa is honoured on two days of the five-day festival, during which innumerable lamps (and in modern times also electric lights) are lighted both in homes and in public places. The fourth day is traditionally one of dicing and gambling and also includes worship and decoration of cattle, associated with Kṛṣṇa Gopāla's lifting of Mt Govardhana. Slightly earlier in the year, the festival of Daśahrā, 'ten days', is celebrated in most of north India by the performance of the Rāmlīlā, already noted, but in Bengal is celebrated as the Durgāpūjā, during which a special image of the goddess is worshipped for nine days and immersed in a river or the sea at its conclusion. During the Durgāpūjā, large numbers of goats are slaughtered in the temple at Kālīghāṭ (Calcutta) and their heads piled before the image of the goddess. This type of sacrifice, quite different from the Vedic sacrifice, is undoubtedly taken over from tribal worship; in it the victim is decapitated in such a way that the blood sprinkles the image of Durgā or Kālī.

The religious life of the ordinary Hindu is expressed through participation in such worship and festivals, without great regard for the elaborate doctrinal structures and systems of thought typical of more intellectual Hinduism. Some aspects of his faith as expressed in such action actually run counter to orthodox thought, representing in some cases extremely archaic as well as popular attitudes. Among the most important rituals are the funeral rites and the memorial ceremonies which follow at periodic intervals; some of these are directed to the ancestors in general, conceived as a group who could be benefited by the offerings made. Since parts of the funeral ritual are drawn from the *Ṛgveda* it is not so surprising that the Vedic view of an after-life is that which is here implicit, as well as in popular beliefs about ghosts (*preta, bhūta*) and the like, despite attempts to bring these views into line with the concept of *saṃsāra*, the perpetual cycle of rebirth. It is incidentally the need to have a son to perform the funeral and memorial rituals which has been one of the strongest incentives leading Hindus to desire so passionately the birth of sons; so important is this ceremony that the offering of the ball of rice, which is the principal feature, gives its name to the rules of inheritance based on family relationship. The emphasis on periodic rituals, annually and on family occasions like weddings, points to the continued existence of the ancestors in their own separate world. The implication clearly is that the dead person is in some after state where these offerings can influence his well-being, which is in itself at variance with the doctrine of *karma*.

A factor which may have influenced this, but certainly cannot be the whole explanation, is that the *bhakti* movement has encouraged the idea that through devotion to the deity one can pass into *mokṣa* at the end of this life or, as they more frequently put it, achieve union of some kind with the deity in his heaven. Indeed, some *bhakti* poets go so far as to suggest that the experience of the deity's presence here and now is to be preferred to liberation. To the extent that doctrines of *karma* and *saṃsāra* are related to the position of the Brāhman in society, there may even be an element of mute protest at his pretensions.

More fundamental are some of the continuing tensions or polarities within Hindu thought. One which has been recognised since the appearance of the concept of *mokṣa* is the opposition between it and the other three ends of man or purposes of life, *dharma*, material well-being and satisfaction of desires. The earlier three are intended to sum up human activity in a scale of ascending value, where each represents a legitimate point of view towards life, and indeed are all to be considered at different times if not necessarily concurrently; to some extent it is the duty of the householder to cultivate prosperity and to raise a family in order to ensure the practice of *dharma*, the aspect of religious merit, including also one's duty. But the fourth aim of liberation is added to the three as one which transcends and in a way is opposed to them. Within this context indeed one might almost say that *dharma*, so often translated religion, is in opposition to the ultimate spiritual value of liberation. A more basic point is that *mokṣa* does replace morality, which is perhaps the best translation of *dharma* in this context; in other words morality has only a limited value in reaching the ultimate goal. This is the ultimate reason for the Vedānta emphasis (based on the Upaniṣads) on knowledge as the most important, indeed sole, factor and for the tantric emphasis on concepts of power.

However, the opposition is not just an irreconcilable contradiction; as with the four stages of life, where the first three are a necessary preparation for the fourth, so in the scheme of the four ends the first three are a precondition to the fourth, which is not opposed to morality but beyond it, as it is beyond all worldly polarities. Whereas the principle of analogy operates within the universe and each individual is himself a miniature replica of the universe, there is a radical dichotomy between the universe and liberation. The principle of organisation expressed in *dharma* at both the cosmic and the human levels is no longer relevant. Even within *dharma*, however, there is a tension between two different levels of *dharma* – the relative morality of one's own particular caste duties and the absolute morality which is valid in any situation.

Hinduism can indeed be seen as a system of such balanced oppositions throughout its history. In the Vedic period the opposition between the Devas and the Asuras is a structural one, based on their conflict for control of the universe, for power. Subsequently, with the elaboration of Sāṃkhya and Yoga concepts, there is the contrast between the proliferation and absorption of the universe. Broadly, in the Sāṃkhya system and in the mythology there is apparent the multiplication of forms leading to an emphasis on the manifold reality of the world in all its external variety; in the Yoga system and contemplative mysticism there is the pursuit of interiorisation and the reduction of the apparent multiplicity back to an original unity. The contrast between the schools and texts which proclaim that unity alone is real and those which seek to discover principles of classification and hierarchy everywhere is one which persists throughout Hindu thought. Nevertheless, the trend towards classification renders possible the emphasis on ultimate correspondences in the other.

Such tendencies begin as early as the divergence between the more impersonal trends found in some late Vedic hymns and early Upaniṣads and the more personal, theistic trend which supersedes the Vedic polytheism in some Upaniṣads and in the epics. The quest for Brahman as first principle by which all phenomena are explained is a continuing influence on Hindu thought and reaches its most abstract development, the most unqualified assertion of unity over against multiplicity, in the Advaita Vedānta of Śaṅkara. Yet Rāmānuja's theology, based on an experience of a personal deity entering into a real relationship with multiple souls, is also justified from the Upaniṣads and presented in philosophical form as the Viśiṣṭādvaita Vedānta. These can be seen as separate developments, simply opposed to one another. But that is not the Hindu view, which prefers to bring them into relationship, not rejecting anything but trying to find a synthesis. Time and again, the *bhakti* movement comes back to the Vedānta, and even its Advaita form, for the explanation of its own experiences. Unity and diversity are for the Hindu not contradictory notions but two ends of a spectrum.

Mythologically, this is perhaps most fully expressed in the contrast between Śiva the yogin and Śiva embracing his *śakti*, the one the symbol of the withdrawal from the world and of its reabsorption, the other the symbol of creation in all its diversity. On the human plane it is the tension between fulfilling one's duties to society, including the need to produce sons, and becoming a *saṃnyāsin*, giving up all sensual pleasures; it is the choice between *dharma* and *mokṣa*. At this level, the resolution of the tension is chronological: first the householder and then the ascetic. However, neither in fact exists in isolation and at the cosmic level these tensions or polarities remain.

Throughout the history of Hinduism, this complex interplay of contrasting elements in the specific situations involved is what has given the religion its unique character. Hinduism is not just one particular approach to life. It is not even for many of its adherents so much a theory as a practice; for many at the lower levels it is a matter of performing certain traditional rituals. But here, as elsewhere, the balance is constantly shifting. Tradition is not always just what it seems, but has constantly been undergoing reinterpretation to accommodate new understandings and changed circumstances. Innovation is not the enemy of tradition but that by which it maintains its relevance. Hinduism does not reject the old in favour of the new but blends the two, expressing new dilemmas in traditional language and accommodating fresh insights to established viewpoints. The ability to adapt itself to changing circumstances has been a mark of Hinduism throughout its history, and the unifying factor bringing together its many diverse threads lies in their common history within this unique weaving together of tradition and innovation. Hinduism is ever the same, yet different.

Bibliography

The purpose of this bibliography is twofold: to suggest suitable books in which the interested reader may pursue the subject further and to indicate those works on which the details given in this book are based. It is confined to books, since articles in periodicals are not easily accessible to most readers, and for the same reason, mostly to those written in English. A first section of general works and collections of translations is followed by more specialised works grouped according to the chapters of this book; however titles are not repeated for subsequent chapters – the listing is cumulative.

GENERAL

Basham, A. L. (ed.), *A Cultural History of India*, Oxford 1975.
Bowes, Pratima, *The Hindu Religious Tradition, a philosophical approach*, London 1978.
Brown, W. N., *Man in the Universe: some continuities in Indian thought*, Berkeley 1966.
Daniélou, Alain, *Hindu Polytheism*, London 1964.
de Bary, W. T. (ed.), *Sources of Indian Tradition*, New York 1958.
Gonda, Jan, *Change and Continuity in Indian Religion*, 's-Gravenhage 1965.
— *Die Religionen Indiens I–II*, Stuttgart 1960–3.
O'Flaherty, W. D., *Hindu Myths*, Harmondsworth 1975.
Renou, Louis, *L'Inde fondamentale*, Paris 1978.
— *Religions of Ancient India*, London 1953.
— (ed.), *Hinduism*, London 1961.
Stutley, M. and J., *Dictionary of Hinduism: its Mythology, Folklore and Development, 1500 B.C.–A.D. 1500*, London 1977.
Zaehner, R. C., *Hinduism*, London 1962.
— (tr.), *Hindu Scriptures*, London 1966.

CHAPTER ONE

Allchin, F. R., *Neolithic Cattle-Keepers of South India: a study of the Deccan ashmounds*, Cambridge 1963.

Dumézil, Georges, *Mitra-Varuṇa: essai sur deux représentations indo-européennes de la souveraineté*, Paris 1940.

Fairservis, W. A., *The Roots of Ancient India: the archaeology of early Indian civilization*, 2nd edn, London 1975.

Gonda, Jan, *Vedic Literature (Saṃhitās and Brāhmaṇas)*, Wiesbaden 1975.

Hauer, J. W., *Der Vrātya; Untersuchungen über die nichtbrahmanische Religion altindiens*, Stuttgart 1927.

Macdonell, A. A., *Vedic Mythology*, Strassburg 1897.

Panikkar, Raimundo, *The Vedic Experience: Mantramañjarī*, London 1977.

Rodhe, Sten, *Deliver us from Evil: studies on the Vedic ideas of salvation*, Lund 1946.

Wasson, R. G., *Soma, Divine Mushroom of Immortality*, New York 1968.

CHAPTER TWO

Edgerton, Franklin, *The Beginnings of Indian Philosophy*, London 1965.

Gonda, Jan, *Notes on Brahman*, Utrecht 1950.

Keith, A. B., *The Religion and Philosophy of the Veda and Upanishads*, Cambridge, Mass. 1925.

Radhakrishnan, Sarvepalli, *Indian Philosophy*, 2 vols, 2nd edn, London 1931.

— (tr.), *The Principal Upaniṣads*, London 1953.

Radhakrishnan, S. and Moore, C. A., *A source book in Indian Philosophy*, Princeton 1957.

Senart, Émile (tr.), *Chāndogya-upaniṣad*, Paris 1930.

CHAPTER THREE

Agrawala, V. S., *Śiva Mahādeva, The Great God*, Varanasi 1966.

Gail, Adalbert, *Paraśurāma, Brahmane und Krieger*, Wiesbaden 1977.

Gonda, Jan, *Aspects of Early Viṣṇuism*, 2nd edn, Delhi 1969.

— *Viṣṇuism and Śivaism*, London 1970.

Held, G. J., *The Mahābhārata: an ethnological study*, London and Amsterdam 1935.
Hiltebeitel, Alf, *The Ritual of Battle; Krishna in the Mahābhārata*, Ithaca 1976.
Hopkins, E. W., *Epic Mythology*, Strassburg 1915.
Jacobi, Hermann, *Das Râmâyaṇa*, Bonn 1893.
The Mahābhārata, tr. and ed. by J. A. B. van Buitenen, Chicago 1973–.
La Mahā Nārāyaṇa Upaniṣad, édition critique, avec une traduction française, une étude par Jean Varenne, 2 tomes, Paris 1960.
O'Flaherty, W. D., *Asceticism and Eroticism in the Mythology of Śiva*, London 1973.
Zaehner, R. C., *Hindu and Muslim Mysticism*, London 1960.
— (ed.), *The Bhagavadgītā*, Oxford 1969.

CHAPTER FOUR

Basham, A. L., *History and Doctrines of the Ājīvikas*, London 1951.
Caillat, Colette, Upadhye, A. N., and Patil, Bal, *Jainism*, Delhi 1974.
Chattopadhyaya, Debiprasad, *Lokāyata: a study in ancient Indian materialism*, New Delhi 1959.
Conze, Edward (ed.), *Buddhist Scriptures*, Harmondsworth 1959.
— *A Short History of Buddhism*, London 1980.
Glasenapp, Helmut von, *Der Jainismus*, Berlin 1926.
Lamotte, Étienne, *Histoire du Bouddhisme Indien des origines à l'ère śaka*, Louvain 1958.
Rahula, Walpola, *What the Buddha taught*, rev. edn, London 1978.
Riepe, Dale, *The Naturalistic Tradition in Indian Thought*, Seattle 1961.
Schubring, Walther, *The Religion of the Jainas*, Delhi 1966.
Schumann, H. W., *Buddhism: an outline of its teaching and schools*, London 1973.
Stietencron, Heinrich von, *Indische Sonnenpriester, Sāmba und die Śakadvīpīya-Brāhmaṇa*, Wiesbaden 1966.

CHAPTER FIVE

Chemparthy, George, *An Indian Rational Theology: introduction to Udayana's Nyāyakusumāñjali*, Leiden 1972.

Dasgupta, Surendranath, *A History of Indian Philosophy*, 5 vols, Cambridge 1922–49.

Deutsch, Eliot, *Advaita Vedānta: a philosophical reconstruction*, Honolulu 1969.

Deutsch, E. and Buitenen, J. A. B. van, *A Source Book of Advaita Vedānta*, Honolulu 1971.

Eliade, Mircea, *Yoga, Immortality and Freedom*, London 1958.

Encyclopaedia of Indian Philosophies, ed. by K. H. Potter, Delhi 1970–.

Feuerstein, Georg (tr.), *The Yogasūtra of Patañjali*, London 1979.

Frauwallner, Erich, *History of Indian Philosophy*, tr. by V. M. Bedekar, Delhi 1973.

Jha, Ganganath, *Pūrva-Mīmāṃsā in its sources*, 2nd edn, Varanasi 1964.

Larson, G. J., *Classical Sāṃkhya: an interpretation of its history and meaning*, Delhi 1969.

Lingat, Robert, *The Classical Law of India*, tr. with additions by J. D. M. Derrett, Berkeley and Los Angeles 1973.

Matilal, B. K., *Nyāya-Vaiśeṣika*, Wiesbaden 1977.

Śaṅkara's Upadeśasāhasrī, critically ed. by S. Mayeda, Tokyo 1973.

Smart, R. N., *Doctrine and Argument in Indian Philosophy*, London 1964.

Staal, J. F., *Advaita and Neoplatonism*, Madras 1954.

Varenne, Jean, *Yoga and the Hindu Tradition*, tr. by D. Coltman, Chicago 1976.

Werner, Karel, *Yoga and Indian Philosophy*, Delhi 1977.

CHAPTER SIX

Beane, W. C., *Myth, Cult and Symbols in Śākti Hinduism; a study of the Indian Mother Goddess*, Leiden 1977.

Bharati, A., *The Tantric Tradition*, London 1965.

Gupta, Sanjukta (tr.), *Lakṣmī Tantra*, Leiden 1972.

Gupta, S., Hoens, D. J., and Goudriaan, T., *Hindu Tantrism*, Leiden 1979.

Kinsley, D. R., *The Sword and the Flute: Kālī and Kṛṣṇa*, Berkeley and Los Angeles 1975.
Lorenzen, D. N., *The Kāpālikas and Kālāmukhas; two lost Śaivite sects*, Delhi 1972.
Rawson, P. S., *The art of Tantra*, London 1973.
Varenne, Jean, *Le tantrisme: la sexualité transcendée*, Paris 1977.

CHAPTER SEVEN

Buitenen, J. A. B. van, *Rāmānuja on the Bhagavadgītā*, Delhi 1970.
Carman, J. B., *The Theology of Rāmānuja*, New Haven 1974.
Desai, P. B., *Basaveśvara and his times*, Dharwar 1968.
Dhavamony, M., *The Love of God according to Śaiva Siddhānta*, Oxford 1971.
Lott, E. J., *Vedantic Approaches to God*, London 1980.
Nilakanta Sastri, K. A., *Development of Religion in South India*, Bombay 1963.
Raghavan, Venkatarama, *The Great Integrators: the Saint-singers of India*, Delhi 1966.
Ramanujan, A. K. (tr.), *Speaking of Śiva*, Harmondsworth 1973.
Siauve, Suzanne, *La Doctrine de Madhva: Dvaita-vedānta*, Pondicherry 1968.
Zvelebil, K. V., *The Smile of Murugan: on Tamil literature of South India*, Leiden 1973.

CHAPTER EIGHT

Barz, R., *The Bhakti Sect of Vallabhācārya*, Faridabad 1976.
Bhattacharya, Deben (tr.), *Love Songs of Vidyāpati*, London 1963.
— *Love Songs of Chandidās*, London 1967.
— *The Mirror of the Sky, songs of the Bāuls from Bengal*, London 1969.
— *Songs of Kṛṣṇa*, New York 1978.
Briggs, G. W., *Gorakhnāth and the Kānphaṭa Yogīs*, Calcutta and Oxford 1938.
Bryant, K. E., *Poems to the child-god; structures and strategies in the poetry of Sūrdās*, Berkeley 1978.
Cole, W. O. and Sambhi, P. S., *The Sikhs: their religious beliefs and practices*, London 1978.

Deleury, G. A., *The Cult of Viṭhobā*, Poona 1960.
Dimock, E. C., *The Place of the Hidden Moon; erotic mysticism in the Vaiṣṇava-Sahajiyā cult of Bengal*, Chicago and London 1966.
Eidlitz, Walther, *Kṛṣṇa-Caitanya: sein Leben und seine Lehre*, Stockholm 1968.
Hein, Norvin, *The Miracle Plays of Mathurā*, New Haven 1972.
Kinsley, D. R., *The Divine Player (a study of Krishna Lila)*, Delhi 1979.
McLeod, W. H., *Gurū Nānak and the Sikh Religion*, Oxford 1968.
Miller, B. S. (tr.), *Love Song of the Dark Lord: Jayadeva's Gītagovinda*, New York 1977.
Tulsīdās, *The Holy Lake of the Acts of Rama, an English translation of Tulsī Dās's Rāmacaritamānasa*, by W. D. P. Hill, Bombay 1952.
— *Kavitāvalī, translated and with a critical introduction* by F. R. Allchin, London 1964.
— *The Petition to Rām*, a translation of *Vinaya-patrikā* by F. R. Allchin, London 1966.
Vaudeville, Ch., *Étude sur les sources et la composition du Rāmāyaṇa de Tulsī-Dās*, Paris 1955.
— *Kabīr*, Oxford 1974.

CHAPTER NINE

Bolle, K. W., *The Persistence of Religion: an essay on Tantrism and Sri Aurobindo's philosophy*, Leiden 1965.
Gandhi, M. K., *The Story of My Experiments with Truth*, 2nd edn, Ahmedabad 1940.
Ghose, Aurobindo, *The Life Divine*, Pondicherry 1955.
Heimsath, C. H., *Indian Nationalism and Hindu Social Reform*, Princeton 1964.
Kopf, David, *The Brahmo Samaj and the Shaping of the Modern Indian Mind*, Princeton 1978.
Nikhilananda, Svami (tr.), *The Gospel of Sri Ramakrishna*, 2nd edn, Madras 1947.
Rai, L. L., *A History of the Arya Samaj*, New Delhi 1967.
Sharma, D. S., *The Renaissance of Hinduism*, Varanasi 1944.

CHAPTER TEN

Babb, L. A., *The Divine Hierarchy: popular Hinduism in Central India*, New York 1975.
Bhardwaj, S. M., *Hindu Places of Pilgrimage in India*, London 1973.
Cohn, B. S., *India: the social anthropology of a civilization*, Englewood Cliffs 1971.
Dimmitt, C., and Buitenen, J. A. B. van, *Classical Hindu Mythology, a reader in the Sanskrit Purāṇas*, Philadelphia 1978.
Dubois, J. A., *Hindu Manners, Customs and Ceremonies*, tr. by H. K. Beauchamp, 3rd edn, Oxford 1906.
Dumont, Louis, *Homo hierarchicus; the caste system and its implications*, tr. by M. Sainsbury, London 1970.
O'Malley, L. S. S., *Popular Hinduism*, Cambridge 1935.
Mitchell, George, *The Hindu temple: an introduction to its meaning and forms*, London 1977.
Singer, Milton (ed.), *Krishna: myths, rites and attitudes*, Hawaii 1966.
— *Traditional India: structure and change*, Philadelphia 1959.

Index